Software Industry
Accounting

Software Industry Accounting

Joseph M. Morris, CPA
Scientific Software-Intercomp, Inc.

Contributing Authors

Richard P. Graff, CPA
Coopers & Lybrand

Francis J. O'Brien, CPA
Ernst & Young

Lynn E. Turner, CPA
Coopers & Lybrand

Edward S. Wittman, MBA
TecConsults (USA) Inc.

John Wiley & Sons, Inc.
New York · Chichester · Brisbane · Toronto · Singapore

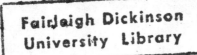
Appendix A. Statement of Position 91-1. Copyright
© 1991 by American Institute of Certified Public Accountants.
Inc. Reprinted with permission.

Statement of Financial Accounting Standards No. 86,
*Accounting for the Costs of Computer Software to Be
Sold, Leases, or Otherwise Marketed* copyright 1985
by Financial Accounting Standards Board is reprinted
with permission. Copies of the complete document
are available from the FASB, 401 Merritt 7, P.O. Box
5116, Norwalk, CT 06856-5116.

Library of Congress Cataloging in Publication Data:
Morris, Joseph M., 1949–
     Software industry accounting / Joseph M. Morris ; contributing
authors, Richard P. Graff . . . [et al.]
          p.   cm.
     Includes index.
     ISBN 0-471-55931-8
     1. Computer software industry—United States—Accounting.
     2. Computer software industry—Accounting—Standards—United States.
     I. Graff, Richard P.   II. Title.
     HF5686.C54M67   1992   92-21904
     657'.834—dc20   CIP

Printed in the United States of America

10   9   8   7   6   5   4

SUBSCRIPTION NOTICE

This Wiley product is updated on a periodic basis with supplements to reflect important changes in the subject matter. If you purchased this product directly from John Wiley & Sons, Inc., we have already recorded your subscription for this update service.

If, however, you purchased this product from a bookstore and wish to receive (1) the current update at no additional charge, and (2) future updates and revised or related volumes billed separately with a 30-day examination review, please send your name, company name (if applicable), address, and the title of the product to:

Supplement Department
John Wiley & Sons, Inc.
One Wiley Drive
Somerset, NJ 08875
1-800-225-5945

This book is dedicated to Lindsay and Katy.

ABOUT THE AUTHOR

Joseph M. Morris is vice president–corporate controller of Scientific Software-Intercomp, Inc., of Denver, Colorado, a provider of high technology software and services to the petroleum and other industries. He was previously a project manager at the FASB, where he had staff responsibility for software industry accounting matters, which included serving as FASB staff liaison and advisor to the AICPA Task Force that developed SOP 91-1, on software revenue recognition.

ABOUT THE CONTRIBUTING AUTHORS

Richard P. Graff is a partner in the Denver office of Coopers & Lybrand, who has significant experience in the auditing of software companies. He specializes in the firm's high-technology practice and serves as an SEC consulting partner. His client base consists primarily of public companies, many of which have international operations.

Francis J. O'Brien is a partner in the West Region office of Ernst & Young, and is technical advisor to Ernst & Young's National High-Technology Group. As a member of the AICPA Task Force on Accounting for the Development and Sale of Computer Software, he was extensively involved in the development of SOP 91-1 and FASB Statement 86, on software costs. Mr. O'Brien recently completed a three-year term as a member of the AICPA Accounting Standards Executive Committee.

Lynn E. Turner is a partner in the Denver office of Coopers & Lybrand, where he specializes in their high-technology practice and SEC consulting matters. Previously, he was a professional accounting fellow in the SEC chief accountant's office, where he was extensively involved in accounting matters related to the software industry. Mr. Turner served as the SEC observer to the AICPA Task Force on Accounting for the Development and Sale of Computer Software during the development of SOP 91-1. He also worked with the FASB staff during the development of FASB Statement 86.

Edward S. Wittman is president of TecConsults (USA) Inc., a firm specializing in contract engineering and technical recruiting for software and other high-technology companies. For the previous eleven years, he was chief financial officer of Scientific Software-Intercomp, Inc., of Denver, Colorado. For part of that time, he also served in a general management role responsible for one of Scientific Software's operating units.

Preface

The software business is characterized by two key activities—development of software products and marketing them. The issuance of AICPA Statement of Position (SOP) 91-1, *Software Revenue Recognition*, in December 1991, completed a long effort by many parties, beginning in the early 1980s, to address accounting principles for both of these key activities. The first segment of this great effort resulted in FASB Statement No. 86, *Accounting for the Costs of Computer Software to Be Sold, Leased, or Otherwise Marketed*.

Our team of authors was uniquely equipped to prepare this book. The team includes individuals who either directly or indirectly participated in the development of both Statement 86 and SOP 91-1, and the team of authors has a background of extensive experience in accounting, auditing, and general management in the software industry.

In regard to Statement 86 and SOP 91-1, the author team has undertaken to share with the software industry its insight into the pronouncements—what the provisions of Statement 86 and SOP 91-1 are, the rationales of those provisions, and the many nuances of their implementation. The authors have been and continue to be on the front line in implementation of the pronouncements in practice, and continue to deal with new questions that arise frequently.

This book is directed to accountants, auditors, controllers, and chief financial officers, as well as investors in and lenders to software companies, analysts, software company general managers, and anyone who can benefit from understanding accounting, financial reporting, and auditing in the software industry.

Prior to this project, I had the professional privilege of working with each of the contributing authors. I would like to express my sincere gratitude to each of them for their outstanding contributions to the preparation of this book.

JOSEPH M. MORRIS

Denver, Colorado
October 1992

Acknowledgments

This book contains various references to and brief quotations from materials contained in pronouncements on accounting and auditing, which are acknowledged as follows:

Copyright by Financial Accounting Standards Board
Statements of Financial Accounting Standards
FASB Interpretations
FASB Technical Bulletins
FASB Invitations to Comment

The references to, and quotations from, the above pronouncements are contained herein with the permission of the Financial Accounting Standards Board. Complete copies of the pronouncements are available from the Financial Accounting Standards Board, 401 Merritt 7, Norwalk, CT 06856.

Copyright by American Institute of Certified Public Accountants
Opinions of the Accounting Principles Board
Statements on Auditing Standards and Codification of Statements on Auditing Standards
Statements of Position Issues Papers

The references to, and quotations from, the above pronouncements are contained herein with the permission of the American Institute of Certified Public Accountants. Complete copies of the pronouncements are available from the American Institute of Certified Public Accountants, 1211 Avenue of the Americas, New York, N.Y. 10036.

Copyright by Digital Information Group
The Software Industry Factbook

The references to and quotations from *The Software Industry Factbook* are included with the permission of the Digital Information Group. Complete copies of *The Software Industry Factbook* are available from Digital Information Group, 51 Bank Street, Stamford, CT 06901.

We thank Judy Ward, partner and computer auditing specialist in the Denver office of Coopers & Lybrand, for her review of and assistance with the sections of Chapter 9 dealing with auditing the technical aspects of software development projects.

We also thank Lee W. Zieroth, Esq., of Cohen Brame & Smith, Professional Corporation Attorneys at Law, of Denver, Colorado, for his assistance in developing the example software licenses and postcontract customer support agreement that are the appendices to Chapter 1.

Contents

CONTENTS

CHAPTER ONE

A General Industry Perspective

Edward S. Wittman
TecConsults (USA) Inc.

1.1 INTRODUCTION: A GENERAL INDUSTRY PERSPECTIVE

This chapter provides a general perspective of the software industry, its relationship with the computer industry as a whole, the various types of software, how software is developed, how it is licensed, and how it is distributed. The software industry is unique, and its special characteristics must be understood to properly apply the industry's specialized accounting practices. The discussion assumes that the reader has some familiarity with computers and computer software.

The computer industry, consisting of computer hardware, computer software, and computer-related services, has become one of the most important industries in the world. Computer software has become an industry in itself, with developments in computer software frequently requiring changes in hardware, just as hardware developments require advances in software. The software industry is worldwide—one often sees newspaper reports of the export of sophisticated computer systems. The computer software industry will continue to grow in importance, particularly as modern business continues to evolve from the old "brick and mortar" era to the modern era based on information and automation technology.

It is almost impossible to estimate the number of computers in use today. Computers and software are found everywhere—in automobile control devices, watches, textile mills, hand-held electronic devices, microwave ovens, and, of course, in homes, on office desks, and in dedicated computer rooms.

1.2 ROOTS OF THE COMPUTER SOFTWARE INDUSTRY

(a) Basics of the Computer Industry

The beginnings of the computer industry can be traced back almost four thousand years to a time when Babylonian mathematicians

The views expressed in this chapter reflect those of the individual author and do not necessarily represent those of the other contributing authors.

developed the first algorithms, or mathematical formulae, to solve numerical problems. In the early seventeenth century, John Napier, a Scottish inventor, found that division could be performed as a series of subtractions and that multiplication could be performed by a series of additions. Approximately 30 years later, Pascal, a Frenchman, developed the first numerical calculating machine, and approximately 30 years after that, Leibniz built the first numerical calculating machine that could multiply and divide as well as add and subtract. In 1780, Benjamin Franklin discovered electricity, completing the discovery of the necessary fundamentals which, with further development and application, ultimately led to the creation of the computer industry and, shortly thereafter, the software industry.

(b) Early Computers and Software Technology

The technology of software itself seems to have had its origin in the middle of the eighteenth century, when Jacquard used perforated cards to manage a weaving loom and Charles Babbage, in the United Kingdom, designed a machine capable of rudimentary analysis that followed logical instructions from a perforated tape. Programs, independent of the machine's inherent functionality, were written for this analytical machine.

Shortly thereafter, George Boole published the basis for the use of the binary system, *The Mathematical Analysis of Logic.* In 1855 in Sweden, the first practical mechanical computer was introduced. In 1887 Herman Hollerith was granted a patent on the first automatic tabulating machine, which utilized punch cards, known then as Hollerith cards and later as IBM cards—the now obsolete, 80-column cards that were used extensively until the early 1980s.

In 1886 William Burroughs introduced the first commercial-grade mechanical adding machine, and in 1890 Hollerith constructed an electrically powered mechanical system, using the perforated cards for tabulating the U.S. census. In 1896 Hollerith founded the Tabulating Machine Company, which then merged with two other firms in 1911 to form the Computer-Tabulating-Recording Company (CTRC). In 1924 CTRC changed its name to International Business Machines Corporation (IBM).

In 1936 Turing, working at Princeton University, published the concept of applying algorithms to the computation of complex mathematical functions and created the idea of independent sets of instruction capable of computing any relationship that can be mathematically described.

The first electrical digital computer is attributed to the work completed in 1939 at Iowa State University. This claim is disputed by some who attribute the first electrical digital computer to George Stibitz, working at Bell Telephone Laboratories.

(c) Acceleration of Computer and Software Development

Following the developments discussed in the preceding sections, the rate of new advances and developments accelerated. In 1945 the idea of stored programs appeared. In 1946 BINAC was introduced—the first computer to perform in real time. At about that time, ENIAC, which used 18,000 vacuum tubes, was commissioned at the University of Pennsylvania, and the predecessor company of Universal Automatic Computer Company (Univac) was formed. In 1948 the first stored-program computer, said by some to be the first true computer, was developed. This was the IBM SSEC (selective sequence electronic calculator), so named because it was software driven. Credit for the original development of the stored program, or software concept, is attributed to the team of von Neumann, Mauchly, Eckert and Goldstine at IBM.

Development of electronic components followed over the next few years, and in 1953 IBM shipped the first commercial stored-program computer, the Model 701, a vacuum-tube, first-generation computer. In 1954 FORTRAN, the first "high level," rather than binary-code computer language, was created by John Backus at IBM, and Gene Amdahl developed the first operating system, which was then used on the IBM 704. Two years later, Automatic Programmed Tool (APT) and Information Processing Language (IPL) were introduced. ALGOL and LISP were released in 1958, and in the same year Seymour Cray completed the first fully transistorized supercomputer for Control Data Corporation.

The first packaged software program was sold by Computer Science Corporation in 1959. In the same year, IBM introduced the Model 1401, of which more than 10,000 units were sold, and the first patents were filed for the integrated circuit. In 1960 the first minicomputer, the PDP 1, was introduced by Digital Equipment Corporation. Intel, the giant integrated circuit microprocessor developer, was formed in 1968, and in that year Data General introduced the predecessor to the personal computer, the first 16-bit computer, the first of the Nova series.

In 1969 IBM began the practice of "unbundling," or charging separate prices for hardware and software—the event that really set the computer software industry loose from the computer hardware industry. In 1975 Microsoft, now the largest independent software supplier, with fiscal 1991 sales of approximately $1.8 billion, was founded.

Computer developments continued at a rapid pace. In 1976 the first CRAY 1, developed by Seymour Cray, was delivered, which was capable of performing calculations at the then extremely fast rate of 100 million floating point calculations per second. Digital Equipment Corporation (DEC) introduced the VAX 11/780 and a new operating system, VAX, in 1977, at the same time that Apple, Commodore, and Tandy released their lines of personal computers. During the late 1970s, electronic spread sheets and word-processing programs developed specifically for the personal computer were released. In 1980 Microsoft licensed the UNIX operating system from Bell Laboratories and released XENIX as an operating system for the scientific use of personal computers.

In 1981 IBM introduced its first personal computer, setting a new standard for personal computer performance. In 1982 Microsoft licensed MS-DOS to approximately 50 personal computer manufacturers for resale with their computers. In 1983 Compaq shipped its first computer; it sold more than $100 million worth in the first year following introduction. Also in 1983, the CRAY 2 was introduced, which was capable of one billion floating point operations per second, representing a tenfold increase in speed over a seven-year period.

It is interesting to note that in 1980 the total number of stand-alone computers in use in the United States was estimated to have been about 1,000,000 units, and that by the end of 1983 more than 10,000,000 were in use. So began the dramatic growth of computer and software technologies and of the software industry.

1.3   THE SOFTWARE INDUSTRY TODAY

(a) Growing Importance of Software in the Computer Industry

Originally, the power of a computer determined the power of the functions that could be performed, as well as how fast those functions could be completed. Over the past 10 years, computer hardware technology has become mature, with many computer hardware manufacturers providing comparable products, as evidenced by the widespread use of the term *clone*—computer hardware seems to be fast developing the characteristics of a commodity. Software now provides much of the value to the features, operating characteristics, and overall functionality of a computer system. A further indication of the increasing dominance of the software component of a computer system can be found in IBM's 1990 annual report, which indicated that user spending on software was growing at twice the rate of spending on hardware.

It is estimated that the software industry will average a 19% annual growth rate during the early 1990s. Following is an analysis of total computer industry revenues of $130 billion during 1990, which was included in the *Software Industry Factbook*, printed here with permission of Digital Information Group.

Computer Industry Revenues for 1990
(in thousands)

Personal computer hardware	$ 37,200,000
All other hardware	54,000,000
All software	29,850,000
LAN	6,400,000
Games	2,640,000
Total computer industry revenues	$130,090,000

Exhibit 1.1 indicates the relative contributions of the above components of the computer industry to total industry revenues in 1990.

EXHIBIT 1.1   1990 Computer Industry Sales

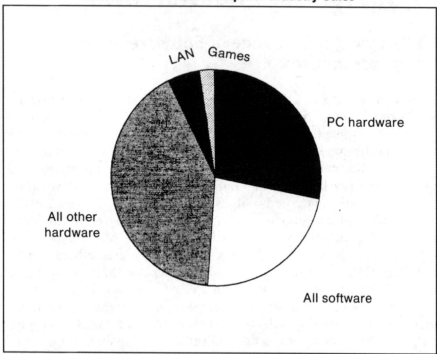

(b) Hardware and Software Vendors in the Software Market

Not only independent software suppliers compete in the software market. Hardware vendors, recognizing the importance of independent software in enhancing hardware sales value, have been investing heavily in software development. In 1990 IBM, the world's leading computer hardware company, reported approximately $10 billion, or 14% of its revenues, from sales of software, a large portion of which was from the marketing of operating systems. IBM has also invested directly in independent software vendors such as Knowledgeware and Easel. DEC, another large hardware supplier, reported sales of $810 million, or 6% of its total revenues, from marketing of software.

By comparison, the largest independent software supplier, Microsoft Corporation, reported sales of $1.8 billion for 1991. Microsoft markets MS-DOS, the disk operating system used extensively in the personal computer market. Microsoft also supplies many different business and home applications software products as well as Windows, a graphic user interface, which has spawned a whole new family of software products with increased ease of use.

1.4   TYPES OF COMPUTER HARDWARE AND SOFTWARE

(a) Types of Computer Hardware

Most view the computer hardware industry as consisting of markets for mainframe computers, minicomputers, and personal computers, including workstations. These distinctions refer to memory size, speed of throughput, and limitation on the amount of data that can be stored on-line.

(b) Types of Computer Software

Software is a series of instructions, written and stored so that it is readily repeatable for directing a computer to function. There are two types of software: system software and applications software.

(c) System Software

System software is required for every computer and can be categorized in the following three groups: (1) operating systems, (2) utilities, and (3) data base managers.

(i) OPERATING SYSTEMS.   Operating systems manage and are essential to the operation of a computer. Nearly all application programs, as well as other types of system programs, rely on the capabilities of the operating system for their own functionality; they are written in strict conformity to the protocol, syntax, and conventions of the host operating system.

(ii) UTILITIES SOFTWARE. Utilities software serves as a development tool in writing, structuring, internally documenting, and maintaining other software programs. High-level programming languages such as COBOL, FORTRAN, and C++ are examples of utilities software, as are the language compilers and interpreters that translate the higher-level languages into machine language directly readable by a computer. Other types of utilities software simplify software development and computer operation, such as the graphical user interfaces supplied with the Macintosh Computer of Apple Computer Company, and Windows, supplied by Microsoft Corporation. Utilities software also includes the software products known as computer-aided software engineering, or CASE systems. CASE consists of sophisticated and powerful software development tools that are used extensively in large software development projects.

(iii) DATA BASE MANAGERS. An example of a data base management system is ORACLE, supplied by Oracle Corporation, the third largest independent supplier of software. Each having its own language, data base managers allow users to create specific custom applications based on the data base management system's ability to create, file, retrieve, and report the data contained within. Although certain conventions are coming into wide use, each data base management system has its own vocabulary and syntax, usually requiring a person with a programming background to implement the data base management system to meet the user's requirements.

(d) Applications Software

Applications software performs the specific functions of information processing requirements. These functions can range from scientific calculations used in weather forecasting, tracking rockets, space probes, and design simulation, to commercial processes such as those used in accounting, payroll, inventory control, and general information processing, to name but a few.

Office automation software, including word-processing software, grew rapidly as the price of computing power decreased during the 1980s. These programs can help with common tasks such as word processing, desktop publishing, file retention, ease of controlling the decision-making process, and electronic mail. Some programs are specifically designed to enhance the educational process and are generally called computer-aided instruction or computer-aided training. Recreational software became popular with the advent of personal computers. Traditional board games, flight and ship simulation, mysteries, and adventure and action games are among the kinds of recreational software marketed for home computers.

(e) Firmware—Another Kind of Software

There is another special and sometimes overlooked form of software known as *firmware*, sometimes called *microprograms*. Firmware is the software that enables automated products to operate. Examples of firmware are the code in a game cartridge, the "computer" that controls the electronic ignition in an automobile, and the controller in a microwave oven that provides push-button ease of use. Firmware is the software that controls, for example, alarm systems and environmental control systems, as well as a number of other processes. Firmware embodies the characteristics and functions of both systems and applications software.

Firmware is encoded on a semipermanent basis into ROM (read only memory), which consists of integrated circuits (chips). To change firmware code requires removal of the ROM and the use of a highly specialized eraser-programmer. Because firmware is so difficult to modify, whereas other software is normally easy to modify, the programming is specialized, with major emphasis on reliability and economy of code.

1.5   GLOSSARY OF KEY TERMS IN THE SOFTWARE INDUSTRY

The software industry, like other highly specialized high-technology industries, has developed a specialized vocabulary. A number of terms have been defined and described in the preceding sections. Following are definitions of additional key words used in the software industry.

(a) Batch Processing

A method by which software performs its function without interfacing with a person during the process is called *batch processing*. A job is submitted by a computer operator for processing by the computer, using additional lines of code written as a special set of instructions in job control language (JCL). The user of the data usually does not have direct interface with the computer. Compare this notion with interactive processing, discussed later in this section.

(b) Bit

Short form of the original term, *binary digit*. A bit is the lowest unit of data, containing either a 1 or 0, implemented by an *electric current on* or *electric current off* condition at that specific electronic media location. This is the most fundamental activity of the computer.

(c) Byte

Consisting of eight bits, a byte is the lowest unit that most software can accept.

(d) Chip

Also identified as an integrated circuit, a chip is wafer of silicon on which a large number of circuits are implanted. These circuits can provide computer memory, signal processing, data handling, or any other function in which electronic circuits are used.

(e) Distributed Processing

A method of software structure in which various functions of the software are performed by separate computing units, generally connected by telecommunication lines, operating interdependently without human intervention.

(f) Integrated Systems

Sometimes known as turnkey systems, integrated systems encompass the hardware, peripherals, operating system software, applications software, and, frequently, the data structures and communications capabilities to meet particular user specifications.

(g) Interactive Processing

Processing with software that allows immediate interaction between the user of data and the computer system is known as *interactive processing*.

(h) Kilobyte (K)

A kilobyte equals 1,000 bytes, the unit of measure commonly used for the measurement of memory capacity in earlier personal computers.

(i) Megabyte (Meg)

A megabyte equals one million bytes, the unit of measure commonly used for data storage, such as for disk drives and tapes for modern personal computers.

(j) Microprocessor

A central processor unit, self-contained on an integrated circuit, is a microprocessor.

(k) MIPS

The acronym MIPS means *millions of instructions per second*, the unit used to measure computer speed.

(l) Platform

The term *platform* refers to the computer system on which software operates or the system software, such as the operating system, or both.

(m) Portability

Portability is a measure of the ease with which a program can be modified, if necessary, to operate on various types of computers or with different operating systems.

(n) Program

A program is the sequence of instructions that direct a computer to complete a function.

(o) Random Access Memory (RAM)

Ram is the main memory of a computer, providing the fastest access time for manipulation of data and processing of a software program. RAM provides data access much quicker than a disk drive is capable of providing.

(p) Read Only Memory (ROM)

Read only memory is the section of main memory dedicated to the most basic functioning of a computer. Read-write access is denied to the user in this area of memory.

(q) Software Architecture

Software architecture is the overall scheme for developing software that describes how data will be identified, stored and retrieved, as well as the organization of the individual functional module to provide for ease of transfer, speed, accuracy, and other features.

(r) Syntax

Vocabulary, punctuation, and other conventions unique to a programming language constitute syntax. In MS-DOS, for example, the length of filenames and use of semicolons are part of the DOS syntax.

1.6   THE SOFTWARE DEVELOPMENT PROCESS

(a) Distinguishing Between Research Activities and Development Activities

In many software companies, the department principally responsible for the creation of new products is referred to as the research and development (R&D) department, even if no research is conducted. The word *research* generally refers to scientific or scholarly investigation. *Development* generally refers to bringing into being or to making active, more available, or effective.

Very few software companies actively engage in research in the sense of its usual meaning. If such research activities are conducted, they are usually associated with an underlying technology, rather than with a software product itself. For example, creation of a software system for process control in the petrochemical arena requires knowledge of the chemical process. The development of that knowledge may require research activities such as sophisticated chemical experimentation, including field studies and laboratory evaluations, and subcontracted university-based analysis.

Although these distinctions are important to understanding the software development process, the words *research* and *development* are not used in accounting literature to describe activities afforded different accounting treatment. Instead, the term *research and development costs* as used in FASB Statement No. 2, *Accounting for Research and Development Costs*, refers to an aggregation of costs that are to be expensed because they meet certain criteria. An ambiguity in accounting terminology is that software development costs meeting certain criteria, called *production costs* in FASB Statement No. 86, *Accounting for the Costs of Computer Software to Be Sold, Leased, or Otherwise Marketed,* must be capitalized.

(b) Six Phases of the Software Development Process

There are six phases in the software development process, as outlined in Exhibit 1.2. The development process described is relatively structured. There are many variations in the process, often depending on the particular experience of those administering it. Often, especially in development of microcomputer software, the process is significantly less structured than the one described here. As discussed in other chapters, the accountant or auditor of a software company must have an understanding of the software development process to be able to identify key events, and to be able to prepare and evaluate the documentation required for accounting for capitalization of software development costs. Each phase is discussed in the following sections. Section i includes an exhibit summarizing the principal activities and types of documentation usually developed during each phase.

(c) Problem Statement

Phase 1 in the software development process may involve many departments, including marketing, product management, engineering, development, and general management. The sources of ideas for software products are legion—ideas can come from existing customers, sales prospects who decided not to buy from the subject company, the software development staff, market research personnel, employee suggestions, or a creative third party. Ideas for software products are usually first evaluated by marketing personnel for economic feasibility, for fit with existing channels of distribution, for possible effects on existing product lines, and for fit with the company's marketing objectives. From this evaluation, a problem statement is prepared—a document outlining the software needs that are to be solved by the capability of the new software product.

Next, the development department evaluates the cost and time assumptions used in the marketing evaluation. A decision is reached early in this phase as to whether, based on the more detailed informa-

EXHIBIT 1.2 Phases of the Software Development Process

1. *Problem Statement* Recognition of the objectives of the product
2. *Design* Evaluation of alternatives, development of fundamental relationships within the product design, completion of a feasibility study, and the development of a prototype and the creation of test plans
3. *Programming and System Development* Coding and testing of the software programs based on the results of Phase 2 above
4. *System Testing* Testing of the overall system in simulated user environments and testing at selected user sites
5. *Release for Production and Distribution* Finalization of the product, including the corrections of errors in coding or design identified in Phase 4 above
6. *Product Enhancement* Products enhanced to expand their application, and to develop new functionalities (note that this effort does not include the efforts to correct identified coding or design errors [bugs])

tion generated by the marketing and development staffs, the project should be pursued further.

(d) Design Phase

From an accounting point of view, the design phase is the most critical, because it is in this phase that the activities relevant to the issue of capitalization of development costs are performed. Design decisions are made, including those relating to system architecture and general design. Also during this phase a working prototype is developed, which is one of the ways of determining technological feasibility for capitalization. The existence of a working prototype does not mean that the product is fully developed, but rather that the technical risk of the development has been minimized. The prototype is a set of code, generally without documentation and without comments, created only for the purpose of demonstrating that the design document incorporating the design decisions remains valid.

The first step in the design phase is preparation of a preliminary design document, which includes a description of the software functionality to be developed and the system configuration, or architecture, which describes the overall data flow through the system. Preliminary design documents may identify existing software, if any, available within the company or from others, that can be used as is or with modification to meet some of the design requirements.

In this stage, many fundamental design decisions about the software product are made, including confirmation of the platform on which the software will run and the computer languages and syntax conventions that will be used. The design phase also includes determining the functionalities of the software that will be library-based, meaning available as a utility subroutine to all programmers working on development of the software product, which will not require rewriting each time the functionality is required.

A feasibility study may be performed concurrent with the development of the preliminary design document, or immediately following its approval, to evaluate the capability of the software company's development team to create a product meeting the requirements of the problem statement, within budgetary cost limitations. A feasibility study may include the first detailed description of areas of technical concern and risk, details and results of experimentation done to demonstrate that the design objectives can be reasonably achieved.

Sometimes a prototype of the product functionality is developed. It is usually not necessary to develop a prototype of an entire product—prototypes are often developed for only portions of functionality in which technical success is not considered certain. Prototypes are usually developed with a minimum of design documentation, that is, without software comments or user documentation, and only to the stage that the technical risk of the functionality being demonstrated is minimized. Usually, a prototype is sufficiently functionally complete that its use demonstrates that the known inputs can be processed to produce predictable and numerically correct results. For a prototype to serve as a working model as contemplated in Statement 86, it should not be necessary that the prototype demonstrate that all combinations of inputs can be processed and that all possible outcomes can be computed—rather, it should be able to demonstrate that the technological risk of its inability to do so is remote.

Upon successful completion of the feasibility study and, if applicable, prototyping, a detail program design may be prepared, which includes all information required for the assignment of specific tasks in the development of the software product. This document includes detailed design information for the modules to be developed or modified from existing modules, the development required for each module, the flow of data required for each module, and the flow of data created by the module. Tasks may be identified for individual system designers, programmers, and coders. In addition, tasks may be assigned to scientific professionals for the development of mathematical formulae, or to hardware professionals to assure maximum utilization of the chosen platform capabilities. Statement 86 requires the capitalization of development costs incurred subsequent to completion of the detail design document.

At this point in the development process, detailed test plans may be developed to assure that the software product will meet quality standards identified in the problem statement phase. Test plans may include five levels of testing. First, each function or subfunction is *unit tested*. The originator of the code is required to test the operation of each function within the full range of use specified in the design document. Second, *integration tests* may be performed to evaluate whether data flows properly between modules, so that the system when integrated and functioning as a whole will operate properly. These tests are generally performed by the product development team.

Third, *alpha testing* evaluates operation of a system in a simulated user environment, employing team members who generally were not previously involved in development of the product. The primary purpose of alpha testing is to identify remaining shortcomings in the software product's design or implementation that could prevent the product from achieving the commercial goals identified in the problem statement. Product refinements and corrections may be made as a result of alpha testing, such as improvements to ease of use, menu clarity, elimination of endless loops, and the addition of help aids. Fourth, the test plan usually identifies potential test sites for *beta testing*, where the software product will undergo extensive testing in live situations at user sites. A beta test plan may specify the extent of testing to be performed and the reporting expected from the testers, the amount of technical support to be provided by the development team, and plans for monitoring the test sites.

The fifth and final test stage is the *acceptance test*, in which internal quality control personnel review all results of previous tests, and review all product documentation, both internal comments to the code to ensuring proper software maintenance, and documentation to be provided with the software product to the end user.

(e) Programming and System Development

Based on the planning, feasibility studies, and testing program determined during the problem statement and design phases, coding and development of the individual components of the system are then completed. During this phase, the project development staff creates a source code for each of the functions specified in the product design, performs unit tests as specified, and incorporates comments in the source code to ensure product maintenance and minimization of future corrective actions. Work on product documentation is usually done simultaneously with the completion of the software product, including on-line, computer-provided aids, as well as hard copy manuals such as user guides, technical reference manuals, packaging, installation procedures, and any other descriptive materials, in any form of media.

When individual modules are completed, they are then integrated into a single system, and the software product takes on its own identity. The system is compiled and data transfers between modules are demonstrated. Integration testing, as discussed earlier, is performed, and refinements, corrections, and modifications are made as necessary to meet the design criteria.

(f) System Testing

During Phase 4, alpha testing at the development team site and beta testing at various user sites is performed. Results of alpha testing or beta testing may require that portions of the development cycle be reiterated because one or more of the system's functions do not meet its design objectives. In addition to the alpha and beta testing of the software product, the product documentation is tested and evaluated for readability, correctness of description, completeness, and usefulness under end user conditions.

(g) Release for Production

Upon successful completion of all testing, quality assurance personnel approve the software product and documentation for production and distribution. The product is now available for general market release, and at this point Statement 86 requires cessation of the capitalization of development costs. The software product and documentation are usually assigned a "version 1.0" release number, and reproduction for marketing and distribution in the marketplace is authorized. Control of the product is transferred from development to customer support.

(h) Product Enhancement

Following the release of a product and its use in the marketplace, future improvements to the product—in the form of enhancements—are defined. Enhancements are distinguished from bug fixes or error corrections in that they often expand the functionality of the software product, adding new capabilities and widening the spectrum of solutions for existing functions. Enhancements may be improvements to the existing functionality that increase the marketability of the product and extend its life.

(i) Chart Summarizing the Software Development Process

Exhibit 1.3 summarizes the activities and documentation usually associated with each of the six phases of the software development process.

EXHIBIT 1.3   The Software Development Process

	Phase	Activities	Documentation
1	Problem Statement	Define problem and required functionality	Basic design concept statement
		Plan the development project	Project plan and budget
		Determine applicable acceptance criteria	Quality assurance requirements

	Phase	Activities	Documentation
2	Design	Prepare preliminary design document	Detailed product design statement
		Determine system architecture	Data flow diagrams, system integration plan
		Determine feasibility of the designed product	Technical description of study, results of experimentation
		Develop prototype	Results of working model demonstration
		Develop final system specification	Final detailed design specification
		Develop test plan	Details of quality assurance program, including unit, integration, alpha, beta, and final acceptance testing

3	Programming and System Development	Code and unit test	Source code, comments, test results, acceptance by software librarian
		Prepare documentation	Drafts of user guides, technical reference manuals, and on-line help screens
		Integrate modules to system specifications	Fully compiled system with data available for transfer or sharing between modules, acceptance of system by software librarian
		Integration testing	Results of testing of the working completed product

4	System Testing	Alpha testing	Test results
		Beta testing	Test results from use of product in an unmanaged environment
		Final acceptance testing	Test results and release of product

5	Release for Production and Distribution	Completion of all documentation and making product and documentation available for reproduction	Documentation release notes, production records, and serial release number

6	Product Enhancement	Depending on magnitude and complexity, the activities and documentation of Phases 1 through 5 may be partially or entirely completed for the enhancement

1.7 MARKETING AND DISTRIBUTION OF SOFTWARE PRODUCTS

(a) How Software Companies Derive Revenues

The preceding sections discuss the software development process—how software companies go about developing their intellectual property. The rest of this chapter discusses how software companies derive revenues from the marketing of that intellectual property. Most software and software-related revenues are derived through the following methods of marketing.

- Issuing software licenses, which are similar to product sales in other industries

- Providing postcontract customer support, or maintenance

- Providing software in projects that combine software with hardware or services or both

- Providing software development services, in which software development activities and revenue generation overlap

- Providing services that accompany software products

- Providing services that use software, such as data-processing services, or consulting services that require specialized software

(b) Software Licenses

Although the terms *software sales* and *leases* are frequently used in the industry, they are generally misapplied. Except in very unusual circumstances, software is almost always licensed. Software is an intangible item consisting of intellectual property, the proprietary rights to which are almost never sold. Instead, the software company, as the owner of the proprietary intellectual property, grants a license for the customer to use the software. A license to use software may be restricted in any of several ways. A defined period of months or years, number of users or number of times a software program can be run, specific users, or nontransferability may be stipulated.

Exhibit 1.4 is a chart of the key terms often included in a software license agreement.

EXHIBIT 1.4 General Provisions in a Software License Agreement

Key Term	General Provisions
Grant of License	States the term and key restrictive elements of the right to use granted to the licensee by the licensor
Consideration	States the amount and terms of the license fee or royalty to be paid to the software supplier
Title to Materials	Provides that all rights, title, and interest in the software and documentation remain with the licensor Includes acknowledgment by the licensee that the software and documentation contain proprietary information of the licensor
Limitation on Use	Limits the software to internal use by the licensee, and may prohibit sublicensing, relicensing, and use in processing data for others for a fee Prohibits transferrability without approval of the licensor
Limited Warranty	Limits modification to eliminating errors (bugs) in the code Includes a specific warranty that the software does not infringe on any patents, copyrights, or trade secrets
Maintenance	Provides for modification to software to correct for errors during the warranty period Sometimes provides for update services to data content Sometimes provides for enhancements Sometimes provides for customer support services

Illustrative software license agreements are provided in Appendices 1-A and 1-B. They are provided only for illustration of how software licenses might be prepared to embody the previously described terms. It is not this contributing author's intent that they be used by any reader in commercial transactions. Software license agreements should be prepared with the advice of legal counsel.

(c) Channels of Distribution for Software Licenses

Software products are generally marketed through the following four channels of distribution.

(i) END USER LICENSING. The software developer provides and licenses the software directly to the end user.

(ii) RETAIL SALES. Most personal computer software is provided by the developer to wholesale or retail distributors, which include mail order companies, retail chains, independent computer dealers, and software stores, who are given the right to pass the license for the software to the end user.

(iii) VALUE-ADDED RESELLER (VAR) LICENSING. The software developer licenses a software program to another software vendor, giving the other vendor the right to relicense the software as part of a system marketed by the VAR that includes the licensed product. This type of arrangement is most common in the incorporation of utility programs into applications software.

(iv) ORIGINAL EQUIPMENT MANUFACTURER (OEM) LICENSING. The software developer licenses the software to a hardware supplier, giving the hardware supplier the right to relicense the software as part of a complete system that the hardware supplier provides to an end user.

(d) Postcontract Customer Support, or Maintenance

What has commonly been referred to in the software industry as "maintenance" has been renamed "postcontract customer support"

(PCS) in the AICPA Statement of Position (SOP) 91-1, *Software Revenue Recognition*. The contributing author believes that the word *maintenance* will continue to be used in the industry, perhaps more frequently than *postcontract customer support*. In this discussion, however, the contributing author will conform to using the new term suggested by the AICPA Task Force.

Postcontract customer support typically includes providing telephone or on-site support of the customer in the use of software, which includes "bug" fixing. Moreover, postcontract customer support often includes providing to customers ongoing product enhancements developed during the term of the postcontract customer support agreement that are far more than routine changes and additions, or updating for current information.

Postcontract customer support is an important source of revenue to software companies because it enables them to continue to derive a revenue stream from existing customers. To the extent that postcontract customer support relates to providing enhancements, software companies are in essence able to "relicense" their products annually to the same customers by simply providing them with an enhanced version of the product they have developed for licensing to new customers. To the extent that postcontract customer support relates to telephone and on site support, the postcontract support customers represent an established customer base for ongoing consulting services. The continuing revenue stream from postcontract customer support arrangements with existing customers can become of increasing importance as products mature and the number of possible new customers declines. At this point the pressure for development of enhancements is generated by existing customers as well as by the desire of the software company to sell to new customers.

Postcontract customer support arrangements cover a defined term, typically ranging from a few months to several years. Most postcontract customer support arrangements are for periods of 1 year, with the software company anticipating annual renewals. Postcontract customer support agreements are generally offered as separate contracts in conjunction with perpetual licenses and are sometimes bundled with limited-term software licenses.

Postcontract customer support arrangements are generally offered through the same channels of distribution as software licenses, which are described in the preceding section.

(e) Providing Software in Projects That Combine Software with Hardware or Services or Both

Some software companies market their software products by providing software to the end user in a "turnkey" package that includes the software and some or all of the following: hardware, installation and commissioning of the software and hardware, integration of the system with the end user's existing systems, and other services. An example of this type of contract is one by which a supplier of an accounting software package also provides the computer hardware, sets up the initial data base and processing, designs and facilitates reports generation, and implements a chart of accounts. Typically, the software company expects to make most of its margin or profit on the software element of the contract. Although other elements, such as hardware and services, are normally priced so as to generate some profit margin, they are usually small in comparison with the gross margin contemplated for the software element. Essentially, a combined contract can be viewed economically as another vehicle for transporting software from the shelf, into the marketplace, and onto the bottom line.

(f) Providing Software Development Services

Sometimes software companies enter into contracts to develop software for an end user. Where services of this type are performed, the software development activities and revenue generation overlap. A software company is often entitled to market the software it develops under a contract to others—this arrangement is typically called a "funded development" contract.

(g) Providing Services That Accompany Software Products

Providing software products to their customers affords software companies the opportunity to sell a great many related services, including installation, training, assistance in integration and implementation, and a host of other services. Although these are generally not large profit margin services, they can make a consistent contribution to a software company's operations. To some extent, such services provide incremental revenue that can, at least in part, be generated by personnel already on the company's payroll.

(h) Providing Services Using Software

Some software companies market their software by providing services in which they use the software for others. Examples are processing of data for others, through data-processing services, and consulting services utilizing specialized software.

APPENDIX 1-A

Illustration of Source Code License Agreement

This book is designed to provide accurate information in regard to the subject matter covered. It is sold with the understanding that neither the publisher nor the authors are providing legal, accounting, or other professional services to readers.

This appendix has been provided to illustrate situations and issues regarding the subject matter covered. Readers will find it informative about issues and contingencies that should be considered, but should consult with their own legal counsel before entering into any contract or business arrangement based on any perceptions derived from review of this illustrative form.

License Agreement

THIS AGREEMENT, made and entered into this _____ day of _____, 19____, by and between _____ (hereinafter "Supplier"), a corporation authorized and existing under the laws of the State of _____ and having its principal offices at _____, and _____ (hereinafter "User"), a corporation existing under the laws of the State of _____ and having its principal offices at _____:

WITNESSETH:

WHEREAS, Supplier desires to grant to User, and

WHEREAS User desires to license certain computer software as hereinafter defined, on the terms and conditions set forth in this Agreement;

NOW, THEREFORE, in consideration of the premises, and obligations made herein, the parties hereto agree as follows:

Section 1

DEFINITIONS

The following definitions shall apply when such terms are used in this Agreement, its exhibits, and any amendments.

1.1 **"Licensed Program."** The computer program including source code, object code and comments or procedural code designated by Supplier as [program], as further defined in Attachment A[not provided].

1.2 **"Licensed Documentation."** The system documentation and the user manuals, currently available from Supplier, for the Licensed Program as further defined in Attachment B[not provided].

1.3 **"Enhancements."** Changes or additions to the Licensed Program or Licensed Documentation that add significant new functions or substantially improved performance.

1.4 **"Errors."** Problems caused by an incorrect operation of the computer code in the Licensed Program or an incorrect statement or diagram in Licensed Documentation that produces incorrect results.

1.5 **"Maintenance Modifications."** Modifications or revisions to the Licensed Program or Licensed Documentation that correct Errors.

Section 2

GRANT OF LICENSE

2.1 **Scope of License.** Supplier hereby grants to User, in perpetuity unless otherwise terminated, a nonexclusive, nontransferrable license (without the right of sublicense), to:

   a. Install, use, and execute the Licensed Program on the computer(s) used by User at its facilities in the United States and as listed in Attachment C [not provided], and only in support of the internal business activities of User; and

   b. Use the Licensed Documentation only in conjunction with installation and use of the Licensed Program.

2.3 **Necessity for Third-Party Software.** User acknowledges that in order to be executed, the Licensed Program requires certain third-party software, described more fully in Attachment D [not provided].

Section 3

TITLE TO MATERIALS

3.1 **Title to Licensed Program and Licensed Documentation.** All rights, title, and interest in and to the Licensed Program and

Licensed Documentation are and shall remain with Supplier. User acknowledges that no such right, title, or interest in or to the Licensed Program and the Licensed Documentation is granted under this Agreement, and no such assertion shall be made by User. User is granted only a limited right of use of the Licensed Program and Licensed Documentation as set forth herein.

Section 4

ROYALTIES AND PAYMENTS

4.1 **License Fee.** In consideration of the licenses granted hereunder, User shall pay Supplier a one-time royalty in the amount of $_____.

4.2 **Payment.** The License Fee set forth in Section 4.1 hereof shall be paid by User within 30 days of Supplier's delivery of the Licensed Program and Licensed Documentation in accordance with the provisions of this Agreement.

4.3 **Taxes.** The License Fee specified in Section 4.1 hereof is exclusive of any federal, state, or local excise, sales, use, and similar taxes assessed or imposed with respect to the computer software licensed hereunder. User shall pay any such amounts upon request of Supplier accompanied by evidence of imposition of such taxes.

Section 5

PROPRIETARY PROTECTION OF MATERIALS

5.1 **Acknowledgment of Proprietary Materials; Limitations on Use.** User acknowledges that the Licensed Program and Licensed Documentation are unpublished works for purposes of federal copyright law and embody valuable confidential and secret information of Supplier, the development of which required the expenditure of considerable time and money by Supplier.

User shall treat the Licensed Programs and Licensed Documentation in confidence and shall not use, copy, or disclose, nor permit any of its personnel to use, copy, or disclose the same for any purpose other than that which is specifically authorized under this Agreement.

5.2 **Secure Handling.** Except for copies of the Licensed Program installed and operated upon its computers as permitted hereunder, User shall require that the Licensed Program and Licensed Documentation be maintained in a manner so as to reasonably preclude unauthorized persons from having access.

5.3 **Proprietary Legends.** User shall not permit any personnel of User to remove any proprietary or other legend or restrictive notice contained or included in any material provided by Supplier, and User shall not permit User personnel to reproduce or copy any such material except as specifically authorized hereunder.

5.4 **User's Obligations Respecting Access.** User shall limit use of and access to the Licensed Program and Licensed Documentation to such personnel of User as are directly involved in the issue thereof by User, and User shall prevent all User personnel from having access to any such information that is not required in the performance of their duties for User.

5.6 **Technical Protections.** Supplier may from time to time prescribe password protection as an additional security measure for the Licensed Program, and User shall cooperate with Supplier with the installation thereof.

5.8 **Survival of Terms.** The provisions of this Section 5 shall survive termination of this Agreement for any reason.

Section 6

LIMITED WARRANTY, LIMITATION OF LIABILITY, AND INDEMNITY

6.1 **Limited Warranty Against Infringement.** Supplier warrants that the Licensed Program and Licensed Documentation as delivered to User do not infringe any third-party rights in patent, copyright, or trade secret in the United States.

6.2 Limited Warranty of Conformity to Specifications. Supplier warrants, for the benefit only of User, that for a period of one year after delivery to User of the Licensed Program, the Licensed Program shall conform in all material respects to the Specifications (except for modifications made by User or by Supplier at the request of User). Supplier assumes no responsibility for obsolescence of the Licensed Program.

6.3 Exclusive Remedy. As the exclusive remedy of User for any nonconformity or defect constituting an Error in the Licensed Program for which Supplier is responsible, Supplier shall use commercially reasonable efforts to provide Maintenance Modifications with respect to such Error. However, Supplier shall not be obligated to correct, cure, or otherwise remedy any Error in the Licensed Program resulting from any (1) modification of the Licensed Program by User, (2) misuse or damage of the Licensed Program other than by personnel of Supplier, or (3) failure of User to notify Supplier of the existence and nature of such nonconformity or defect promptly upon its discovery.

6.4 Disclaimer. EXCEPT AS SPECIFICALLY SET FORTH HEREIN, SUPPLIER MAKES NO WARRANTIES, WHETHER EXPRESS OR IMPLIED, REGARDING OR RELATING TO THE LICENSED PROGRAM OR LICENSED DOCUMENTATION OR TO ANY OTHER MATERIALS FURNISHED OR PROVIDED TO USER HEREUNDER. SUPPLIER SPECIFICALLY DISCLAIMS ALL IMPLIED WARRANTIES OF MERCHANTABILITY AND FITNESS FOR A PARTICULAR PURPOSE WITH RESPECT TO SAID MATERIALS OR THE USE THEREOF.

6.5 Limitation of Liability. Except with respect to liability arising from claims of infringement of third-party rights in the United States in copyright, trade secret, or patent, in no event shall Supplier be liable under any claim, demand, or action arising out of or relating to its performance or lack thereof under this Agreement for any special, indirect, incidental, exemplary, or consequential damages, whether or not Supplier has been advised of the possibility of such claim, demand, or action.

6.6 **User Indemnification.** User shall and does hereby agree to indemnify, hold harmless, and save Supplier from liability against any claim, demand, loss, or action (1) resulting from User's use or modification of the Licensed Program and Licensed Documentation and (2) alleging that any Maintenance Modifications made by User infringe any third-party rights in the United States respecting copyright, trade secret, or patent. The foregoing indemnification is predicated upon Supplier (1) fully cooperating with User in the defense or settlement or such actions and (2) giving User prompt written notice of any claim, demand, or action for which indemnification is sought.

6.7 **Supplier Indemnification.** Supplier shall and does hereby agree to indemnify, hold harmless, and save User from liability against any claim, demand, loss, or action alleging that the Licensed Program and Licensed Documentation or any Maintenance Modifications or Enhancements made by Supplier infringe any third-party rights in the United States respecting copyright, trade secret, or patent. The foregoing indemnification is predicated upon User fully cooperating with Supplier in the defense or settlement of such actions and User providing Supplier with prompt written notice of any claim, demand, or action for which indemnification is sought.

Section 7

TERM AND TERMINATION

7.1 **Term.** This Agreement shall commence on the date and year first above written and shall continue until terminated in accordance with the terms thereof.

7.2 **Termination by User.** User may terminate this Agreement at any time upon written notice to Supplier.

7.3 Termination by Either Party. Either party may terminate this Agreement upon 30 days' written notice to the other party if the other party commits a breach of any term hereof and fails to cure said breach within the 30-day period. Such notice shall set forth the basis of the termination.

7.4 Actions upon Termination. Upon termination of this Agreement for any reason, User shall immediately cease use of, and return immediately to Supplier, all copies or portions of copies of the Licensed Program and Licensed Documentation.

Section 8

MISCELLANEOUS

8.1 Entire Agreement. The provisions herein constitute the entire agreement between the parties with respect to the subject matter hereof and supersede all prior agreements, oral or written, relating to the subject matter of this agreement. No amendment or modification of any provision of this Agreement will be effective unless such is in writing and is executed by both parties hereto.

8.2 No Assignment. User shall not sell, transfer, assign, or subcontract any right or obligation hereunder without the prior written consent of Supplier.

8.3 Force Majeure. Excepting provisions of this Agreement relating to payment of royalties and protection of Supplier's Proprietary Information, neither party shall be in default of the terms hereof if such action is due to a natural calamity, act of government, or similar causes beyond the control of such party.

8.4 Governing Law. The validity and performance of this Agreement shall be governed by the laws of the State of _____.

8.5 Severability. If any provision of this Agreement is held by a court of competent jurisdiction to be contrary to law, the remaining provisions of this Agreement will remain in full force and effect.

8.6 **Notice.** Any notice required by either party under this Agreement shall be made in writing and delivered by hand or by certified mail, postage prepaid, addressed as first set forth above or to such other address as either party shall designate by written notice provided to the other party.

IN WITNESS WHEREOF, the parties have caused this Agreement to be executed as set forth below.

[Supplier]   [User]

By: _____   By: _____

Title: _____   Title: _____

Date: _____, 19____   Date: _____, 19____

Illustration of "Shrink-Wrap" License Agreement

This book is designed to provide accurate information in regard to the subject matter covered. It is sold with the understanding that neither the publisher nor the authors are providing legal, accounting, or other professional services to the readers.

This appendix has been provided to illustrate situations and issues regarding the subject matter covered. Readers will find it informative about issues and contingencies that should be considered, but should consult with their own legal counsel before entering into any contract or business arrangement based on any perceptions derived from review of this illustrative form.

LICENSE AGREEMENT

"Shrink-Wrap"
STOP!
READ THIS BEFORE YOU OPEN THIS PACKAGE!

READ THE TERMS AND CONDITIONS OF THIS LICENSE AGREEMENT CAREFULLY BEFORE OPENING THE PACKAGE CONTAINING THE PROGRAM DISKS AND THE ACCOMPANYING USER DOCUMENTATION. OPENING THIS PACKAGE INDICATES YOUR ACCEPTANCE OF THESE TERMS AND CONDITIONS.

THIS LICENSE AGREEMENT REPRESENTS THE ENTIRE AGREEMENT CONCERNING THE PROGRAM BETWEEN YOU AND _____ (REFERRED TO AS LICENSOR), AND IT SUPERSEDES ANY PRIOR PROPOSAL, REPRESENTATION, OR UNDERSTANDING BETWEEN THE PARTIES. IF YOU DO NOT ACCEPT AND AGREE TO THE TERMS OF THIS LICENSEE AGREEMENT, YOU SHOULD PROMPTLY RETURN THE UNOPENED DISK PACKAGE AND ALL ACCOMPANYING DOCUMENTATION TO THE PLACE WHERE YOU OBTAINED THEM FOR A REFUND OF YOUR MONEY. NO REFUNDS WILL BE GIVEN FOR RETURNS THAT HAVE AN OPENED DISK PACKAGE OR MISSING DOCUMENTATION.

   1. **License Grant**. Licensor hereby grants to you, and you accept, a nonexclusive, nontransferable license to use the computer software Program and the accompanying user Documentation only on a single computer owned, leased, or otherwise controlled by you; or in the event of the inoperability of that computer, on a backup computer selected by you. You agree that you will not assign, sublicense, transfer, pledge, lease, rent, or share your rights under this License Agreement.

   Upon loading the Program into your computer, you may retain the Program Disks for backup purposes. In addition, you may make one copy of the Program on a second set of diskettes solely for the purpose of backup in the event that the Program Disks are damaged or destroyed. You must reproduce and include the copyright notice on the backup copy. Except as authorized under this paragraph, no copies of the Program may be made by you or any person under your authority or control.

2. **Licensor's Rights**. You acknowledge and agree that the Program consists of proprietary, unpublished products of Licensor, protected under U.S. copyright law and trade secret laws of general applicability. You further acknowledge and agree that all rights, title, and interest in and to the Program are and shall remain with Licensor.

3. **Term**. This License Agreement is effective upon your opening of this package and shall continue until terminated. Licensor my terminate this License Agreement upon the breach by you of any term or condition hereof. Upon such termination by Licensor, you agree to return to Licensor the Program, Documentation and all copies end portions thereof.

4. **Limited Warranty**. Licensor warrants, for your benefit alone, that under normal use the Program Disks in which the computer software Program is embedded and the User's Manual shall, for a period of 90 days from the date of commencement of this License Agreement (referred to as the Warranty Period), be free from defects in material and workmanship.

Licensor further warrants, for your benefit alone, that during the Warranty Period the Program shall operate substantially in accordance with the specifications in the User's Manual, provided that the Program is properly used on the machine for which it was designed. If, during the Warranty Period, a defect in the Program Disks or User's Manual appears, You lay return the defective item to Licensor for either replacement or, if so elected by Licensor, refund of the amount paid by you under this License Agreement. You agree that the foregoing constitutes your sole and exclusive remedy for breach by Licensor of any warranties made under this Agreement.

Licensor does not warrant that the function contained in the Program will meet your requirements or that the operation of the Program will be uninterrupted or error free or will function properly in every hardware environment.

EXCEPT FOR THE WARRANTIES SET FORTH ABOVE, THE USER'S MANUAL AND PROGRAM DISKS, AND THE SOFT-

WARE CONTAINED THEREIN, ARE LICENSED "AS IS," AND LICENSOR DISCLAIMS ANY AND ALL OTHER WARRANTIES, WHETHER EXPRESS OR IMPLIED, INCLUDING (WITHOUT LIMITATION) ANY IMPLIED WARRANTIES OF MERCHANT-ABILITY OR FITNESS FOR A PARTICULAR PURPOSE.

SOME STATES DO NOT ALLOW THE EXCLUSION OF IMPLIED WARRANTIES, SO THE ABOVE EXCLUSION MAY NOT APPLY TO YOU. THIS WARRANTY GIVES YOU SPECIFIC LEGAL RIGHTS, AND YOU MAY ALSO HAVE OTHER RIGHTS WHICH VARY FROM STATE TO STATE.

5. **Limitation of Remedies**. Licensor's cumulative liability and your exclusive remedy for any loss or damages resulting from any claims, demands, or actions arising out of or relating to this Agreement shall be limited to replacement of any defective item, subject to Licensor's Limited Warranty, or refund of the license fee paid to Licensor by you for the use of the Program. In no event shall Licensor be liable for any indirect, incidental, consequential, special, or exemplary damages or lost profits, even if Licensor has been advised of the possibility of such damages.

SOME STATES DO NOT ALLOW THE LIMITATION OR EXCLU-SION OF LIABILITY FOR INCIDENTAL OR CONSEQUENTIAL DAMAGES, SO THE ABOVE LIMITATION OR EXCLUSION MAY NOT APPLY TO YOU.

6. **Trademark**. _____ is a registered trademark of Licensor. No right, license, or interest to such trademark is granted hereunder, and you agree that no such right, license, or interest shall be asserted by you with respect to such trademark.

7. **Governing Law**. This License Agreement is governed by the laws of the State of _____.

Illustration of Postcontract Customer Support Agreement

This book is designed to provide accurate information in regard to the subject matter covered. It is sold with the understanding that neither the publisher nor the authors are providing legal, accounting, or other professional services to the readers.

This appendix has been provided to illustrate situations and issues regarding the subject matter covered. Readers will find it informative about issues and contingencies that should be considered, but should consult with their own legal counsel before entering into any contract or business arrangement based on any perceptions derived from review of this illustrative form.

SUPPORT AGREEMENT

This Support Agreement ("this Agreement") is made and entered into this _____ day of _____, 199__, by and between _____ (hereinafter "Vendor"), a corporation with principal offices at _____, and _____ (hereinafter "User"), a corporation with principal offices at _____.

WITNESSETH:

WHEREAS, Vendor and User entered into a license (the "License") to use certain computer software and related user documentation (the "Licensed Program") on certain terms and conditions;

WHEREAS, Vendor desires to offer User certain services with respect to the Licensed Program on the terms and conditions set forth herein;

NOW THEREFORE, in consideration of the premises hereof, the parties intending to be legally bound, hereby agree as follows:

Section 1

DEFINITIONS

For the purpose of this Agreement, the following definitions shall apply to the respective capitalized terms:

1.1 **"Licensed Program."** The computer software described in Exhibit A hereto [not provided].

1.2 **"Agreement Term."** An initial period of _____ year(s), commencing on the first day following the warranty period that applies to the Licensed Program. Thereafter, the Agreement Term shall automatically renew for successive periods of one year each unless otherwise terminated.

1.3 **"Error Correction."** Either a software modification or addition that, when made or added to the Licensed Program, establishes material conformity of the Licensed Program to the functional specifications.

1.4 **"Enhancement."** Any modification or addition that, when made or added to the Licensed Program, materially changes its functional capability.

1.5 **"Normal Working Hours."** The hours between _____ A.M. and _____ P.M. on the days _____ through _____, excluding regularly scheduled holidays of Vendor.

1.6 **"Releases."** New versions of the Licensed Program, which new versions may include both Error Corrections and Enhancements.

Section 2

SCOPE OF SERVICES

2.1 During the Agreement Term, Vendor shall render the following services in support of the Licensed Program, during Normal Working Hours, subject to the compensation fixed for each type of service in Vendor's rate schedule provided in Exhibit B [not provided].

a. Vendor shall maintain a facility capable of receiving computer-generated reports, and by telephone or network transmission, user reports of system problems.

b. Vendor shall be responsible for using all reasonable diligence in correcting verifiable and reproducible Errors when reported to Vendor in accordance with Vendor's standard reporting procedures. Following completion of the Error Correction, Vendor shall provide the Error Correction operating instructions to implement the Error Correction.

c. Vendor shall consider and evaluate the development of Enhancements for the specific use of User and shall respond to User's requests for additional services pertaining to the Licensed Program, provided that such assistance shall be subject to supplemental charges.

Section 3

FEES AND CHARGES

3.1 User shall pay Vendor its fees and charges based on the rate schedule and timeliness set forth in Exhibit B [not provided).

3.2 User shall reimburse Vendor for travel expenses (i.e., transportation, lodging, and meals) and telephone expenses incurred by Vendor in providing services to User.

3.3 User shall be responsible for procuring, installing, and maintaining all equipment, communication interfaces, and other hardware necessary to operate the Licensed Software and to obtain from Vendor the services called for by this Agreement.

Section 4

DISCLAIMER WARRANTY AND LIMITATION OF LIABILITY

4.1 EXCEPT AS EXPRESSLY SET FORTH IN THIS AGREEMENT, VENDOR EXPRESSLY DISCLAIMS ANY AND ALL WARRANTIES CONCERNING THE LICENSED PROGRAM OR THE SERVICES TO BE RENDERED HEREUNDER, WHETHER EXPRESS OR IMPLIED, INCLUDING (WITHOUT LIMITATION) ANY WARRANTY OF MERCHANTABILITY OR FITNESS FOR A PARTICULAR PURPOSE.

4.2 In no event shall Vendor be liable for any loss of profit, indirect, special, incidental, or consequential damages, even if Vendor has notice of the possibility of such damages.

4.3 Vendor's liability, if any, for damages (including but not limited to liability arising out of contract, tort, or patent or copyright infringement) shall be limited to the greater of $_____ or the charges which would be due for twelve months of Licensed Program services hereunder, for the specific License Program that is directly related to User's cause of action. This limitation shall not apply to personal injury or tangible personal property claims caused solely by Vendor's negligence.

Section 5

TERMINATION

5.1 This Agreement may be terminated as follows:

a. This Agreement shall immediately terminate upon the termination of the License.

b. This Agreement may be terminated by either party upon the expiration of the then-current term of this Agreement, provided that at least _____ days' prior written notice of intention to terminate is given prior to the end of the then-current term.

c. This Agreement nay be terminated by either party upon _____ days' prior written notice if the other party has materially breached the provisions of this Agreement and has not cured such breach within such notice period.

Section 6

MISCELLANEOUS

6.1 This Agreement is governed by the laws of the State of

_____.

6.2 In the event that any provision of this Agreement is held invalid, the remaining provisions shall be enforced to the maximum extent permitted by applicable law.

6.3 Neither party may assign its rights or duties under this Agreement without the prior written consent of the other party, except to a successor of all or substantially all of its businesses and properties.

6.4 This Agreement constitutes the entire contract between the parties and supersedes all existing agreements between them, whether oral or written, with respect to the subject matter hereof. No change, modification, or amendment of this Agreement shall be of any effect unless in writing and signed by both parties.

6.5 The failure by either party to enforce any term or condition of this Agreement shall not be deemed to constitute a waiver thereof nor of any further or additional right that such party may hold under this Agreement.

IN WITNESS WHEREOF, the parties have caused this Agreement to be executed by their duly authorized representatives as set forth below.

[Vendor]   [User]

By: _____   By: _____

Title: _____   Title: _____

Date: _____, 19___   Date: _____, 19___

CHAPTER TWO

The AICPA Task Force on Accounting for the Development and Sale of Computer Software

Francis J. O'Brien
Ernst & Young

2.1 BACKGROUND

(a) Historical Perspective

The events that led to the formation and work of the AICPA Task Force on Accounting for the Development and Sale of Computer Software can be traced back to about 1969 when International Business Machines Corporation (IBM) began unbundling, or charging separate prices for hardware and software. IBM also began charging separate prices for other computer hardware and software related services such as systems engineering and education. Until that time, computer hardware vendors generally provided their customers with software along with the hardware.

(b) FASB Statement No. 2

The software industry was still quite young in 1974 when the FASB issued FASB Statement No. 2, *Accounting for Research and Development Costs*. Respondents to the exposure draft of Statement 2 raised the question of whether development of computer software was within the definition of research and development costs contemplated in the

The views expressed in this chapter reflect those of the individual author and do not necessarily represent those of the other contributing authors.

FASB project. In paragraph 31 of the Basis for Conclusions section of Statement 2, the FASB held that whether certain activities should be defined as research and development had to be evaluated in terms of the guidelines of Statement 2, and went on to say

> Efforts to develop a new or higher level of computer software capability for sale (but not under a contractual arrangement) would be a research and development activity encompassed by this Statement.
> —FASB Statement No. 2, paragraph 31

The predominant practice of software companies after the issuance of Statement 2 was to expense costs of developing software products as incurred, either identifying them as research and development costs or simply expensing them because that was the common industry practice.

Questions about application of Statement 2 in the software industry persisted, and some objected to expensing of all software development costs. In February 1975 the FASB issued FASB Interpretation No. 6, *Applicability of FASB Statement No. 2 to Computer Software*, which was generally interpreted to exclude certain software product enhancements from the definition of research and development costs in Statement 2. In 1976 the Association of Data Processing Service Organizations (ADAPSO*), a leading industry organization, requested the FASB to reassess Statement 2 as applied to software development costs, and met with the FASB in 1978. In 1979 the FASB decided not to undertake the requested project, but did state in FASB Technical Bulletin No. 79-2, *Computer Software Costs*, that not all costs incurred in developing software products or processes are necessarily research and development costs.

In the meantime, the software industry grew rapidly. Other than the pronouncements just discussed, it had no specific accounting literature to provide guidance on the two most significant items impacting

---

*ADAPSO changed its name to Information Technology Association of America (ITAA) in November 1991.

measurement of financial performance of software companies—revenue recognition and software development costs. As often happens when unique industries develop without specific accounting guidance, a diversity of accounting practices developed.

(c) ADAPSO Exposure Draft

In 1982 ADAPSO issued an exposure draft, *Accounting Guidelines for the Computer Services Industry*. It discussed revenue recognition and software development costs, with the objective of encouraging its membership and others to adopt consistent accounting practices to enable reasonable comparison between software companies. Although many supported ADAPSO's objective, respondents from the accounting profession generally believed that some of ADAPSO's views on accounting practices that should be used in the industry were not in conformity with existing generally accepted accounting principles and they maintained that the setting of standards should be left to the FASB.

(d) Formation of the AICPA Task Force

Despite the somewhat negative response to the ADAPSO exposure draft, it contributed to the formation of a joint Task Force of the AICPA Accounting Standards Executive Committee (AcSEC), ADAPSO, and the National Association of Accountants (NAA), to address issues of accounting for software. The Task Force initially consisted of three members from the accounting profession, three from ADAPSO, and one from the NAA. Accounting profession members were Joseph D. Lhotka, chairman, James I. Gillespie, and the contributing author. ADAPSO members were James R. Porter, who had been patiently pursuing the issues with the FASB for years, William M. Graves, and Lawrence J. Schoenberg. Messrs. Porter and Graves were later succeeded by Paul K. Wilde and I. Sigmund Mosely, Jr. Penelope A. Flugger was the original NAA member. After several changes, the NAA position was replaced with a fourth representative of the accounting profession, Naomi S. Erickson.

All members of the Task Force had insight into the accounting issues facing the software industry. Although they held differing ideas about the right accounting answers, all approached the issues with open minds. A common thread was that none of the members was predisposed against capitalization of software development costs. The Task Force held its first meeting in late 1982.

2.2 CAPITALIZATION OF SOFTWARE DEVELOPMENT COSTS

(a) Acceleration of Addressing the Capitalization Issue

Shortly after the formation of the Task Force, the staff of the Securities and Exchange Commission (SEC) began to consider placing a moratorium on capitalization of software development costs by public companies. The Task Force then decided to split its work in software accounting into two parts—capitalization of software development costs and revenue recognition—and to accelerate its work on capitalization of costs. It decided to defer work on software revenue recognition until the first part of the project was completed. The long-term objective of the Task Force was to prepare an issues paper for each part of the project and to provide them to the FASB in order to stimulate projects leading to the development and issuance of appropriate accounting standards. It was planned that the issues papers would trace the background and history of each relevant accounting issue, analyze relevant existing accounting literature, study and describe the process of designing, developing, and marketing software, and present the recommendation of the Task Force and AcSEC.

(b) SEC Moratorium on Capitalization of Software Development Costs

In April 1983 the SEC proposed to prohibit capitalization of internal costs of developing computer software for marketing to others by public companies that had not previously disclosed that practice. The proposal was adopted in August 1983, as SEC Financial Reporting Release No. 12, and the SEC stated that it would be automatically rescinded upon the issuance of guidance on the subject by the FASB. The SEC was concerned about increasing diversity in accounting for software development costs, and about the capitalization of significant amounts by an increasing number of companies. Because it was anticipated that this issue would be addressed by the Task Force, AcSEC, and, ultimately, the FASB, the SEC concluded that it did not need to develop definitive accounting guidelines in view of the pending actions by the other groups.

(c) Issues Paper on Capitalization of Software Development Costs

The Task Force prepared an Issues Paper, *Accounting for the Costs of Software for Sale or Lease*, which addressed the following questions:

- Can some costs of producing computer software for sale or lease be capitalized as an asset?

- If so, which costs are they?

- How does one assess the recoverability of capitalized costs?

The Task Force quickly concluded that some capitalization of software development costs was appropriate; however, the Task Force perceived the need to be conceptually consistent with Statement 2, which requires that research and development costs be charged to expense as incurred.

The Task Force concluded that technological, market, and financial feasibility should be established before any software development costs are capitalized. This would include completing all product planning and design activities and solving any high-risk technological issues. Costs incurred after those criteria were met, including the cost of a detail program design, coding, testing, and packaging, would be capitalized if recovery of the costs was probable. Capitalized costs would be subject to a recoverability assessment under FASB Statement No. 5, *Accounting for Contingencies*, and no specific new literature for the assessment of recoverability was considered necessary by the Task Force.

In February 1984 the Issues Paper was unanimously approved by AcSEC and sent to the FASB, which added a project on capitalization of software development costs to its agenda the next month.

(d) Exposure Draft of the FASB Statement

The FASB undertook a complete examination of the issues and the conclusions reached by the Task Force and AcSEC, and generally agreed with those conclusions except in one significant respect. The FASB concluded that costs of producing a detailed program design should be accounted for as research and development costs. Several other differing conclusions of lesser importance were also reached by the FASB. The FASB expanded the scope of the project to include software purchased for marketing to others. It also decided to be more specific about the ongoing assessment of recoverability of capitalized software costs by requiring a net realizable value test as normally applied to inventories. The FASB met with the Task Force several times while developing its exposure draft to review the software development process, and issued the exposure draft in August 1984.

(e) Response to the FASB Exposure Draft

The FASB received 210 letters of comment on its exposure draft, many of which disagreed with the FASB's conclusions. As a result of these letters, the FASB convened two educational meetings with industry representatives in March and April 1985 and held public hearings in May 1985. The following three primary points of view emerged.

1. Support for the exposure draft as written
2. Support for the exposure draft as written, with modification to include the costs of detail program design in capitalizable costs
3. Support for expensing all software development costs as incurred

The FASB was faced with a difficult task, partly because no one group appeared to express a uniform view. Software companies, industry organizations, the investment community, and accounting firms were all divided. Those preferring expensing all software development costs used some of the same arguments as those preferring capitalization, both citing improvement in comparability and better industry access to capital markets. At the FASB hearings there was discussion of cost-benefit considerations, and whether the exposure draft was so subjective that it would, in effect, create an optional standard that could be manipulated by maintaining or not maintaining required documentation. Whether the costs of detailed program design work should be capitalized or expensed was also a primary discussion point at the public hearings.

After the public hearings, the FASB board members appeared to be split. Three board members preferred the AcSEC recommendations; three preferred a hybrid method under which capitalization would begin when a detail program design was completed or when a working model of the software product was completed, whichever was earlier; and one preferred expensing all costs of software development.

(f) Issuance of FASB Statement No. 86

After further work, in August 1985 the FASB issued FASB Statement No. 86, *Accounting for the Costs of Computer Software to be Sold, Leased, or Otherwise Marketed*. Its conclusions are understandable in light of the different views of the board members following the public hearings, as well as the FASB's conclusion that objective evidence of technological feasibility must be available before the research and development phase can be considered complete and the production phase to have begun. The FASB concluded that completion of a detail program design was the earliest point at which technological feasibility could be considered established for capitalization purposes. They allowed for use of an alternative criterion of technological feasibility—the completion of a working model, if a detail program design is not used in the software development process. Other provisions of Statement 86 relating to purchased software, amortization of capitalized costs, software inventory costs, and the continuing evaluation of capitalized costs, differed in some respects from AcSEC's recommendations and the FASB exposure draft. The differences, however, were not considered significant or controversial.

(g) Retrospective

Little has happened on the subject of software capitalization since the issuance of Statement 86. The FASB's Emerging Issues Task Force (EITF) addressed a few transition and implementation issues in EITF Issue No. 85-35. The FASB staff, in a Status Report publication, provided some unofficial guidance in question-and-answer format. One could interpret the low level of official activity in regard to software capitalization to mean that there has not been much difficulty in applying Statement 86 in practice; however, that is not the case. The degree to which software development costs have been capitalized varies substantially among companies, and some believe the differences are attributable in part to how much of the costs a company wants to capitalize, rather than to different circumstances.

The software industry has continued to develop, and there have been changes in the software development process since the publication of Statement 86 in 1985. The principal change in the software industry that impacts accounting results under Statement 86 is that use of a detail program design as an explicit step in the software development process is becoming less common. This trend stems from advances in software development tools and, to a lesser degree, from the evolution of methodology in the software development and production process. As a result, an increasing number of companies are unable to capitalize the major portion of their software production costs unless they unnecessarily add a detail program design to the development process.

To the extent that there have been changes in the software development process, some provisions of Statement 86 may be less relevant today than when it was published. Although at some time there may be a need to revisit the conclusions and provisions of Statement 86, this author does not perceive any enthusiasm in the standard-setting community to do so at this time.

2.3 SOFTWARE REVENUE RECOGNITION

(a) Issues Paper on Software Revenue Recognition

The AICPA Task Force expected that addressing software revenue recognition issues would be more difficult than addressing capitalization of software development costs. Most software companies had not capitalized software development costs before the publication of Statement 86, and the issue for them was only to what extent to capitalize in the future. In contrast, all software companies were recognizing revenue on a basis with which they were comfortable, and narrowing the alternatives would significantly affect many of them. For example, software companies were recognizing software license revenue upon contract signing, delivery, installation, acceptance, or payment, and some were recognizing portions of the revenue on a software license at several of those points. Although the AICPA Task Force had little difficulty in agreeing that capitalization of software development costs was appropriate, it was initially deeply divided on several basic revenue recognition issues. Because of the necessity to resolve these differing views and because of other delays, it took more than 6 years to deal with software revenue recognition, as compared with less than 3 years to deal with capitalization.

The AICPA Task Force organized the project by dividing issues into the following categories.

1. The point at which revenue should be recognized in a transaction involving only a software license—contract signing, delivery, or some other point

2. The effect of obligations other than delivery of the software, and whether it makes a difference if they are insignificant or significant

3. Pricing terms of licenses with non-end users

4. Contract accounting issues

5. Postdelivery customer-support services (i.e., "maintenance")

6. Data services companies

Many in the industry believed that using a matching concept justified recognition of software license revenue at contract signing. They believed that delivery of software that is available is incidental to the earnings process and that essentially all the significant costs related to the transaction, ranging from software development to marketing, had been incurred and generally expensed prior to contract signing. They did not believe that the limited capitalization of software development costs under Statement 86 provided much relief in this regard. Others believed that delivery of software should be required prior to revenue recognition, as in the requirements under generally accepted accounting principles for product sales.

Moreover, many in the industry believed that most of the costs of maintenance were either incurred prior to a maintenance agreement or were sufficiently insignificant when measured incrementally, and that maintenance revenue should be recognized at the inception of the term of the maintenance agreement. Others believed that maintenance obligations were principally discharged over a period of time and that no accounting other than amortization of maintenance revenue over the maintenance period was justified.

The AICPA Task Force started work on the revenue recognition issues immediately after completion of its work on capitalization of software development costs. The Task Force met with AcSEC in October 1985 and again in February 1986. After considerable discussion among Task Force members, and with AcSEC, the following majority views of the Task Force emerged:

1. Software license revenue should be recognized on delivery.

2. Software license revenue should not be recognized on delivery if significant vendor obligations remain.

3. Nonrefundable fixed fees should be recognized as revenue immediately for software licenses to reproduce and distribute copies, even if a license is for limited quantities or for limited periods of time.

4. Contract segmentation criteria required by the AICPA Statement of Position 81-1, *Accounting for Performance of Construction-Type and Certain Production-Type Contracts*, should be modified for software companies because of unique factors in the industry.

5. Maintenance revenue should be deferred and recognized over the maintenance period.

AcSEC accepted the views of the Task Force, although not unanimously, and voted at the September 1986 AcSEC meeting to forward the proposed Issues Paper, *Software Revenue Recognition*, to the FASB. At that point, however, the project ran into a delay. There was considerable debate at that time about whether "advisory conclusions" of

AcSEC should be included in AICPA issues papers, and, as drafted, the software revenue recognition issues paper included advisory conclusions. The concern with advisory conclusions was that the FASB believed that issues papers published with AcSEC's advisory conclusions might inappropriately influence practice. It took until April 1987 for this situation to be sufficiently resolved that the Issues Paper could be sent to the FASB, with advisory conclusions and a request that the FASB undertake a project on software revenue recognition.

(b) FASB Reaction to the Issues Paper

In February 1988 the FASB concluded that it would not undertake a project on software revenue recognition. In part, the decision was based on the FASB's general preference to address broad issues that affect many or all industries, rather than a topic as narrow as revenue recognition in one industry. The possibility of a broad project on revenue recognition in general is often discussed when new projects are considered at the FASB, with the observation that it could be an enormous project.

The FASB encouraged the AICPA to develop industry guidance for software revenue recognition, similar to the practice guidance the AICPA has provided for other industries in its statements of position and accounting and audit guides. FASB members offered informal comments about the Issues Paper. It appeared that the general direction of the advisory conclusions was endorsed; the only major objection was that the FASB board members disagreed with modification of contract segmentation criteria for software companies.

(c) Preparation of Statement of Position No. 91-1

The Task Force initially believed that preparing a statement of position based on the Issues Paper would be a straightforward effort, requiring only conversion from the "issues and conclusions" format of an issues paper to the plain text format used in statements of position. The preparation of SOP 91-1 was far more complex and tedious than anyone imagined it could be.

First, the conclusions in the Issues Paper were stated in broad terms. They needed to be completely rewritten to make them operational and precise enough to be usable by software companies in a consistent manner.

Second, the Task Force decided it needed to reexamine the definition of *significant vendor obligations other than delivery of software* and to give more guidance on how to account when significant vendor obligations are present. The Issues Paper contained numeric criteria as to significance, which the Task Force concluded had been useful in defining the issues but could not be used to describe the way in which a broad spectrum of transactions should be accounted for. It was also decided that accounting for service transactions that are separable from software licenses should be addressed, and these were not discussed in the Issues Paper at all.

Third, considerable difficulty was encountered in providing coherent guidance for contract accounting by software companies. The principal advisory conclusions in the Issues Paper were that software companies should generally use the percentage-of-completion method, and that the contract segmentation criteria included in SOP 81-1 should be modified for software companies. Although both AcSEC and the Task Force believed that modification of the contract segmentation criteria was appropriate, based on the unofficial reactions of the FASB board members to the Issues Paper, there was concern that the FASB would ultimately object to this proposal. The concern was well founded, as the FASB ultimately did object. Because of this concern, the Task Force expended considerable effort in analyzing alternatives, available within the boundaries of SOP 81-1, to the use of both input and output measures of progress-to-completion. The Task Force concluded that use of output measures would give software companies some relief from the distortion caused by the inability of most of them to meet SOP 81-1's criteria for segmentation. Software companies would need guidance in the use of output measures to apply them in practice. Because there was very little existing literature on the use of output measures, the Task Force was in some respects charting new ground, although it entirely based its effort on the fundamental ideas of SOP 81-1.

Fourth, the Task Force revisited its conclusions on accounting for maintenance, reviewing in particular the question of whether initial year maintenance bundled with a software license needed to be unbundled for accounting purposes. Some were concerned with the practicality of unbundling, and others believed that the cost of unbundling was not worth the benefit.

Finally, the issue concerning accounting for data service companies was dropped from the scope of the project. The topic had been included in the Issues Paper because it had been included in the 1982 ADAPSO exposure draft. The Task Force concluded, however, that its membership did not have sufficient expertise to deal with the issue, and dropped it rather than delay the project.

After much work, the Task Force resolved these issues to its satisfaction, and in September 1989 AcSEC voted to expose a proposed SOP for public comment after clearance by the FASB.

During the long process of preparing the SOP, certain FASB staff members periodically met with members of the Task Force as observers and to assist in informal discussions, particularly at meetings of the drafting committee of the Task Force held to review and discuss the developing sections of the draft SOP.

Throughout the entire process of developing the draft SOP, the Task Force also received input from the SEC staff, which had observed several practices it believed should be addressed in the SOP. In late 1988 the SEC staff provided a letter to the Task Force, and the Task Force believed it had appropriately addressed all the issues raised in the letter. However, in late 1989, the Task Force received another letter from the SEC staff, which raised several new issues, as well as additional comments about some of the issues raised in the previous letter. Generally, these areas of concern related to the need for several clarifications to avoid ambiguities and misinterpretation, distinguishing between significant and insignificant other vendor obligations, and measurement of progress-to-completion under contract accounting. In addition, the SEC staff disagreed with the Task Force's recommendation to modify the contract segmentation criteria of SOP 81-1 for software companies.

The Task Force generally agreed with the SEC staff's comments and made changes in the draft SOP to accommodate them, except for those concerning the proposal for modified contract segmentation criteria.

(d) FASB Review of the Draft Proposed SOP

The draft of a proposed SOP, *Software Revenue Recognition*, was finally sent to the FASB in August 1990 for clearance before exposure for public comment. At an open meeting of the FASB on November 14, 1990, the FASB advised that it would not object to the public exposure of the draft SOP if the proposal for modified contract segmentation criteria was deleted. The FASB reiterated its unofficial comment, previously made in respect to the Issues Paper, that it believed contract segmentation criteria should be applied uniformly in all industries. The Task Force disagreed with the FASB, but concluded that trying to overcome the FASB's objection would result in substantial delay in the issuance of a final SOP. At its December 1990 meeting, AcSEC acquiesced to the objections of the FASB and the SEC staff and deleted the proposed provision for modified contract segmentation criteria from the proposed exposure draft. However, in view of the concern about whether accounting results could be obtained that corresponded with the value of the various contractual elements of contracts in the software industry, the Task Force decided to solicit views from the public on the segmentation of software contracts.

(e) Exposure Draft of the Software Revenue SOP

The exposure draft of the SOP was issued on January 16, 1991, with a 4-month exposure period. In all, 49 comment letters were received, the majority of which supported the exposure draft or did not object to it. Many of the letters commented on specific provisions of the exposure draft. As a result of the comments and upon further study of the issues raised by the comments, several refinements to the exposure draft were made, principally in the following areas:

1. Clarification that software under lease should be accounted for as described in the SOP, even if the lease includes other items, such as hardware

2. Clarification of requirements concerning postcontract customer support and provision that in certain limited circumstances, revenue for initial-year postcontract customer support can be recognized as part of the software license fee

3. Changes and clarifications to provisions for postcontract customer-support arrangements not offered separately from software licenses

4. Addition of a requirement to disclose accounting policies

5. Addition of the requirement to obtain signed contracts before recognition of revenue if signed contracts are normally obtained

6. Clarification of accounting for returns and exchanges

7. Addition of guidance for arrangements providing for rights to multiple copies of two or more software products under site licenses or reseller arrangements

Respondents showed little interest in the idea of modified contract segmentation criteria, so the Task Force decided to do nothing more with that issue.

The most significant issue discussed during the exposure period concerned postcontract customer support. ITAA, formerly ADAPSO, strongly believed that postcontract customer support, particularly if bundled with a software license, for the initial period should be recognized at the beginning of the license term, rather than over the period of the license. The draft SOP was modified to permit this practice in the limited circumstance where the postcontract customer support for the initial term, including enhancements, is not significant. Not many companies are expected to qualify for this exception.

The Task Force was pleased with the quality of the comment letters. Although only 49 were received, a small number in comparison with the number of comment letters received by the FASB on its controversial projects, the letters were well thought out and presented. For that reason the Task Force was able to accommodate many of the comments seeking clarification of the precise requirements of the SOP.

(f) Issuance of SOP 91-1 and Effective Date

At its September 1991 meeting, AcSEC approved the SOP for issuance, subject to final clearance by the FASB. At its open meeting on November 20, 1991, the FASB voted unanimously not to object to the issuance of the final SOP, which was then issued on December 12, 1991, almost exactly 9 years after the first meeting of the Task Force.

The last change to the SOP was its effective date. The SOP is effective for financial statements issued after March 15, 1992, for fiscal years and interim periods in fiscal years beginning after December 15, 1991. Previously, it had been proposed that the SOP be effective for financial statements (including interim periods) for years beginning after December 15, 1991. The change in effective date was made so that the SOP would be included among the pronouncements that must be adhered to under a new hierarchy of generally accepted accounting principles, which was published as Statement on Auditing Standards No. 69, *The Meaning of "Present Fairly in Conformity With Generally Accepted Accounting Principles" in the Independent Auditor's Report*. This new hierarchy had been undergoing revision throughout 1991 and is effective for periods ending after March 15, 1992. Under the new hierarchy, a statement of position must be adhered to unless there is superior literature issued by the FASB. Under hierarchy transition provisions, however, a company could be "grandfathered"—that is, allowed to continue its past practice, notwithstanding the provisions of an SOP, if the SOP had an effective date prior to the effective date of the new hierarchy. The Task Force would have preferred to make the SOP effective for financial statements for periods beginning after March 15, 1992, but the SEC staff was concerned about any further delay in the effective date of the SOP and urged the Task Force and AcSEC not to change the December 15, 1991, effective date. Thus the SOP ended up with a rather convoluted effective date in order to prevent grandfathering of any software companies.

The distinction is not significant for public companies, inasmuch as the SEC would expect them to follow SOP 91-1 anyway. Nonpublic companies, however, will not have a choice—they will have to comply with SOP 91-1 just as will public companies.

2.4 FINAL COMMENTS: A PERSPECTIVE

From the contributing author's perspective, working on the Task Force was invigorating and rewarding. However, as anyone who has been involved in the standard-setting process can understand, at times it was frustrating. Different participants in the process can each have the "right" answer to an issue, but these answers are often not the same. Thus, the process becomes one of persuasion and compromise.

As commented earlier, not much has happened with the issue of capitalization of software development costs since the issuance of Statement 86. The software revenue recognition SOP is new, and significant implementation issues will arise because the SOP deals with principles and does not try to identify and solve the array of revenue recognition questions that can surface in individual transactions. To answer all those questions would have been impossible. Software companies should focus on the broad principles and intent of the SOP, and not seek loopholes to obtain accounting results that are not consistent with the intent of the broad principles of the SOP. The Task Force did not include in the SOP exhaustive guidance on specific types of transactions and thereby attempt to challenge the creativity of those who structure transactions in ways that achieve inappropriate accounting results. If software companies and their advisors apply the principles of the SOP in good faith, the goal set by ADAPSO in 1982— to assure consistent accounting that enables reasonable comparisons between companies in the software industry—will be achieved for software revenue recognition.

CHAPTER THREE

The Securities and Exchange Commission

Lynn E. Turner
Coopers & Lybrand

3.1 BACKGROUND

(a) Organization of the Securities and Exchange Commission

It is useful for software companies to have an understanding of the Securities and Exchange Commission (SEC) organization and how it functions as related to accounting matters and ongoing registration statements.

The SEC consists of five commission members and the commission's staff. The commissioners are all presidential appointees who serve 5-year terms. The president designates one of the commissioners as chairman, who determines the key matters to be focused on by the commission, and to whom the staff reports.

The staff consists of divisions, such as the Divisions of Enforcement and Corporation Finance, which are operations-oriented, and offices, such as the Office of General Counsel and the Office of the Chief Accountant of the Commission, which provide policy advice to the

The views expressed in this chapter reflect those of the individual author and do not necessarily represent those of the other contributing authors.

commission. See Exhibit 3.1, which provides a chart of the organizational structure of the SEC. As an illustration of the roles of the divisions, the Division of Corporate Finance (see Exhibit 3.2) reviews ongoing filings, and in an extreme case might recommend enforcement action for any number of reasons, which would be investigated by the Division of Enforcement, and, if necessary, prosecuted by the Office of General Counsel. The Office of the Chief Accountant of the SEC also recommends enforcement actions for accounting-related cases.

Public filings with the SEC by software companies, such as those using Forms S-1, S-3, 10-K, and 8-K, are routed by the filing desk to the Division of Corporation Finance, which is divided into 13 industry-specialized branches. For example, Branches 9 and 10 review the filings of software and insurance companies, and Branches 1 and 2 review the filings of financial institutions.

EXHIBIT 3.1   Organization of the Securities and Exchange Commission Staff

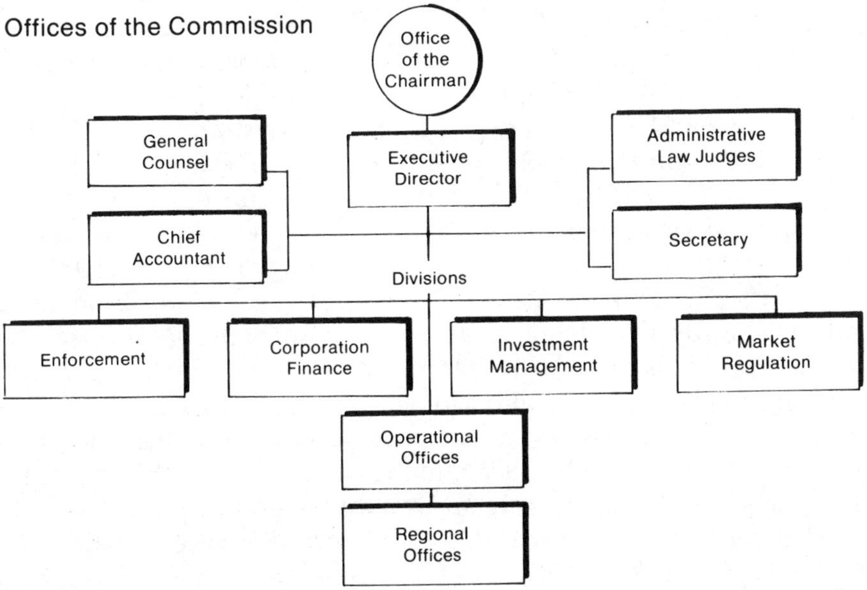

EXHIBIT 3.2 Securities and Exchange Commission
Division of Corporation Finance

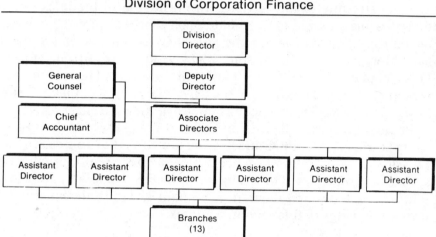

Each branch has four to six branch accountants and a number of attorneys who report to a branch chief, and usually two assistant chief accountants who report to both the branch chief and to the chief accountant of the Division of Corporation Finance. The branch accountants and attorneys review filings by registrants and, if necessary in their opinion, prepare draft comments. The accounting comments are reviewed by an assistant chief accountant and included with the legal comments prepared by the attorneys in a final comment letter to the registrant, which is signed and issued by the branch chief.

The chief accountant of the Division of Corporation Finance is responsible for supervising the accounting staff of the division, resolving accounting issues arising from reviews of filings by the staff, and assisting the SEC in rule making for accounting and filing matters. The chief accountant is assisted by a deputy chief accountant and approximately five associate chief accountants. The associate chief accountants are generally responsible for overseeing a specific branch.

The chief accountant of the SEC is the primary counsel to the SEC on accounting matters. If a registrant disagrees with a position taken on an accounting matter by the chief accountant of the Division of Corporation Finance, the registrant may appeal the issue to the Office of

the Chief Accountant of the SEC. The chief accountant has responsibility for setting SEC staff policy on such appeals, and registrants
may contest the chief accountant's decision only by appealing to the
commissioners of the SEC. Such appeals are extremely unusual and
seldom successful in overturning the SEC staff's position.

Oversight of the accounting standards set by the FASB and AICPA is
also the responsibility of the chief accountant. Representatives of the
Office of the Chief Accountant often work closely with the standard-
setting organizations as important new pronouncements are being
developed. The SEC staff followed with keen interest the development
of FASB Statement No. 86, *Accounting for the Costs of Computer Software
to Be Sold, Leased, or Otherwise Marketed,* and AICPA Statement of Position 91-1, *Software Revenue Recognition.* The contributing author was
the SEC observer assigned to work with the AICPA Task Force during
the development of SOP 91-1.

(b) Enforcement Cases Involving Software Companies

Several SEC Accounting and Auditing Enforcement Releases (AAERs)
have involved software companies, including their management and
auditors. Among these are AAER No. 190 (Cali Computer Systems,
Inc.), AAER No. 205 (Intex Software Systems, International Ltd.),
AAER No. 225 (Systems and Computer Technology Corporation),
AAER No. 265 (Desk Top Financial Solutions), and AAER No. 271
and AAER No. 351 (both related to 3CI, Inc.).

Typically, SEC enforcement actions have been taken in response to
improper revenue recognition or to capitalization of research and
development costs that should have been expensed. In particular, the
cases cited in the preceding paragraph involved the following:

- Revenue recognition prior to the existence of a binding executed
  agreement

- Recognition of revenue when there were uncertainties over customer
  acceptance of the product, and when "side" or "out" agreements
  existed, enabling the customer to void the transaction

- Improper capitalization of research and development expenses
- Misstated quarterly and annual financial statements

Several of these matters were addressed in SOP 91-1 as a result of discussion of the SEC staff's concerns with the AICPA Task Force. Several other portions of SOP 91-1, such as additional guidance on determining whether a fee is fixed, recognition of revenue on software development contracts prior to the determination of technological feasibility and the ability to make reasonable estimates on contracts, were influenced by ongoing SEC enforcement cases.

3.2 CAPITALIZATION OF SOFTWARE DEVELOPMENT COSTS

(a) Concern and Moratorium on Capitalization

Shortly after formation of the AICPA Task Force, the SEC became concerned about software companies' accounting for the costs incurred in development of software products. There was diversity in the extent of capitalization of software development costs by software companies as a result of diverse application of various pronouncements issued by the FASB, including FASB Statement No. 2, *Accounting for Research and Development Costs*; FASB Interpretation No. 6, *Applicability of FASB Statement No. 2 to Computer Software*; and FASB Technical Bulletin No. 79-2, *Computer Software Costs*. Effective April 1983, the SEC placed a moratorium on the capitalization of software development costs until the FASB issued a pronouncement providing further guidance.

(b) SEC Views on and Implementation of FASB Statement 86

There has been significant diversity in the implementation and application of Statement 86 by software companies. Software development costs capitalized by software companies have ranged from zero to very high percentages of total research and development expenditures. Although the SEC had wanted an accounting standard that would eliminate this broad range of accounting results, it has not challenged the diversity. The reason is, in part, that the SEC believes that Statement 86 has placed limits for determining how much software development can be capitalized and therefore, Statement 86 should be preventing abuses. The broad range of percentages of software costs that are capitalized is also due in part to the variety of software development processes.

The SEC, however, has been focusing on the net realizable value test for capitalized costs. It would not be unusual for a publicly held software company with amounts of capitalized software development costs that significantly exceed industry norms, or that uses a long amortization life, to be asked to justify to the SEC staff the recoverability of the capitalized costs. In some cases registrants have been requested to provide their net realizable value analyses for review by the SEC staff.

Another way that the SEC staff monitors capitalized software development costs is through reviews of Management's Discussion and Analysis. The SEC staff looks for trends that could affect the recoverability of capitalized costs. Registrants can anticipate that if a significant write-off of capitalized costs or a significant change in amortization rates is necessary, the SEC staff would challenge the adequacy of current and prior disclosures in Management's Discussion and Analysis if known trends which resulted in the write-down or change in amortization were not previously discussed.

(c) Amortization of Capitalized Software Costs

In FRR No. 12, the SEC stated the following:

> Computer software (whether internally developed or purchased) is an area characterized by both rapid technological development and increased industry competition and growth. Therefore, the use of very short amortization periods is indicated. Further, the Commission reminds registrants that have capitalized such costs that careful periodic evaluation of the recoverability thereof is necessary.

The SEC staff has indicated it will typically challenge amortization of capitalized software costs over periods longer than 3 to 5 years for personal-computer-based (PC) software products, and 5 to 7 years for other software products. The SEC staff has advised that registrants preferring to use amortization periods longer than these should consider discussing the basis for longer amortization periods with the SEC staff on a prefiling basis.

3.3 SOFTWARE REVENUE RECOGNITION

(a) SEC Involvement in SOP 91-1

Between 1985 and 1990, the Task Force worked on developing an exposure draft of an SOP on software revenue recognition, to be issued for public comment. As early as 1983 the SEC staff had a great deal of interest in software revenue recognition and the related AICPA project, because of the diverse industry accounting practices, the broad implications of any project on revenue recognition, and the various SEC enforcement actions taken against software companies. As a result, the SEC staff closely monitored the progress of the project. In November 1988, July 1989, and November 1989, the staff issued letters to the Task Force expressing concerns about the following.

- Recognition of software license revenue prior to delivery and completion of significant vendor services
- Accounting for postcontract customer support
- Accounting for software licenses with deferred payment terms
- The proposal for amended contract segmentation criteria for software companies
- Early recognition of contract revenues when input or output measures are used for hardware elements of contracts
- Premature recognition of revenue on customer-funded software development contracts

After the Task Force completed the exposure draft of the SOP for review by the FASB, the SEC sent another letter to the FASB expressing many of the same concerns expressed earlier to the Task Force. The SEC staff indicated that it might issue its own guidance for public companies if the staff's concerns were not adequately addressed in an AICPA SOP. After much discussion between the SEC staff and the

Task Force, most of the issues were resolved and various modifications to the draft SOP were made to the satisfaction of the SEC staff. With regard to the last of the listed concerns, the Task Force decided not to address the issue because of time constraints and because it would have required dealing with contract costs as well as contract revenues, which was deemed to be beyond the scope of SOP 91-1.

As the exposure draft of the SOP was being prepared, the SEC staff reviewed the filings of many software companies and engaged in various prefiling discussions with registrants on revenue recognition issues. The staff was concerned about the number of registrants who were using accounting practices that it believed were not in accordance with generally accepted accounting principles. Beginning in the late 1980s, these accounting practices had become much more diverse and, in some cases, abusive, during a time when the SEC staff was not challenging software revenue recognition practices. In particular, the SEC staff believed that software companies were recognizing revenue before delivery or completion of services, demonstrating that an exchange had occurred, and without assurance of collectibility. Moreover, the SEC staff was concerned because some software companies accounted for postcontract customer support in a manner different from that set forth for similar products in the then newly issued FASB Technical Bulletin No. 90-1, *Accounting for Separately Priced Extended Warranty and Product Maintenance Contracts*. The subject had been of much interest to the SEC staff, as the Technical Bulletin and related EITF Issue consensus dealing with revenue recognition for extended warranties were the result of disagreements between the SEC staff and registrants. In 1988 and 1989, the SEC staff had challenged the revenue recognition policies of certain electronics products retailers who were recognizing revenue from maintenance contracts upon signing the contracts.

In addition, various newspaper and journal articles printed in 1990 and early 1991, as well as the *Software Business Practices Council White Paper*, issued in October 1990, were very critical of accounting practices in the software industry.

As a result of its growing concerns about accounting and reporting by software companies, the SEC staff sent letters to several software companies requesting they revise their accounting practices and improve the information provided in the Management Discussion and Analysis. This resulted in something of an uproar in both the software industry and the accounting profession. For example, in one case the SEC staff challenged and objected to a registrant's changing revenue recognition from ratable recognition over the contract period, to recognition on contract signing with accrual of future costs. The SEC staff believed it was inappropriate to recognize revenue when the contract required the registrant to continue to provide services—it believed that revenue should be recognized as the services were performed or over the period of the contract.

The SEC staff was urged to delay taking action against software companies until the software revenue recognition SOP was completed and issued, which the AICPA had agreed to do by the end of 1991. The staff agreed to delay further action on software revenue recognition issues except for extreme cases, as long as specified disclosures were made by registrants, and provided that the Task Force completed the SOP and issued it by the end of 1991, with an effective date not later than January 1, 1992. The SEC staff did, however, continue to consider enforcement actions in cases in which it was clear that license revenue was recognized prior to completion of the earnings process, such as when "minimum" fixed licensing fees were recognized, but amounts not paid by the end of the year were renegotiated as part of the following year's license fee.

At a December 1991 meeting with representatives of the AICPA SEC Regulations committee, the SEC staff said that it agreed with the newly issued SOP 91-1, and would apply strict interpretations of the SOP in its reviews of registrant filings. The SEC staff said that, if necessary, it would issue a Staff Accounting Bulletin, reinforcing the principles set forth in SOP 91-1. At the January 1992 annual SEC Current Developments Conference, the SEC staff reiterated its support of SOP 91-1 and its intent to require full compliance with the statement by registrants.

(b) SEC Views on Other Vendor Obligations

In considering the issue of whether remaining vendor obligations are significant, the SEC staff focused on the likelihood of successful completion of the obligations and the effect on acceptance of the product by the customers if the obligations are not fulfilled. In its November 1989 letter to the Task Force, the SEC staff said the following.

In considering whether an obligation is significant or not, a vendor should also consider such factors as the relative values and costs attributable to the completed and uncompleted obligations and the ability of the customer to reject the contract if a remaining obligation is not completed satisfactorily.

Further, the SEC staff indicated to the Task Force that it believed that many of the remaining vendor obligations described in paragraph 70 of SOP 91-1, such as testing, porting, system integration, and data conversion, would usually be significant other obligations, precluding software license revenue recognition until their completion. The Task Force rejected this view in the final SOP, but does note in the SOP that consideration of whether other vendor obligations are significant requires judgment and assessment of their effect on customer acceptance.

Factors that the SEC staff is likely to consider in assessing whether a vendor obligation is significant or insignificant include the following.

- The significance to the license revenue of the costs to be incurred to complete the obligations—the 1987 AICPA Issues Paper defined *significant* as 15 percent or more of the contract price. However, this notion was not included in SOP 91-1. The SEC staff has commented that it believes costs equal to (and perhaps less than) 15 percent of the license price would be considered significant. Determining whether remaining vendor obligations are significant based solely on the 15 percent test, as defined in the Issues Paper, would not be appropriate.

- Whether the services involve new technology with which the software vendor has limited or no experience.

- The historical experience of the software vendor in completing similar services.

- Other potential risk factors particular to the contract that could adversely affect the customer's acceptance of the product.

(c) Inability to Make Reasonable Estimates of Progress-to-Completion on Contracts

As a result of a comment in a July 1989 letter from the SEC staff to the Task Force, paragraph 82 of SOP 91-1 highlights the requirement that, in assessing whether reasonable estimates can be made for use of the percentage-of-completion method, software companies should consider technological risks of projects and reliability of cost estimates. The SEC staff requested this be included as a result of its concern, arising from an enforcement action, that some software companies were recognizing revenue on software development contracts prior to the establishment of the technological feasibility of the software. The SEC staff believed that if there is uncertainty about the ability to successfully develop a software product, the software company should use the completed contract method or, if it can be assumed that no loss exists, the zero gross profit method of contract accounting until the uncertainty is eliminated. The SEC staff also noted that Statement 86 provides useful guidance with respect to assessing when the development of a software product should be considered to be in the research stage and when technological feasibility has been established. In reviewing such situations, the SEC staff is likely to focus on whether all significant uncertainties that might affect the success of completion of the product development have been clearly resolved. The SEC staff will have hindsight available when reviewing filings including contract accounting issues.

(d) SEC Views on Use of Output Measures

The SEC staff has indicated that it believes paragraph 90 of SOP 91-1 requires using the method that best measures progress-to-completion on elements of contracts for software. A registrant may use either input- or output-based measurements as long as the method chosen best reflects progress and performance on the elements of the contract. The SEC staff has expressed concern about the use of contract accounting to accelerate revenue recognition when actual performance has not been rendered by the contractor. For example, the SEC staff would challenge a registrant that includes the value of hardware delivered at the vendor's or customer's site in measurement of progress-to-completion prior to installation.

At the request of the SEC staff, the AICPA Task Force amplified the guidance provided in SOP 91-1 for the use of output measures, such as milestones and value-added measures. The output measures applied in assessing percentage-of-completion need to be objectively measurable and reflect progress on the contract. In the case of off-the-shelf software, the AICPA Task Force concluded that measurement of progress-to-completion could be based on the value of the off-the-shelf software. This conclusion was based on the fact that off-the-shelf software is a product typically sold without modification, resulting in an objective value for measuring the value added to a contract. However, the SEC staff has challenged the use of output measures of off-the-shelf software if modifications are made to its functionality during installation. In that situation, the SEC staff and FASB staff have both indicated that they believe the software is not off-the-shelf software for that transaction. Instead, the software should be regarded and accounted for as core software. Progress-to-completion for core software must be measured as the customization work is performed or upon completion of installation.

The SEC staff will also challenge the use of output measures using the value of off-the-shelf software if remaining obligations associated with the software could preclude revenue recognition in accordance with paragraph 100 of SOP 91-1. Accordingly, the SEC staff believes that if output measures are used, there should be clearly defined criteria or milestones that have been achieved and documented, with demonstration of acceptance of that portion of the contract by the customer. Registrants who are unable to document achievement of such milestones may be well advised to consult with their accounting advisors and the SEC staff.

(e) General Summary of Expected SEC Application of SOP 91-1

The SEC staff believed that some accounting practices used in the software industry prior to the issuance of SOP 91-1 were not in accordance with generally accepted accounting principles. The staff wanted more strict revenue recognition guidelines than SOP 91-1 provides, such as those that might address remaining vendor obligations. Accordingly, it is unlikely that the SEC staff will compromise on application of SOP 91-1. The contributing author expects the SEC to apply SOP 91-1 with relatively strict and conservative interpretations.

The SEC staff has expressed a number of views on how it would apply selected aspects of SOP 91-1. These views are described in the following paragraphs.

(i) DELIVERY. Software may be delivered that is not the final version the customer is paying for and accepting. For example, demonstration versions of software are often reviewed by customers prior to ordering or accepting the final products. Sometimes a customer is initially provided a copy of the software that has much the same functionality as the final version to be delivered, or that requires a software key or code to operate fully in an authorized mode. Providing a customer with a demonstration or other version of the software, one that does not have the same functionality as the final product to be licensed would not constitute delivery. The SEC staff has indicated that delivery will not be considered to have occurred until delivery of the final version of the software that the customer is licensing, including any required software keys.

During the development of SOP 91-1, the SEC staff informed the AICPA Task Force that it had become aware of software deliveries being made to third-party warehouses, pending the customer's taking final delivery of the software or the delivery of the required hardware. These transactions were considered similar to "bill and hold" arrangements for which revenue should not be recognized unless the criteria of AAER No. 108 are met. The SEC staff emphasized that as stated in SOP 91-1, for revenue to be recognized, delivery must be to the customer's site or to another site specified by the customer, and that if payment is not due until delivery to a specified site, revenue should not be recognized until delivery to that site.

(ii) APPLICATION OF FASB STATEMENT NO. 48. SOP 91-1 indicates that revenue should not be recognized prior to the existence of persuasive evidence that a sales agreement exists. The inclusion of this requirement in SOP 91-1 was influenced by the SEC staff's becoming aware of two registrants who had recognized revenue prior to obtaining executed contracts. A written contract is usually sufficient persuasive evidence of the existence of a sales agreement. If the contract contains customer cancellation or termination clauses, however, such as a municipality's fiscal funding clause or a clause permitting cancellation if the contract is not approved by legal counsel, revenue should not be recognized until such clauses lapse. The SEC staff concluded that FASB Statement No. 48, *Revenue Recognition When Right of Return Exists*, is not applicable to such clauses and that accounting for such clauses by recognizing revenue and providing allowances for expected returns or cancellations, is not appropriate. The SEC staff noted that Statement 48 addressed transactions where a binding contract existed and goods were shipped and then returned, as opposed to a cancellable contract for which goods have not been shipped. Some believe that if a contract with a **governmental** agency contains a fiscal funding clause, an assessment may be made as to the likelihood of exercise of that clause, consistent with the guidance in FASB Technical Bulletin No. 79-10, *Fiscal Funding Clauses in Lease Agreements*. For example, if the fiscal funding clause in the software contract with the government were the same as used in the government contracts, it may be supportable to conclude the likelihood of the contract being cancelled was remote. However, if the cancellation clause in the government contract was not standard to all of the governmental agency's contracts (e.g., AAER Nos. 271 and 351), then analogy to Technical Bulletin 79-10 may be inappropriate.

Footnote 3 of Statement 48 says that exchanges of products for similar products by **end** users are not considered exchanges for which an allowance for returns must be provided. Consistent with that directive, SOP 91-1 states that an allowance for exchanges of software by end users for a product with a similar price and functionality, need not be accrued when the revenue is recorded. For example, the exchange of a spreadsheet product that runs on Unix for the same program for a DOS environment would not require the anticipation of an allowance for returns.

Sales returns or exchanges by resellers must be susceptible to reasonable estimation and recorded when the product's revenue is recognized. These would include exchanges under "stock balancing" arrangements that do not involve products with similar prices or functionality, such as a word-processing program exchanged for spreadsheet program. Such exchanges by resellers would require estimation of an allowance for returns. In recent comment letters issued to registrants, the SEC staff has required them to provide historical data on product returns so that the SEC staff can assess the reasonableness of amounts recorded for product return allowances.

(iii) DISCOUNTING. During 1990 the SEC staff noted some software licenses involving payment terms that were not normal and customary in relation to the software vendor's typical payment terms. The SEC staff indicated revenues from such arrangements should be discounted in accordance with APB Opinion No. 21, *Interest on Receivables and Payables*, if the discounting would be significant to the financial statements, even if the payments are due in less than 1 year. The SEC staff indicated public companies should be cognizant of this provision in SOP 91-1 and Opinion 21 as to the impact of discounting on quarterly financial statements. In one case, a company filing with the SEC for an initial public offering was required to recirculate its "red herring" prospectus after completing its public offering road shows, the day before it was expecting its filing to become effective, because of the material effects of discounting on the interim financial statements included in the filing.

(iv) BUNDLING AND UNBUNDLING OF MAINTENANCE FEES. Fees for maintenance services are often included or "bundled" into the initial software license price. The SEC staff and AICPA Task Force expected that few software companies would meet the criteria set forth for bundling maintenance fees with initial license fees, as it was perceived that most software companies offer all enhancements to their licensees. A company that has (a) past patterns of offering enhancements that are more than minimal to its initial licensees, or (b) expects to offer its initial licensees within a postcontract customer support contract period a more than minimal enhancement, does not meet the criteria for bundling initial maintenance fees with the software license. A company that meets the criteria during the current reporting period for recognizing the postcontract customer support revenue on product delivery, but does not meet the criteria in a later period, should change to ratable recognition and may report an accounting change in the period in which it does not meet the criteria. Software companies that may otherwise qualify for bundling of postcontract customer-support fees with initial license fees may decline to do so as a result of the impact of changes in accounting required from one period to another.

Some software companies offer postcontract customer support only in their software license and do not market postcontract customer-support arrangements separately. For example, some companies market annual licenses to use a product that include both the software license and the postcontract customer support arrangement. If the software company can meet the same criteria for bundling postcontract customer support with initial licenses, the company can recognize the postcontract customer support revenue in delivery of the product. If the company cannot meet those criteria, but can obtain sufficient information to determine a separate price for the two components, revenue for the software component should be recognized on delivery and the postcontract customer support revenue should be generally recognized ratably over the term of the postcontract customer support arrangement.

Software companies may sell annual licenses at a significant discount from the amount typically charged for an initial license. Such licenses are presumed to be for postcontract customer support, unless the software company has objective evidence of pricing for separate license and postcontract customer-support components in subsequent years.

What constitutes sufficient objective evidence for separating license and postcontract customer support is not discussed in detail in SOP 91-1. Sales of postcontract customer support to other customers for similar products, or in limited circumstances postcontract customer support fees charged by competitors for similar products, may be adequate evidence. The SEC staff has indicated that adding a normal profit margin to postcontract customer support costs or using industry averages to determine the postcontract customer-support component would not be sufficient information. The SEC staff has also challenged the use of a competitor's pricing when there was not **persuasive** and objective evidence that the competitor's product had the **same** functionality and pricing characteristics as the registrant's product.

3.4 SIGNIFICANT SEC REPORTING ISSUES

(a) Regulation S-X

Regulation S-X, Article 5-03, requires registrants to separately disclose revenues from tangible products, services, and other sources, for each of those categories that exceeds 10 percent of total revenues. In addition, for categories of revenues that are required to be disclosed, the related costs must be separately disclosed on the face of the income statement.

Accordingly, public software companies are required to separately disclose postcontract customer-support revenues and related costs on the face of the income statement, if those revenues are more than 10 percent of total revenues. If postcontract customer-support revenues exceed 10 percent of total revenues, the related costs must be disclosed separately on the face of the income statement, even if the costs are less than 10 percent of total costs. An inability to determine the costs of postcontract customer support may be indicative of an accounting system that does not provide sufficient evidence to support the accrual of postcontract customer support costs and up-front recognition of post-contract customer support revenue in the limited instances in which that accounting treatment is permitted.

(b) Increased Scrutiny of Management's Discussion and Analysis

The SEC staff has increased its scrutiny of Management's Discussion and Analysis sections of filings by software companies since the release of Financial Reporting Release (FRR) 36 in 1989, and with changing trends in the industry. FRR 36 states the following.

> MD&A [Management's Discussion and Analysis] is intended to give the investor an opportunity to look at the company through the eyes of management by providing both short- and long-term analysis of the company. The Item (MD&A) asks management to discuss the dynamics of the business and to analyze the financials.

Many SEC staff comments have been received by software companies with significant increases in revenues, where cash flows did not similarly increase because of increases in receivables. The SEC staff has noted that software companies have tended to discuss the increases in revenues, but have often not discussed the increases in receivables, which have in some cases significantly impacted the liquidity of the registrant. The SEC staff has indicated that it believes software companies should discuss the impact on operations and liquidity of significant increases in, and trends with respect to, the aging of receivables. The SEC staff recommends using the data in the statement of cash flows as a tool in discussing these trends, and they should be used to reconcile the increases in revenue in the income statement, to increases in receivables in the balance sheet.

The SEC staff has indicated Management's Discussion and Analysis should discuss historical and expected effects of trends in postcontract customer support revenues affecting operating income and liquidity, such as when revenues are constant or declining and related accrued costs have not yet been paid.

In reviewing filings, the SEC staff often looks for prior discussions in the Management's Discussion and Analysis about the possibility of changes in the business that may result in future effects on trends or results of operations. This would apply to trends in product sales that could affect the recoverability of capitalized software development costs. The SEC staff has urged registrants to consider carefully the adequacy of such information provided in quarterly, as well as annual, filings.

The SEC staff will continue to review many software industry filings in developing its perceptions about the industry and its trends, such as changing products and market consolidations. Software companies should consider reviewing the filings of competitors, as well as those of others in the industry, to ensure that can explain and justify perceptions of the industry and market trends in light of statements made by others.

(c) Product Descriptions Consistent with Accounting and Matters Discussed

The SEC staff has indicated software companies should ensure that the description of products in the foreparts of annual reports is consistent with the accounting used for the products. For example, if the cost of a newly acquired product is expensed as research and development in the financial statements, then it is expected that the Management's Discussion and Analysis section would include the status of the research and development, market uncertainties, and significant impacts on liquidity from further commitments required to develop the final marketable product.

(d) Quarterly Adjustments

Many software companies have reported significant fourth-quarter adjustments in recent years. In 1992 the AICPA issued its Statement on Auditing Standards (SAS) No. 71, *Interim Financial Information.* This new standard includes a section which resulted from two enforcement actions taken by the SEC when registrants' auditors were aware of significant misstatements in clients' interim filings with the SEC, but did not discuss the misstatements with the clients' boards of directors and request the clients to restate their filings. The SEC authorized the SEC staff to draft a rule to address this problem, but the SEC also gave AICPA's Auditing Standards Board the opportunity to respond with its own guidelines, which resulted in SAS 66, which was superceded by SAS 71.

SAS 71 requires auditors who become aware of probable misstatements in interim filings with regulators, as a result of performing any interim-review-related procedures, including merely discussing interim financial statements with a client, to discuss the probable misstatements with representatives of the board of directors and, in essence, resign if the filing is not corrected. Any such resignation would trigger the SEC's Form 8-K filing requirements, and the misstatement would in that way be communicated to the SEC.

(e) Escrow Share Arrangements

The SEC staff has addressed accounting for escrow arrangements involving the stock of a company at or near the time of its initial public offering. The typical transaction involves some or all shareholders of the previously private company (some or all of whom also may be employees) placing a portion of their shares in an escrow account, somewhat analogous to a reverse stock split. The escrow shares generally are legally outstanding and may continue to have voting and dividend rights. The shares are to be released from escrow based on the attainment of certain performance measures by the company in subsequent periods, such as specified earnings or market price levels. If the levels are not achieved, the escrow shares are returned to the company and canceled.

Depending on facts and circumstances, the SEC staff believes that the subsequent release of shares from escrow could be viewed as a compensatory arrangement. The primary factors the Staff would consider is whether the escrow arrangement includes only those shareholders who are also employees of the company versus all shareholders of the company, whether the recipient has to fulfill an employment contract period and whether the distribution is "across the board." Registrants can expect the SEC staff to challenge the release of escrow shares to management and other employees, which are not treated as compensatory. The SEC staff believes that even though the escrow shares have dividend or voting rights, a compensatory situation may still exist. The SEC staff also has concluded that an escrow arrangement involving shares owned by a corporate parent that also provides management services to the subsidiary should be considered "compensatory" (e.g., management fee expense).

Escrow share arrangements in an initial public offering also have earnings per share consequences. Although the escrow shares are legally outstanding and should be presented as such in the balance sheet, the SEC staff believes the shares should be considered as "contingently issuable" for earnings per share purposes. In general, under APB Opinion No. 15, *Earnings Per Share*, the shares are reflected as outstanding for earnings per share purposes only when the conditions for issuance are currently being met or it will be issued upon the mere passage of time. If a registrant has treated such shares as outstanding for EPS purposes even though the conditions for issuance are not being met, it should discuss the matter with the Staff.

(f) Stock Compensation

Staff Accounting Bulletin (SAB) Topic 4D notes that consistent with APB Opinion No. 25, *Accounting for Stock Issued to Employees*, registrants **must** recognize compensation expense for any issuances of stock and warrants to employees for less than fair value. Paragraph 25(b) of Opinion 25 states the quoted market price must be used to measure cost related to issuing both restricted (or letter) and unrestricted stock through stock option, purchase or award plans. The SEC staff has challenged registrants who have issued stock or stock options to employees at a price significantly below the public offering price, shortly before going public, when compensation was not recorded. They have also challenged accounting for stock issuances when the option exercise price or value placed on the shares was significantly lower than the prices paid for similar stock, issued at approximately the same time. Items affecting the Staff's decision on whether to challenge the compensation recorded (or lack thereof) will include:

a. Whether there were any equity or convertible security transactions for cash within a reasonable period of time of the grant to the employee, and the size and nature of such transactions;

b. Changes in the company's business that would indicate there has been a change in the value of the business, such as new contracts or sources of revenues, more profitable operations, etc.;

c. The length of time between the grant to the employee(s) and the date of the public offering, and

d. Adequate documentation from the date of the grant or earlier that supports the valuation used by the company at that time.

The SEC staff has not accepted "haircuts" of, say, 25% or 50% from the IPO price, or earlier cash price, without **persuasive** evidence supporting the valuation methodology and value used.

In one situation, a registrant granted stock options to management about ten days before filing the registration statement, but set the exercise price at 50% of the initial public offering price. They argued that a 50% haircut was appropriate given the normal uncertainty about whether the offering would be completed successfully. They felt that at the grant date, the stock was worth much less than the IPO price, since without the offering proceeds they couldn't repay high-coupon debt or expand operations. The Staff agreed in principle that the value of a company immediately before an IPO may be something less than after a successful offering. However, in this case the Staff objected to a 50% haircut only days before filing of the registration statement. The Staff ultimately did not object to measurement of compensation expense using a much smaller haircut to determine fair value. The Staff will continue to resolve these issues on a case by case basis.

(g) Preferred Stock

Many software companies have received funding from venture capitalists and other investors in the form of redeemable or convertible preferred stock. In an October 1987 letter, the SEC staff took the position that preferred stock that automatically converts into common stock on the **effective** date of an initial public offering should be reflected in the stockholders' equity section of the historical financial statements as being converted as of the earliest period presented, with the conversion also taken into consideration in the computation of earnings per share. The SEC staff had also indicated that for preferred stock converted into common stock on the **closing** date of an initial public offering, earnings per share, should be provided on the face of the income statement for all periods presented **in lieu of** historical earnings per share. The SEC staff noted that in periods subsequent to the initial public offering closing, the preferred stock would be converted into common stock and, therefore, historical earnings per share for all subsequent periods presented would be comparable to the pro forma earnings per share. The Staff had noted their position was consistent with SAB Topic 1(B)(2) (SAB 55).

In spring of 1992, the SEC staff changed its position as to preferred stock that converts into common upon the closing or the effective date of registration. In general, they now require the preferred stock to be reflected as such until the date the conversion occurs. Upon conversion, prior period financial statements should not be restated to show the preferred stock as common stock. Generally, the historical balance sheet or statement of operations should not be revised to reflect conversions or term modifications of outstanding securities that become effective **after** the latest balance sheet date presented in the filing, although pro forma data presented along side of the historical statements would generally be required if the conversion or modifications have a dilutive effect. If the registrant and its independent accountants elect to present a modification or conversion as if it had occurred at the date of the latest balance sheet (with no adjustment permitted to earlier periods), the SEC staff ordinarily will not object. However, if the original instrument legally accrues interest or dividends or accretes toward redemption value after that balance sheet date, or if the terms of the conversion do not confirm the historical carrying value at the latest balance sheet as current value, the registrant should not adjust the historical financial statements prior to the actual stock conversion. Instead the effect of the conversion should be shown in a pro forma column presented alongside the historical balance sheet and in the earnings per share data.

If a conversion or term modification of outstanding equity securities will occur subsequent to the date of the latest balance sheet and the new terms result in a material reduction of permanent equity, the filing should include a pro forma balance sheet (excluding effects of offering proceeds) **presented along side** of the historical balance sheet giving effect to the change in capitalization. Pro forma earnings per share and capitalization should be provided preferably on the face of the balance sheet and income statement, to show the effect of conversions of preferred stock into common stock (but not the offering) upon either the effective date of the registration statement or the closing date of the offering. The SEC staff has noted its position is consistent with SAB Topic 1B(2).

Rule 5-02 of Regulation S-X states that redeemable preferred stock is not to be included in amounts reported as stockholders' equity, and that the redemption amounts are to be shown on the face of the balance sheet. This rule requires the preferred stock to be reported as "mezzanine" capital so long as the redemption privilege is outside the control of the company. This **includes** situations when redemption is not currently probable such as preferred securities which give the holder the right to put them back to the company upon a change in control or death of the shareholder.

3.5 BUSINESS COMBINATIONS

(a) Amortization of Goodwill of Acquired Software Businesses

The SEC staff has indicated that it believes that rapid obsolescence and competition in the software industry should be considered in evaluating the period for amortization of goodwill related to the acquisition of software businesses. The SEC staff has indicated in its 1992 training manual, *Accounting Disclosure Rules and Practices*, that it will challenge amortization of goodwill of a software business over a longer period than 7 to 10 years a period of 5 to 7 years may be necessary if a company is dependent on a single high technology product. The staff has also indicated that it will challenge purchase-price allocations in which little or no cost is allocated to software. In addition, the SEC staff has publicly stated that there is an SEC staff presumption that the amortization and allocation methods used currently for identifiable intangibles for income tax reporting purposes should also be used for financial reporting purposes.

(b) Research and Development Acquired in a Business Combination

Software companies typically have research and development projects in progress, as evidenced by the expenses classified as Research and Development in their income statements. Statement 86 establishes criteria for determining when a software development project is considered to be in the research and development stage and when it has achieved technological feasibility and is in the production stage. APB Opinion No. 16, *Business Combinations*, requires that the purchase price paid for a company be allocated to tangible and identifiable intangible assets. Any unallocated portion of the purchase price is then allocated to goodwill. In addition, FASB Statement No. 2, *Accounting for Research and Development Costs*, and FASB Interpretation No. 4, *Applicability of FASB Statement No. 2 to Business Combinations Accounted for by the Purchase Method*, require that the purchase price be allocated to identifiable intangible assets, including any resulting from research and development activities of the acquired enterprise, or to be used in research and development activities of the combined enterprise. The intent of Statement 2 was to account for the costs of intangibles purchased in a business combination similar to those that are constructed or acquired for research and development projects. The subject was also addressed in EITF Issue 86-14.

Software companies that acquire an entity with research and development in process should follow the guidance in these pronouncements by allocating a portion of the purchase price to the research and development in process. The allocation should be based on fair value and should not be made so as to minimize or to avoid recording goodwill. The SEC may challenge a registrant that allocates a significant portion of a purchase price to acquired research and development but, in discussing the acquisition in a business description, Management's Discussion and Analysis, or notes to financial statements, indicates that the acquisition was completed primarily to obtain completed projects that are already being marketed. The SEC staff may also comment on a filing if there is no discussion of the impact on liquidity of the need for funds to complete the research and development in process at the acquisition date.

(c) Postcontract Customer Support Obligations Assumed in an Acquisition

An acquisition of a software business may include assumption of obligations to perform services under postcontract customer-support agreements, when the acquired business has already received payment. To some extent, as permitted by SOP 91-1, the postcontract customer support revenue may have been recognized and the related costs accrued, and in most cases the revenue would have been deferred and amortized to revenue over the terms of the agreements.

The SEC staff has indicated it believes that in purchase price accounting, obligations to provide future postcontract customer-support services should be recorded as a liability at present value of amounts to be paid in accordance with paragraph 88(h) and (i) of Accounting Principles Board (APB) Opinion No. 16, *Business Combinations*. This results in no profit margin being recognized in postacquisition income statements for assumed postcontract customer support obligations.

Some have expressed the view that such contracts are similar to inventory or construction contracts in progress, and that they should be accounted for so that the acquirer reports a normal profit margin upon completing the obligations. This viewpoint is based on the theory that the acquiror should be able to report a profit on the PCS services it renders and that the purchase price negotiations take such services into consideration. The SEC staff to date has not accepted this view. The staff has noted that postcontract customer support, unlike a product such as inventory, is not being developed for sale, rather an obligation for future performance is being incurred. The SEC staff has also noted that such accounting results in the recognition of a gross profit, even though it will never be realized through a subsequent collection of cash, because the cash has typically already been collected by the seller. As a practical matter, the profit on any acquired PCS contracts, to be earned by the acquiror may be small and difficult to determine and very judgemental. Accordingly, any registrant who records such profits should consider discussing such accounting with the SEC staff prior to any filings.

(d) Pooling of Interests of Software Companies

Some combining software companies prefer to have pooling-of-interests business combinations rather than purchase combinations.

Most of the value of many software companies is imbedded in their software, an intangible asset, and as a result the combining parties often wish to obtain warranties and representations. However, they may cause the transaction to fail the pooling criteria. Interpretation No. 30 of Opinion 16 provides, and position of the SEC staff is, that in a pooling, any general representations or warranties must be resolved or expire at the date of the first postbusiness combination audit or in 1 year, whichever date is earlier. Specific warranties and representations may extend for longer periods.

Software companies should evaluate any representations and warranties in a business combination for which pooling-of-interests accounting is contemplated to be sure they do not violate the conditions for pooling. Specific warranties related to a specific product may qualify, yet not preclude pooling.

Issuances of new stock options or changes in terms of existing option agreements (such as a repricing) would be considered a violation of the pooling rules if done in contemplation of the business combination. Generally, to overcome the presumption that such changes done within two years of the merger were in contemplation of the combination, a company will need to provide sufficient evidence of the business purpose for the stock option changes or issuances. Board of Director minutes, studies by outside compensation consultants and evidence of industry comparisons, done at the time of the change to the plan, are examples of documentation the SEC staff typically asks for. The one exception to this general rule is that if a stock option agreement contains a *preexisting* clause that **requires** acceleration of vesting of stock options upon a change in control (but not a cash-out provision), then the acceleration would not be considered to have been done in contemplation of the merger.

3.6 FOREIGN OPERATIONS: MARKETING ENTITIES

Some software companies interested in expanding their marketing efforts into foreign markets, such as Europe, are faced with the need for capital. There has also been a desire to do so by some software companies, without having to report initial losses incurred in establishing the foreign marketing operations.

A new type of entity has been invented to deal effectively with both objectives. Typically, a foreign entity is formed with capitalization by venture capitalists in the United States and Europe. A United States software company contributes a minor amount of capital. They may have a nonvoting position on the entity's board of directors. The software company receives a right of first refusal to acquire all the stock of the foreign entity at a predetermined price and time, and may enter into a contract to provide certain administrative support to the entity. The entity is licensed to market the software company's products. If the software company does not exercise its right to acquire all the stock of the entity at the predetermined time, the foreign entity retains the license to market the software company's software and may market other products as well.

The needed capital is obtained to establish the U.S. company's foreign marketing effort. Also, venture capitalists with expertise, who sometimes have established networks in the foreign markets, are available for assistance.

Under present consolidation practice, the software company does not have to consolidate the entity because it does not have majority ownership or control of the board of directors and foreign company. In addition, the venture capitalists have significant capital at risk. The SEC staff has indicated that the software company may account for its investment in such entities by either the cost or equity method. Since the software company's investment is minimal, there is a limit to the amount of losses the software company would have to recognize in using the equity method.

A drawback to this type of entity, however, is that the SEC staff has indicated that it is not be "poolable," unless it is considered to be independent from the sponsoring company. If the software company is not poolable, and it exercises its right of first refusal, the purchase price is allocated to assets acquired, usually with an allocation to goodwill as a result of the established marketing organization. To overcome the SEC staff's concerns, the sponsoring company should not exercise significance influence over the sponsored entity, such as through a management contract or significance voting rights, and may only have a right of first refusal, not an option to acquire the entity. The marketing entity must clearly demonstrate it is independently operated in order to be poolable.

3.7 CONCLUSION

The SEC has been significantly involved in the development of accounting principles affecting software companies. This involvement began in the early 1980s, with accounting for software development costs, and has continued through the completion of SOP 91-1 in 1991. It can be expected that the SEC's keen interest in the software industry will continue into the foreseeable future, as the SEC staff monitors the implementation of SOP 91-1 and continues to focus on Management's Discussion and Analysis information of software registrants. Because of the SEC staff's unprecedented level of involvement in the development of SOP 91-1, registrants who do not report within the boundaries it establishes are likely to be challenged by the SEC.

CHAPTER FOUR

Software Revenue Recognition Overview and Types of Transactions

4.1 GENERAL

(a) SOP 91-1 Based on Existing Generally Accepted Accounting Principles

SOP 91-1, *Software Revenue Recognition*, provides guidance for accounting for revenue recognition on transactions that include software. The guidance of SOP 91-1 is based on existing generally accepted acounting principles. Its development was not an attempt to establish new generally accepted accounting principles, but to clarify how existing generally accepted accounting principles should be applied to software transactions.

Over the years, several accounting practices evolved in the software industry that varied from the generally accepted accounting principles in most industries. For example, some software companies recognized revenue from software licenses upon contract signing, which varies from the general practice of recognizing revenue on delivery for product sales. Some used an "unbundling" approach to accounting for contracts for software combined with hardware or services or both, that achieved the same result as contract accounting using segmentation, even though the criteria for segmentation of SOP 81-1 were not met. SOP 91-1 establishes that accounting principles for revenue recognition in the software industry should be the same as those in other industries.

(b) Different Types of Transactions

One has to decide what is being accounted for before determining how to account for it. A key initial step in accounting for software revenue is to determine the nature of the subject transaction. Although that is a simple task in many cases, there are many transactions in the software industry that can be difficult to distinguish. The decision is important, because different ways of accounting apply to various types of transaction. The rest of this chapter discusses the different kinds of software revenue transactions and how to distinguish between them. Chapters 5 and 6 discuss accounting for those transactions.

Substantially all software revenue transactions fall into one of the categories listed in Exhibit 4.1.

4.2 IDENTIFYING THE TYPE OF TRANSACTION

(a) Software Licenses

Software licenses are analogous to sales of products in other industries. A software product transaction may include ancillary services connected with the providing of the product, such as installation, integration with existing software systems or modules in use, software bug fixing, warranty support, training, and other ancillary services. Minor amounts of enhancement or customization may also be required. However, if enhancement or customization activities that modify or add to the functionality of the software are significant, the transaction is probably not a product transaction. It may be a software development project that falls into the category of a contract for software combined with hardware or services or both, subject to contract accounting, or, in some cases, it may constitute separate software license and service transactions contained in the same agreement.

EXHIBIT 4.1   Type of Revenue Transaction

1.	Software licenses
2.	Postcontract customer support
3.	Software license and postcontract support bundled together
4.	Contracts for software combined with hardware or services or both
5.	Separate software license and service transactions included in a single agreement
6.	Service transactions with a software element

NOTE: Postcontract customer support may be bundled with the software portions of transaction types 4, 5, and 6. The requirements of accounting for postcontract customer support bundled with a software license should be considered for these portions of the transactions.

Software licenses are often issued relative to software developed for a customer in a software development project. Such transactions are not software licenses in the sense of being product transactions accounted for as license (or product) revenue.

Software companies market software in product transactions to both end users and resellers. See the discussion in Chapter 1 (1.7.c) about the most prevalent channels of distribution for product transactions by software companies. In this sense, software companies may sell both to a retail market and to a wholesale market. Sometimes software is licensed to resellers for inclusion in larger systems or for marketing along with hardware by the reseller.

Because software consists of intellectual property and is easily reproduced, software companies generally retain the proprietary rights to it, and in the license agreement convey to the customer the right to use or resell specified numbers of copies of the software. Software licenses accounted for as product transactions may be short-term (such as month-to-month or quarter-to-quarter), medium-term (such as for a 1- or 2-year term), or perpetual, meaning that the customer receives the right to use or resell the software for an unlimited or virtually unlimited period.

Sometimes software is leased as part of a package that includes computer equipment or other property, plant, and equipment. Unless the software is incidental to the property, plant, and equipment, the portion of the lease attributable to the software, based on an allocation of fair market values of the components of the lease, constitutes a software license that should be accounted for as a product sale.

Some transactions structured as postcontract customer support arrangements (discussed in the following section) are substantively software licenses that should be accounted for as product sales. This can occur if the arrangements are essentially subscriptions to annual updates of the software product, and if the following conditions are met.

(a) The vendor takes on an explicit obligation to provide the updates,

(b) The utility of the product becomes severely limited with the passage of time for reasons other than technological changes, and

(c) The primary objective of the updates is not to incorporate new technology or improve operating performance.

—SOP 91-1, paragraph 127

(b) Postcontract Customer Support

Postcontract customer support, referred to in SOP 91-1 as "PCS," is the accountant's new word for what has been commonly referred to in the industry as maintenance. Maintenance is defined in FASB Statement 86 as follows:

> Activities undertaken after the product is available for general release to customers to correct errors or to keep the product updated with current information. Those activities include routine changes and additions.
> —FASB Statement 86, paragraph 52

The AICPA Task Force concluded that Statement 86's definition of maintenance did not cover all the activities contemplated by the type of software revenue transaction being considered, and therefore developed the new term *postcontract customer support*. Paragraph 24 of SOP 91-1 says:

> PCS arrangements generally have three distinct elements: telephone support, bug fixing, and product enhancements.

The FASB definition may have been sufficient to describe the activities being contemplated as to error correction, bug fixing, and routine updates for current information. In the software industry, however, postcontract customer support often includes the providing of product enhancements to customers that are more than routine changes and additions. Substantial enhancements are often provided in postcontract customer support arrangements, including those that add to the breadth of functionality, enabling a software product to do more, and depth of functionality, enabling a software product to perform better, such as by speeding up processing. Moreover, postcontract customer support typically includes providing telephone or on-site support of the customer in the use of the software, which is not contemplated in the FASB definition of maintenance.

Postcontract customer-support arrangements cover a defined term, typically ranging from a few months to several years. Most arrangements are made for periods of 1 year, with the software company anticipating annual renewals. Postcontract customer support agreements are generally offered as separate contracts in conjunction with perpetual licenses and, as discussed in the following section, are sometimes bundled with software licenses.

Postcontract customer support is generally performed pursuant to agreements that clearly indicate the enhancement and services to which the customer is entitled. Occasionally, however, a software company as a matter of practice provides similar enhancements and services to certain customers without a separate agreement. In such cases, a postcontract customer support arrangement exists.

(c) Software Licenses Bundled with Postcontract Customer Support

Software license arrangements often provide that during the first year the customer receives rights to product enhancements and services that are later provided in separate postcontract customer support arrangements. In addition, short-term and medium-term licenses often provide the customer with the same rights to postcontract customer support that are purchased by perpetual-license customers on an ongoing basis under separate contracts. A bundled software license and postcontract customer support package is a separate type of software revenue transaction which, as explained in Chapter 5, requires division into components for separate accounting.

If, after the initial term of a bundled software license and postcontract customer-support arrangement, a software company charges substantially less than the initial fee for renewal, there is a presumption that the renewal is entirely a postcontract customer support arrangement, even if the license would lapse if the customer does not pay the renewal fee. If a customer purchases a perpetual license but must continue to pay an annual fee in order to continue using the software, the annual fees are sometimes called "usage and maintenance fees." If the software company can demonstrate that it charges less than the amount of the renewal fee for separate postcontract customer-support arrangements with other customers, it can consider part of the renewal fee to be a software license.

Software included in a lease may consist of a bundled hardware lease and software license, and may as well include a postcontract customer-support arrangement.

(d) Contracts for Software Combined with Hardware or Services or Both

Contracts for software combined with hardware or services or both should be accounted for by contract accounting. They include software development contracts, turnkey system contracts, and other transactions in which a software company provides software combined with hardware or services or both. A turnkey system is defined in SOP 91-1 as follows.

> *Turnkey system.* An integrated group of hardware and software that is built, supplied, or installed complete and ready to operate. Many contracts for turnkey systems define solutions in terms of meeting functionality and performance criteria; others specify basic hardware and software configurations. The vendors represent to the users that the systems will perform stipulated tasks; significant customization of software is often required.
>
> —SOP 91-1, paragraph 11

Contracts for software combined with hardware or services or both are generally transacted in one agreement, with a single fixed fee for the entire contract or, sometimes, a variable fee. The contract may allocate the fee to specific elements, but the contract price generally relates to all the elements of the contract collectively. Sometimes the software, hardware, and services are contracted for in more than one agreement. Consideration should be given and judgment exercised in determining whether the business activities structured in several related agreements substantively constitute a single project that should be accounted for by contract accounting.

The following is helpful in identifying software revenue transactions that fall into this category.

> If a contract to deliver software or a software system, either alone or together with other products, requires significant production, modification, or customization of software, a system, or the other products, that contract should be accounted for in conformity with Accounting Research Bulletin (ARB) No. 45, *Long-Term Construction Type Contracts*, using the relevant guidance in SOP 81-1, *Accounting for Performance of Construction-Type and Certain Production-Type Contracts*.
>
> —SOP 91-1, paragraph 38

Another relevant guideline for identifying transactions that should be accounted for by contract accounting is contained in Accounting Research Bulletin (ARB) No. 45.

> In general the type of contract here under consideration is for construction of a specific project.
>
> —ARB No. 45, paragraph 1

SOP 81-1 provides the following ideas that are useful in identifying transactions subject to contract accounting.

> Contracts covered . . . are binding agreements between buyers and sellers in which the seller agrees, for compensation, to perform a service to the buyer's specifications. . . . Performance will often extend over long periods. . . . The service may consist of designing, engineering, fabricating, constructing, or manufacturing related to the construction or the production of tangible assets.
>
> —SOP 81-1, paragraph 12

Although today's contracts for software combined with hardware or services or both were not explicitly covered by SOP 81-1, paragraph 81 of SOP 91-1 refers to contracts described in SOP 81-1 that are similar to such software contracts.

> - Contracts to design, develop, manufacture, or modify complex . . . electronic equipment to a buyer's specification or to provide services related to the performance of such contracts.
> - Contracts for services performed by . . . engineers . . . or engineering design firms.
>
> —SOP 81-1, paragraph 13

The decision regarding whether to use contract accounting should be based on evaluation of the transaction in light of the guidance provided in ARB 45, SOP 81-1, and SOP 91-1 and by considering whether the characteristics of the transaction identify it more appropriately as a transaction that should be accounted for by other than contract accounting.

(e) Distinguishing Between a Product Sale and a Contract for Software Combined with Services or Hardware or Both

There are a variety of accounting methods that can be used for a particular transaction, depending on whether it is determined to be a software license (accounted for as a product sale) or a contract for software combined with hardware or services or both (accounted for by contract accounting). If a software license accounted for as a product sale also requires the software company to perform services, and those services are determined to be other significant vendor obligations or unreasonably delay the delivery of the software product, the software company is precluded from recognizing revenue for the software license until the remaining obligations are no longer significant. However, if the transaction is determined to be a contract for software combined with hardware or services or both, accounted for by contract accounting, revenue can usually be recognized at an earlier point by using one of the percentage-of-completion conventions. SOP 91-1 addresses the possible abuse of characterizing a product sale as a transaction to be accounted for by contract accounting, highlighting the importance of properly identifying a transaction as one of the two.

> Transactions that are normally accounted for as product sales should not be accounted for as long-term contracts merely to avoid the delivery requirements for revenue recognition normally associated with product sales.
>
> —SOP 91-1, paragraph 80

SOP 91-1 identifies the following types of services that may typically be considered other vendor obligations related to a software license accounted for as a product sale.

- *Installation*. Compiling, linking, and loading software modules into hardware or software platforms so that the software product will execute properly on the system.

- *Testing*. Executing installed software products, applying test routines and data, and evaluating the results against desired or expected results. It may involve adjusting installation or application parameters until the desired or expected results are achieved.

- *Training.* Educating users or resellers to operate or maintain a software system or to teach others to operate or maintain the system. For purposes of this definition, users may consist of personnel who will be operating the system, in-house technical support staff, or both.

- *Data Conversion.* Making data from different sources compatible by changing the presentation format or the physical recording medium.

- *Interface.* Establishing communication between independent elements, such as between one program and another, between a computer operator and the computer, and between a terminal user and a computer.

- *System integration.* Organizing a sequence of data-processing steps or a number of related data-processing sequences to reduce or eliminate the need to duplicate data entry or processing steps.

- *Porting.* Translating a computer program from one machine language to another so that software designed to operate on one platform can operate on another platform.

—SOP 91-1, paragraph 70

Some or all of these services may also be included in a contract for software combined with hardware or services or both, to be accounted for by contract accounting. In addition, contract accounting situations often include software development services or other services connected with the creation of a turnkey hardware and software system. In distinguishing between product sales transactions and contract accounting transactions, one must consider the nature and magnitude of the services, the time period over which the services are performed, and other aspects of the transaction.

(f) Separate Software License and Service Transactions Included in the Same Agreement

SOP 91-1 provides that a separate service transaction exists in conjunction with a software license if

> in addition to the obligation to deliver the software, the sales or licensing agreement includes obligations to perform services that (a) are not essen-

tial to the functionality of any other element of the transaction and (b) are separately stated and priced such that the total price of the agreement would be expected to vary as a result of the inclusion or exclusion of the services.

—SOP 91-1, paragraph 39

If such a separate service transaction is present, SOP 91-1 provides that the software license and the service transaction should be accounted for separately. If services are required as part of or in conjunction with a software license agreement, it will be necessary to decide whether a transaction is a software license with remaining vendor obligations, a transaction to be accounted for by contract accounting, or a separate software license and service transaction contained in a single agreement. SOP 91-1 gives one example of a service transaction.

An example of a service transaction with a discrete service element is one in which a vendor agrees to evaluate and redesign the user's account structure and in the same transaction agrees to provide off-the-shelf software to make a minor enhancement in the report preparation software already in use by the customer.

—SOP 91-1, paragraph 110

Most transactions in the software industry that include services are either software licenses with remaining vendor obligations or transactions to be accounted for by contract accounting. There are, however, services performed in conjunction with software licenses that meet the criteria of a separate service transaction. An example that has been suggested is one in which a software company provides software and, in the same contract, agrees to perform systems integration work and data conversion services that are unrelated to the software. In illustrating the notion of separate product and service transactions in the same agreement, most tend to give examples that clearly show little or no relationship between the software and the services. As the relationship between the software and services becomes greater, the greater is the concern that the contract could not be considered separate product and service transactions in a single agreement.

Perhaps a better threshold illustration is where in a single agreement a customer (1) licenses an existing software product for immediate delivery and use and (2) contracts with the software company to develop enhancements to the product, to be included in an enhanced version of the product that will be delivered to the customer at a later date. Some are concerned that this situation is analogous to providing the customer with a demonstration model of the software, while accepting an order from the customer for the next version of the software currently under development, to be delivered at a later date. In those situations, however, the customer may not be obligated to pay for the demonstration software—payment may be required only when the new version of the software is developed and delivered. The author believes that the demonstration software situation is not analogous to the separate software product and service transaction if the customer's acquisition of the current version of the software is genuine, the software is functional, and the customer is obligated to pay for the software independent of the enhancements to be developed. If those conditions are met, the fee paid for the initial software is not refundable, and the payments for developing the enhancements are reasonable in relation to the services, then the author believes that the provision of the initial software should be accounted for as a product transaction and the development of the enhancements should be accounted for as a service transaction. It should make no difference that the two transactions are included in one contract. Circumstances must be carefully evaluated to determine whether the customer's acquisition of the initial software is a genuinely separate transaction with a separate obligation to pay. If it is not, or if the circumstances are too vague to enable a conclusion as to the existence of separate product and service transactions, the author believes that contract accounting should be used to account for the entire contract as one transaction.

(g) Service Transactions with an Incidental Software Element

Paragraph 112 of SOP 91-1 describes a transaction that includes software, in which the software should be ignored for revenue recognition purposes. If a software company provides software and services together, and if including or excluding the software would not affect the total price of the transaction, the software is incidental to the services and all revenue should be accounted for as service revenue.

CHAPTER FIVE

Software Revenue Recognition—Software Licenses, Postcontract Customer Support, and Service Transactions

5.1 PROBABILITY OF COLLECTION— AN OVERRIDING CONDITION

Appearing throughout the revenue recognition criteria of SOP 91-1 is the general condition that collectibility must be probable. Paragraph 37 of SOP 91-1 provides that if a software company cannot estimate collectibility of a receivable, it should use either the installment method or the cost recovery method in accounting for the receivable. Under the installment method, as funds are collected, a pro rata portion of the revenue and costs of the transaction are recognized. Under the cost recovery method, funds collected are first applied to offset costs of the transaction and profit is recognized only as funds in excess of the total costs of the transaction are collected.

The requirement that collection be probable is an overriding condition, in addition to those for revenue recognition, discussed elsewhere in this book. This condition will not be repeated in the discussions in this chapter. Therefore, the reader should keep in mind that even if all other conditions are met, if collectibility is not probable, revenue should not be recognized until it can be determined that collectibility is probable.

5.2 SOFTWARE LICENSES

(a) Three Principal Criteria for Revenue Recognition

SOP 91-1 provides three principal criteria for revenue recognition of software license revenue, as listed in Exhibit 5.1.

The criteria included in Exhibit 5.1 relate to software licenses accounted for as product transactions. As to the third criterion, other significant vendor obligations could remain in transactions accounted for as service transactions or by contract accounting, in which revenue could be recognized even though other significant vendor obligations remain.

(b) Noncancelable Agreement and Fee Obligation

SOP 91-1 focuses extensively on the revenue recognition criteria requiring delivery and those requiring that no other significant remaining vendor obligations exist. It briefly covers the criterion most difficult to meet—getting the signed contract. Delivery is a simple matter and, in fact, sometimes occurs before a contract is signed. SOP 91-1's reference to the need for signed contracts is as follows.

> Some software licenses are evidenced by a written contract signed by the vendor and customer. Even if all other requirements set forth in this SOP for recognition of revenue are met, revenue should not be recognized on those licenses until persuasive evidence of the agreement exists. Such evidence is usually provided by the signed contract.
> —SOP 91-1, paragraph 50

If all other criteria are met, revenue may be recognized for the amount that the customer is unconditionally obligated to pay by the contract. If the license is noncancelable for an extended term (for example, 2, 3, or more years), and payments are required periodically over the term (for example, at the beginning of each year), the entire amount the customer is obligated to pay may be a fixed fee that should be recognized upon delivery. Paragraphs 57 and 58 of SOP 91-1 provide that license fees with extended payment terms should be evaluated as to enforceability of the agreement, the customer's credit rating, or the possibility that the software company might be reluctant to pursue

EXHIBIT 5.1 Criteria for Software License Revenue Recognition

1.	An enforceable agreement obligating the customer to pay for the software exists, and collectibility is probable.
2.	The software and documentation have been delivered.
3.	There are no remaining other significant vendor obligations.

collection. This passage further indicates that there should be a presumption that a fee is not fixed if payment is not due until the end of the license term or more than 12 months after delivery. Paragraph 57 provides that this presumption can be overcome by persuasive evidence to the contrary. If, for example, a software company has a history of collection of software license fees with deferred payment terms, the customer has an adequate credit rating, and other circumstances indicate that the entire fee will be collected, the author believes that the fee can be determined to be fixed, and the entire fee recognized on delivery. In practice, a convention that is sometimes referred to as a "12 month moving window" is considered appropriate for some transactions. Under this approach, noncancellable fees extending beyond one year are recognized as each payment comes due within 12 months.

For noncancelable software licenses with deferred payment schedules, a software company should consider discounting the software license revenue to present value and reporting a portion of the revenue as interest income.

Software licenses may be perpetual in term, for limited periods such as 1 year, or restricted to the reproduction, distribution, or use of a limited number of copies. Such contractual restrictions on a reseller or user do not change the nature of the transaction as a product sale, entirely recognizable when delivery and other criteria for revenue recognition have been met.

Sometimes software licenses are signed for, possibly, a 2- or 3-year term, with annual license fees payable at the beginning of each year. A customer may have a right to cancel the license upon giving notice, for example, 30 days before each anniversary of the inception of the license. If such notice is not given, the license is automatically renewed. An arrangement of this type is sometimes referred to as a cancelable license with an automatic renewal clause. In such cases, revenue should be recognized 1 year at a time, at the inception of each 1-year term if the customer does not cancel. Sometimes customers forget to cancel within the required time, even though it is their intent to do so, and the software company may be notified only when, upon receipt of an invoice, the customer requests cancelation. In such cases, although the software company may have a legally enforceable right to the next year's fee, the revenue should not be recognized unless the software company intends—one way or another—to collect the fee over the objections of the client. In many cases, as a practical matter, a software company does not pursue such collections, especially if the company wants continuing business with the customer for other products.

Fixed software license fees are the amounts of guaranteed payments to the software company, and may be recognized as software license revenue when all other conditions for revenue recognition are met. Variable fees are amounts payable to the software company contingent on certain conditions, and may be recognized as software license revenue when the events upon which payment is contingent occur and the amounts to be paid have been determined. Such terms often exist in licenses with resellers, in which the reseller agrees to pay a fixed fee plus additional amounts based on units sold or revenues realized by the reseller. Fixed fees in such arrangements should be recognized on delivery, and variable fees recognized when earned.

Sometimes reseller licenses may state an amount characterized as an obligation to pay a fixed fee, but timing of payments to the software company is contingent on transactions between the reseller and its customers. In such arrangements, the fees should be considered variable fees and the software company should not recognize revenue until the transactions between the reseller and its customers have occurred so as to obligate the reseller to pay the software company.

If a software company can be required to refund a portion of a software license fee contingent on the number of units sold by a reseller or used by a user, then any amount that could be repaid should not be recognized as revenue until that contingency is eliminated. Conversely, whenever there is a contingency that provides that the software license fee could be reduced or that the software company could be required to refund a portion of the license fee, whether variable or fixed, the software company may recognize as revenue the minimum amount that the customer is unconditionally obligated to pay, which is not subject to any refund contingency.

If a customer has the right to cancel a software license transaction, revenue should not be recognized until the cancellation rights have expired. Normal trade practices such as routine warranties and short-term rights of return should not be accounted for as cancellation rights, but should be accounted for as required by FASB Statement No. 5,

Accounting for Contingencies, and FASB Statement No. 48, *Revenue Recognition When Right of Return Exists*. However, these arrangements tend to apply generally to high-volume, lower-priced software products. For software companies with fewer transactions of higher-priced products, it may be appropriate to evaluate each transaction separately in terms of cancellation rights or rights of return.

Some software licenses give resellers or users the right to exchange one software product for another. Exchanges of software are returns and should be accounted for under the provisions of FASB Statement No. 48. There is, however, an exception: if a user exchanges one product for another of similar price and functionality, the transaction is not viewed as a return under Statement 48. SOP 91-1 provides that return accounting does not apply if, for example, a program is exchanged for

- The same program designed to run on another platform

- A slightly modified version of the program with minimal enhancements

- The same program on a different software medium of approximately the same cost, such as a different size floppy disk.

—SOP 91-1, paragraph 55

(c) Special Business Concerns Regarding License Obligations of Some Resellers

SOP 91-1 highlights some special business issues that should be considered when a software company licenses software to resellers for further marketing to ultimate users. A reseller may agree to an unconditional obligation to pay a software company for a software license, but as a practical matter, the reseller's ability to pay may be contingent on its success in marketing the software product. In such cases, revenue should not be recognized by the software company until realization is determined to be probable. This determination should be made in light of the reseller's operating history and other factors. The software industry is a young one, and many new resellers are established who will not be able to continue in business and honor the commitments made to their software suppliers.

Sometimes license fees from resellers are variable, based on the number of units sold. Sometimes a reseller's timing of payments to a software company is based on transactions between the reseller and the reseller's customers. For example, a reseller may agree to pay license fees up to $100,000 for the right to market a software product, payable as amounts are collected from the reseller's customers. In such cases, revenues represent variable fees and should be recognized only when transactions between the reseller and the reseller's customers give evidence that collection is probable.

(d) Delivery

SOP 91-1 establishes that software licenses are similar to product sales in other industries and that, therefore, the point at which the earnings process is considered complete is upon delivery, as in other industries.

Delivery of a software product is defined as follows.

Delivery. A transfer of software accompanied by documentation to the customer. It may be by—

a. A physical transfer of tape, disk, integrated circuit, or other medium;

b. Transmission by telecommunications;

c. Making available to the customer software that will not be physically transferred, such as through the facilities of a computer service bureau;

d. Authorization for duplication of existing copies in the customer's possession.

If a licensing agreement provides a customer with the right to multiple copies of a software product in exchange for a fixed fee, delivery means transfer of the product master, or the first copy if the product master is not to be delivered.

—SOP 91-1, paragraph 4

If the software is to be shipped, as in other industries, delivery ordinarily occurs when the product is handed over to a common carrier for shipment to the customer's place of business or to another site specified by the customer. This determination presumes that delivery of the software to the customer's place of business, or to another site specified by the customer, constitutes the completion of the software product transaction between the parties and that the customer will then pay the license fee within normal trade terms. If a substantial portion of the license fee is not payable until delivery to another site following the initial shipment, then revenue should not be recognized until the software is delivered to that site.

Delivery for purposes of recognition of software license revenue can be achieved even though the customer may not use the software immediately on delivery because further events in connection with the product sale are necessary, such as installation of the product and training of the customer's personnel in use of the software. This is similar to practices in other industries in the sale of tangible assets, whereby a machinery vendor would recognize product revenue on delivery of a manufacturing machine even though the machinery vendor must still install the machine and train the plant workers in its operation. As in the software and manufacturing machinery examples, even if the final acceptance of the product in operating order has not occurred, under generally accepted accounting principles the vendor may recognize product revenue on delivery, provided that it is expected that the remaining aspects of the transaction, such as installation and training, will be completed in a timely and orderly manner.

Payment terms for a software product may provide for payment after acceptance. For example, a software license fee may be billable on acceptance and payable 30 days later. Even if payment terms are linked to acceptance, or to a similar event other than delivery, product revenue for a software license should be recognized on delivery if the transaction is expected to be completed in a timely and orderly manner. If, however, there is uncertainty for any reason about whether a customer will accept software that has been delivered, revenue recognition should be deferred until there is no significant uncertainty.

For a summary of guidelines in regard to delivery as a criterion for software license revenue recognition, see Exhibit 5.2.

The following sections discuss consideration of whether other vendor obligations are insignificant, in which case it can be assumed that a software license transaction will be completed in a timely and orderly manner; or if they are significant, in which case software license revenue should not be recognized upon delivery.

EXHIBIT 5.2 Guidelines on Delivery as a Criterion for Software License Revenue Recognition

Delivery is the transfer of a software product and documentation to the customer.
Delivery may be accomplished by transfer of tape, disk, integrated circuit, or other medium; transmission by telecommunications; or making software available to a customer, such as through a service bureau.
Delivery is providing the customer with a product master if the customer has the right to make multiple copies of the software without additional charge.
Delivery is delivering the first copy if the vendor will reproduce the software.
If the product is shipped, delivery normally occurs when the software product is handed over to a common carrier for delivery to the customer.
If delivery is to a site other than the customer's place of business, and a substantial portion of the license fee is not payable until delivery to another site (such as the customer's place of business), then revenue may not be recognized until delivery to that other site.
Delivery completes the earnings process for the software license as a product sale—even if insignificant vendor obligations remain—if it is expected (partly based on history) that the insignificant vendor obligations will be completed and customer acceptance obtained in a timely and orderly manner.
If there is significant uncertainty about whether a customer will accept a software product, revenue should not be recognized upon delivery.
Delivery completes the earnings process—even if payment terms are linked to acceptance—if acceptance is expected to be obtained (partly based on history) in a timely and orderly manner.

(e) Evaluating Whether Other Vendor Obligations Are Significant or Insignificant

If, upon delivery, other vendor obligations (such as installation, testing, training, data conversion, interfacing, integration, and porting) must be completed, the software company must assess whether the obligations are significant or insignificant. Assessment should be based on the factors outlined in Exhibit 5.3.

If a software company is not able to estimate the costs of completing the other vendor obligations, they should be presumed to be significant. Exhibit 5.4 lists factors, cited by SOP 91-1, that could impair the ability of a software company to make an estimate of the cost of completing other vendor obligations. The presence of one or more of these circumstances could lead to a conclusion that other vendor obligations are significant.

EXHIBIT 5.3 Factors in Assessing Other Vendor Obligations:
Significant or Insignificant

Potential risks
Estimates of related costs
Probability that the vendor will be able to fulfill the obligations within cost estimates

EXHIBIT 5.4 Circumstances Possibly Indicating Other
Vendor Obligations Are Significant

Absence of historical experience in fulfilling similar kinds of obligations
History of inability to fulfill similar kinds of obligations to the satisfaction of customers
Absence of a history of relatively homogeneous contracts to be used as a measure of past performance
Relatively long performance periods

The assessment of whether other vendor obligations are significant or insignificant is judgmental. The presence, to some degree, of one or more of the circumstances listed in Exhibit 5.4 does not necessarily lead to a conclusion that obligations are significant. Conversely, there could be other circumstances that lead to a conclusion that other vendor obligations are significant. The fact that a task may be complex may not result in a significant other vendor obligation if the software company has the technical capability to perform the task in an orderly manner, and a history of doing so.

(f) Accounting If Other Vendor Obligations Are Insignificant

If it has been determined that other vendor obligations are insignificant, and fees for the insignificant other vendor obligations are not separately stated, the software company may either defer a portion of the software license revenue, to be recognized as the obligations are completed, or the software company may recognize all the software license revenue and accrue the estimated costs of completing the obligations.

SOP 91-1 permits the use of either of these alternatives because both are found to be in current use in other industries.

Sometimes other vendor obligations are separately priced. For example, assume that a software license agreement includes a $25,000 software license fee and a $5,000 installation and training fee. Assume further that the software company has a history of successful and orderly installation of the product, enabling the determination that these are insignificant other vendor obligations. The most sensible accounting practice for such a transaction would be to recognize the $25,000 software license revenue on delivery, and to recognize the revenue of $5,000 and the related expenses for the installation and training as those tasks are performed.

In some software license transactions, a software company agrees to license to a reseller or user a specified or unlimited number of copies of a software product in exchange for a fixed fee. Sometimes the software company provides the reseller or user with a product master from which the reseller or user may reproduce the software in accordance with the agreement. In such circumstances, the software company should recognize license revenue for the fixed fee upon delivery of the product master.

In some instances, a software company retains the product master and reproduces additional copies for the reseller or user, as requested. Software companies sometimes require this arrangement to ensure the quality of their products in the marketplace and to control the number of copies reproduced. The reproduction of software products by a software company in such circumstances is generally considered an insignificant other vendor obligation, and software license revenue should be recognized when the first copy of the software has been delivered to the user or reseller.

Some fixed-fee software licenses enable the reseller or user to obtain copies of two or more software products up to the amount of the total fixed fee. Sometimes the license gives the customer the right to choose copies of one or more products that do not exist at inception of the arrangement, but which will be developed later. In such arrangements, the software company should recognize the fixed fee proportionately as the customer indicates which products are to be taken under the arrangement and delivery of the copies of the products occurs. Delivery for this purpose is determined to be the point when the customer reproduces copies of the software from a product master, or when the software company delivers copies of the software to the customer (whichever is applicable). Amounts recognized should be equal to the specified prices of the individual products in determining how much of the fixed fee has been consumed by the customer. If the arrangement terminates and the customer has not consumed the entire fixed fee, any unrecognized portion of the fixed fee paid by the customer or that the customer is obligated to pay should be then recognized.

(g) Accounting If Other Vendor Obligations Are Significant

If other vendor obligations are determined to be significant, a transaction should be evaluated to see whether contract accounting applies or whether it should be accounted for as a separate software license and service transaction. If it is determined that the transaction should be accounted for as a software license with other significant vendor obligations, software license revenue should not be recognized until sufficient work has been performed on completing the obligations so that remaining obligations are not significant. At that point, if delivery has occurred and all other conditions for software license revenue recognition are met, the software license revenue should be recognized.

5.3 POSTCONTRACT CUSTOMER SUPPORT

(a) Ratable Recognition of Revenue

SOP 91-1 provides that revenue from postcontract customer support arrangements should be recognized ratably over the term of the arrangement. When the term of the postcontract customer support contract commences, such as upon acceptance of the product or when the software company begins providing services, the software company should begin recognizing postcontract customer support revenue on a monthly and quarterly basis.

Theoretically, postcontract customer support revenue should be recognized pro rata as the related expenses are incurred. However, because maintaining such costs records is not practicable in the industry, SOP 91-1 indicates that postcontract customer support revenue should generally be recognized on a straight-line basis. A software company is, however, permitted to use a basis other than straight-line if it can demonstrate that its expenses related to postcontract customer support are incurred in a different pattern.

(b) Unbundling of Software Licenses That Include Postcontract Customer Support

Software licenses and postcontract customer support are often bundled together in a software license agreement, in that the software company, as part of a license agreement, commits to provide the same services and enhancements that are provided in postcontract customer support arrangements. This is often seen in first-year software licenses, with the software company charging separately for postcontract customer support in subsequent years. It is also seen in continuing licenses that are renewed periodically.

Unless certain conditions (discussed in the following section) are met, allocation of an appropriate amount of revenue should be made to postcontract customer support and recognized over the period in which the postcontract customer support is provided. Allocation of revenue should be made between the license component and postcontract customer-support component, using the best information available. Several approaches for consideration in allocating between software license revenue and postcontract customer support are as follows:

1. If the software company provides separate software licenses and postcontract customer support, allocate the bundled price to the two components in proportion to the separate selling prices.

2. If the software company provides separate postcontract customer support for perpetual licenses but does not provide separate software licenses on an annual or other renewable basis, use the price charged for perpetual license customers as a surrogate price for postcontract customer support to be unbundled.

3. Allocate to postcontract customer support an amount that covers the costs plus a reasonable profit margin. Note that the SEC will not accept allocation based on this method, but that it can be used as a cross-check of the reasonableness of amounts otherwise determined.

4. Use another basis of determining a fair market value allocation for the two components.

In using amounts charged for separate postcontract customer support as a surrogate price for making the allocation, care should be taken to ensure that the services and enhancements are comparable. For example, the level of postcontract customer support services and enhancements provided to software licensees of object code versions of a product could be less than those for software licensees of source code versions of the product.

Sometimes the level of postcontract customer support that is bundled in an initial-year license is less than postcontract customer support offered in subsequent years under a separate contract. The allocation of revenue to first-year postcontract customer support may take this reduced level of services and enhancements into consideration, resulting in a reduced allocation.

If postcontract customer support that is bundled in a software license is not significant, SOP 91-1 permits accounting that does not unbundle the software and postcontract customer support elements, and allows the recognition of all the revenue when the criteria for recognition of the software revenue are met. This applies to postcontract customer support both bundled with an initial license and bundled with continuing licenses. The criteria listed in Exhibit 5.5 must be met to use this accounting.

For purposes of testing against the criteria in Exhibit 5.5, minimal enhancements are improvements to software products that include minor changes to product functionality and features. The history of offering minimal enhancements must be a predominant pattern covering at least several years. A history of offering significant enhancements in some years but not in others would not meet these criteria, nor would it support an expectation that enhancements will be minimal in the future.

If these criteria are met and revenue attributable to postcontract customer support is recognized when the software license revenue is recognized, the costs of providing the postcontract customer support should be accrued at the time the software license is recognized. Such costs should include the costs of postcontract customer support services,

EXHIBIT 5.5 Conditions for Not Unbundling Postcontract Customer Support Arrangements Included in Initial Year and Continuing Licenses

The estimated cost of providing the postcontract customer support is not significant.
Enhancements offered are expected to be, and have historically been, minimal.
The postcontract customer support obligation not to be unbundled must be for one year or less.

research and development expenses for development of enhancements, and amortization of enhancements, if applicable. Paragraph 6 of FASB Statement 86 provides that if any of the postcontract customer support costs are incurred prior to recognition of the software revenue, they should be charged to expense when incurred.

It is important that a software company have or develop a basis for allocating costs to the elements of bundled licenses and postcontract customer support arrangements. If there is no basis, the default position is unpleasant. SOP 91-1, paragraph 120, provides that if an allocation cannot be made, all revenue on a contract for a software license that includes postcontract customer support should be recognized over the period of the postcontract customer support arrangements.

5.4 SEPARATE SOFTWARE LICENSE AND SERVICE TRANSACTIONS INCLUDED IN A SINGLE AGREEMENT

When a software license and service transactions are included in a single agreement, two separate transactions are considered to be contracted for in one agreement. One is a software license and the other is a service transaction. In considering how software companies should account for service transactions, the AICPA Task Force relied on the work of the FASB staff in preparing a 1978 Invitation to Comment, *Accounting for Certain Service Transactions*. No pronouncements were issued by the FASB as a result of that project, but the Invitation to Comment provides an indication of current generally accepted accounting principles for service transactions.

Revenue attributable to the service portion of these agreements

> should be recognized as the services are performed or, if no pattern of performance is discernible, ratably over the period during which the services are performed.
>
> —SOP 91-1, paragraph 40

Generally, service revenue is recognized on an hourly basis if the fees are based on the hour, or on a percentage-of-completion basis if the fee is fixed.

The software license portion of these agreements, which should include only off-the-shelf software, should be accounted for as a product sale. The revenue recognition requirements delivery of software licenses with no significant remaining other vendor obligations would apply. The accounting for a software license that is part of separate software license with service transactions included in a single agreement ought not to be confused with contract accounting, in which measures of progress-to-completion other than delivery could apply.

5.5 SERVICE TRANSACTIONS WITH AN INCIDENTAL SOFTWARE ELEMENT

Paragraph 112 of SOP 91-1 says that if software is incidental to a service transaction, the transaction should be accounted for as a service transaction, and all revenue should be attributed to the services.

Contracts for Software Combined with Hardware or Services or Both

6.1 Methods of Contract Accounting
- (a) The Percentage-of-Completion Method and the Completed Contract Method
- (b) Circumstances in Which to Use the Percentage-of-Completion Method
- (c) Circumstances in Which to Use the Completed Contract Method

6.2 Application of the Percentage-of-Completion Method
- (a) Key Aspects of Applying the Percentage-of-Completion Method
- (b) Segmentation
- (c) Single-Cost-Center Contracts
- (d) Measuring Progress-to-Completion
- (e) Cost-to-Cost Measures of Progress-to-Completion
- (f) Input Hours-to-Hours Measures of Progress-to-Completion
- (g) Output Value Added Measures
- (h) Off-the-Shelf Software, Core Software, and Value Added Output Measures
    - (i) Type 1 Contracts
    - (ii) Type 4 Contracts

6.1 METHODS OF CONTRACT ACCOUNTING

(a) The Percentage-of-Completion Method and the Completed Contract Method

Contracts for software combined with hardware or services or both should be accounted for by contract accounting, using either the percentage-of-completion method or the completed-contract method. The determination of which method to use should be guided by paragraphs 21 through 33 of SOP 81-1. The two methods are not alternatives for the same circumstances, and percentage-of-completion is generally preferable. Guidance for application of the percentage-of-completion AICPA audit and accounting guide method and the completed-contract method is provided in the *Construction Contractors*.

Within the percentage-of-completion method, revenues and costs of a contract are recognized as progress-to-completion is achieved. Paragraph 25 of SOP 81-1 provides that if a contractor can estimate contract revenues and costs, those amounts should be used in applying percentage-of-completion accounting. If the contractor can estimate contract revenues and costs only within a range and can determine the amounts that are most likely to occur, those amounts should be used. If only ranges can be estimated, but no amounts of revenues and expenses within the ranges are considered most likely, then the lowest probable profit margin should be used in accounting until better estimates can be determined. If the final outcome of a contract cannot be estimated other than that a loss will not occur, a zero profit margin should be used to account for progress-to-completion by recording equal revenues and costs until better estimates can be determined. If that way of accounting is used, and the contractor changes from the zero-profit-margin approach when a better estimate is available, this constitutes a change in estimate.

Under the completed-contract method, revenues and costs of the contract are recognized only when the contract is completed.

(b) Circumstances in Which to Use the Percentage-of-Completion Method

The percentage-of-completion method is preferable if reasonably dependable estimates can be made and all the following conditions are met.

- Contracts executed by the parties normally include provisions that clearly specify the enforceable rights regarding goods or services to be provided and received by the other parties, the consideration to be exchanged, and the manner and terms of settlement.

- The buyer can be expected to satisfy his obligations under the contract.

- The contractor can be expected to perform his contractual obligations.
  —SOP 81-1, paragraph 23

Paragraph 24 of SOP 81-1 indicates that if a company has significant contracting operations, it should be presumed that the company is able to make reliable estimates, and therefore the percentage-of-completion method will generally be required. Two reasons for the presumption are that (1) making reliable estimates is an essential part of the contracting business, and that (2) reliable estimates are needed to comply with the requirement of generally accepted accounting principles to measure and record anticipated losses on uncompleted contracts. Persuasive evidence to the contrary is necessary to overcome the presumption that dependable estimates can be made by a company if contracting represents a significant portion of the company's business. The presence of business risks, hazards, or other uncertainties do not automatically overcome the presumption that reliable estimates can be made. The uncertainty caused by these factors must be so significant that there is specific, persuasive evidence to indicate that using the percentage-of-completion method is not preferable.

(c) Circumstances in Which to Use the Completed-Contract Method

The completed-contract method is preferable for contracts that do not meet the criteria for use of the percentage-of-completion method, such as when dependable estimates cannot be made or when business risks, hazards, or uncertainties are so substantial that the outcome of the contract is uncertain. In addition, the completed-contract method may be used for contracts of short duration if the results approximate the results achieved by the percentage-of-completion method.

The rest of this chapter deals with application of the percentage-of-completion method to contracts for software combined with hardware or services or both.

6.2 APPLICATION OF THE PERCENTAGE-OF-COMPLETION METHOD

(a) Key Aspects of Applying the Percentage-of-Completion Method

Applying the percentage-of-completion method to contracts for software combined with hardware or services or both involves a certain decision path, as illustrated in Exhibit 6.1.

The following sections discuss each of the aspects of the percentage-of-completion method shown in Exhibit 6.1 and illustrate their application to accounting for contracts for software combined with hardware or services or both.

(b) Segmentation

In segmentation, a contract is divided into elements, and revenues and expenses of each element are accounted for discretely by using principles of contract accounting. A gross margin is computed for each element; therefore, over the life of a contract, gross margin percentages will vary depending on the accounting periods in which revenues are recognized for each element.

EXHIBIT 6.1 Applying the Percentage-of-Completion Method

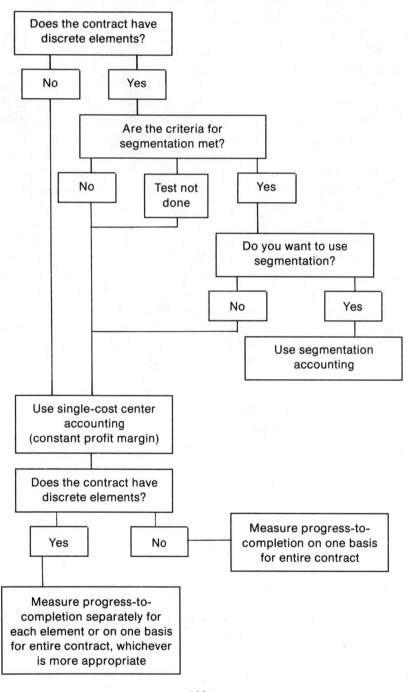

In the past, some software companies have accounted for contracts for software combined with hardware or services or both, by using an accounting approach that yields a result similar to segmentation, in which they unbundled the contracts for accounting purposes. Revenue for the software element of the contracts was recognized at or near the beginning of the contract as revenue for a software license. Some of these software companies had not considered whether contract accounting applied to these transactions and had, therefore, not considered whether they met the criteria of SOP 81-1 for use of segmentation.

The AICPA Task Force believed that segmentation provided the most representationally faithful accounting for contracts for software combined with hardware or services or both, but concluded that most software companies would not meet the stringent segmentation criteria of SOP 81-1. In the initial proposed draft of SOP 91-1 provided to the FASB for review, the AICPA Task Force recommended modification of the segmentation criteria when applied to the software industry to enable more software companies to qualify for segmentation. However, the FASB disagreed, saying that the segmentation criteria of SOP 81-1 should be applied uniformly to all industries. SOP 91-1, paragraph 85, makes clear that for a software company to use segmentation accounting, it must meet the segmentation criteria of SOP 81-1. Under SOP 81-1, a transaction can qualify for segmentation under two sets of conditions. The first is contained in paragraph 40.

A project may be segmented if all the following steps were taken and are documented and verifiable:

a. The contractor submitted bona fide proposals on the separate components of the project and on the entire project.

b. The customer had the right to accept the proposals on either basis.

c. The aggregate amount of the proposals on the separate components approximated the amount of the proposal on the entire project.

Alternatively, segmentation may be used if the criteria in paragraph 41 of SOP 81-1 are met.

a. The terms and scope of the contract or project clearly call for separable phases or elements.

b. The separable phases or elements of the project are often bid or negotiated separately.

c. The market assigns different gross profit rates to the segments because of factors such as different levels of risk or differences in the relationship of the supply and demand for the services provided in different segments.

d. The contractor has a significant history of providing similar services to other customers under separate contracts for each significant segment to which a profit margin higher than the overall profit margin on the project is ascribed.*

e. The significant history with customers who have contracted for services separately is one that is relatively stable in terms of pricing policy rather than one unduly weighted by erratic pricing decisions (responding, for example, to extraordinary economic circumstances or to unique customer-contractor relationships).

f. The excess of the sum of the prices of the separate elements over the price of the total project is clearly attributable to costs savings incident to combined performance of the contract obligations (for example, cost savings in supervision, overhead, or equipment mobilization). Unless this condition is met, segmenting a contract with a price substantially less than the sum of the prices of the separate phases or elements would be inappropriate even if the other conditions are met. Acceptable price variations should be allocated to the separate phases or elements in proportion to the prices ascribed to each. In all other situations a substantial difference in price (whether more or less) between the separate elements and the price of the total project is evidence that the contractor has accepted different profit margins. Accordingly, segmentation is not appropriate, and the contracts should be the profit centers.

g. The similarity of services and prices in the contract's segments and services and the prices of such services to other customers contracted separately should be documented and verifiable.

*In applying the criterion in paragraph 41(d), values assignable to the segments should be on the basis of the contractor's normal historical prices and terms of such services to other customers. The division considered but rejected the concept of allowing a contractor to segment on the basis of prices charged by other contractors, since it does not follow that those prices could have been obtained by a contractor who has no history in the market.

—SOP 81-1, paragraph 41

Software companies generally do not do business in the way described in paragraph 40 of SOP 81-1. As to the second set of criteria, in paragraph 41, most software companies would have difficulty in complying with subparagraphs (b), (d), and (e), partly because of the short life of the software industry in comparison with other industries. Their limited existence does not enable many software companies to demonstrate the required significant history of separately bidding, negotiating, and providing the separable phases or elements. Moreover, some software companies are contractually prohibited from selling computer hardware separately by agreements with their computer hardware suppliers, which prevents compliance with the criterion of paragraph 41(b). Most software companies are not in the business of selling hardware separately.

As provided in SOP 81-1, segmenting is an option a contractor may use if a project meets the segmentation criteria.

> A project . . . with segments that have different rates of profitability *may* be segmented if it meets the criteria [emphasis added].
> —SOP 81-1, paragraph 39

Accordingly, a software company may meet the criteria for segmentation, yet decide to account for its contracts as single-cost-center contracts. That will in some cases defer profitability, because a lower gross margin is recognized in connection with revenue for the software element of the contract. To demonstrate that segmentation criteria have been met may be a difficult task and, in respect to satisfying auditors and possibly the SEC, simply not worth the effort.

Some have confused segmentation with accounting for separate software and service transactions contained in a single agreement. This is evidenced by the presumption that revenue for the software element of a contract accounted for by using segmentation would be recognized as based on the delivery criteria for revenue recognition on a software license. Conceptually, it is important to note that the only distinction between segmentation and single-cost-center contract accounting is the recognition of different gross margins for each element of a contract under segmentation, whereas under single-cost-center contract accounting, a constant gross margin is recognized for all contract revenue.

Segmentation is still contract accounting, and the basis of recognition of contract revenue under segmentation is no different than for revenue of a contract with discrete elements accounted for as a single cost center using a constant gross margin, based on progress-to-completion. Progress-to-completion is a contract accounting notion, whereas delivery of a software product is a notion related to software licenses as product sales. Although the delivery criterion applicable to software license revenue can be used as the basis for measuring progress-to-completion for the software element of a contract accounted for by segmentation, it is by no means the only basis. For example, as discussed later in this chapter, contract activities sometimes take place at the software vendor's site rather than at the customer's site, and progress-to-completion for the software element may occur before delivery to the customer.

Example 6.1 illustrates segmentation accounting for a contract with discrete elements of off-the-shelf software, services, and computer hardware, with typical revenues, costs, and gross margins.

EXAMPLE 6.1 Example Contract Revenues and Costs by Element

	Revenues	Cost Amount	Cost Pct.	Gross Profit Amount	Gross Profit Margin
Off-the-shelf software	$ 400	$ 40	10%	$ 360	90%
Services	250	200	80%	50	20%
Hardware	350	300	86%	50	14%
Contract totals	$ 1,000	$ 540	54%	$ 460	46%

Revenues are recognized for each element in the accounting periods indicated in Exhibit 6.2, using appropriate measures of progress-to-completion. Application of various measures of progress-to-completion for contract accounting in the software industry are discussed in later sections of this chapter.

EXHIBIT 6.2 Illustration of Segmentation Accounting for a Combined Contract for Off-the-Shelf Software, Hardware, and Services

		Accounting Period			
	Total	1	2	3	4
Revenues					
Element					
Off-the-shelf software	$400		$400		
Hardware	350			350	
Services	250	$50	100	$75	$25
Total revenues	1,000	50	500	425	25
Costs					
Costs incurred and recognized					
Off-the-shelf software	40		40		
Hardware	300			300	
Services	200	40	80	60	20
Costs incurred and recognized	540	40	120	360	20
Gross profit reported	$460	$10	$380	$65	$5
Gross profit margin	46%	20%	76%	15%	20%

The illustrations in this chapter are primarily applicable to software companies that acquire hardware from a supplier to include in a contract. If a hardware company provides a turnkey system containing software and hardware, and constructs hardware as part of the contract, percentage-of-completion accounting may be applicable to the hardware element. In that case, revenues and costs applicable to the hardware element would be recognized over the periods of performance, rather than in one period (as in the illustrations in this chapter).

(c) Single-Cost-Center Contracts

Most contracts for software combined with hardware or services or both will not meet the segmentation criteria, requiring the use of single-cost-center contract accounting. Under this method of contract accounting, the entire contract is viewed as a single cost center, establishing a link between all contract revenues and all contract costs. When each dollar of revenue is recognized, a proportionate amount of the total contract cost is recognized; therefore, each dollar of revenue recognized on the contract is accounted for at a constant gross margin.

For example, assume the facts in the illustration on page 177, but that the transaction is accounted for as a single-cost-center contract. Even though the revenues, costs, and gross profits attributed to the elements of the contract by the software company in pricing the contract bid yield different gross margins when looked at separately (off-the-shelf software, 90 percent; services, 20 percent; and hardware, 14 percent), all revenue on the contract must be burdened by cost recognition that yields the gross margin for the entire project (44 percent). Because the timing of costs incurred will not match the timing of costs to be recognized as expenses in the income statement, adjusting cost accruals and reversals must be recognized in order to maintain the constant gross margin.

Those who believe that single-cost-center contract accounting in the software industry does not yield a sensible result view the reporting of gross profits that way as distorted. Significant profits may be reported in periods that include progress-to-completion for the hardware element of the contract. Software companies that are not hardware manufacturers generally contemplate a small gross margin on the hardware element of a contract in relation to other elements of a contract, and higher gross margins on the off the software element of a contract.

The elements of contracts in the software industry are different from those of most contracts contemplated when SOP 81-1 was written, in that the software and hardware elements usually contribute vastly different gross margins to the contract. The software gross margins are quite high and the hardware gross margins are comparatively low. The AICPA Task Force believed that these circumstances, which were essentially unique to the software industry, justified fresh consideration of how to approach some aspects of contract accounting for the software industry. The Task Force was concerned about the inability of single-cost-center contract accounting to provide a rational gross profit and representation of the earnings process by accounting period in relation to progress-to-completion on the individual elements. This concern led to the AICPA Task Force recommendation, which was rejected by the FASB, for modification of the segmentation criteria for software companies.

(d) Measuring Progress-to-Completion

Measures of progress-to-completion can be divided into two major categories: input measures and output measures. Input measures define progress in terms of efforts expended (such as the percentage of total-contract labor hours incurred) or costs incurred within a particular contract. Output measures define progress based on results achieved. Milestones and value-added measures, the two output measures mentioned in SOP 81-1, are the most applicable to the software industry. Input measures have been used predominantly in contract accounting over the years. They are suitable for measuring progress-to-completion in the construction industry and other industries in which contract accounting has been most common.

Measuring progress-to-completion solely on an input basis may not be appropriate for some contracts in the software industry, because the earnings process on a contract attributable to preexisting software is not adequately measured by input measures because of the low cost of software charged as expense to a given project. As a result, it is more likely in the software industry that different measures of progress-to-completion should be considered for different elements of a contract.

The following sections discuss application of various input and output measures to contracts for software combined with hardware or services or both.

(e) Cost-to-Cost Measures of Progress-to-Completion

Under the cost-to-cost convention of measuring progress-to-completion, contract costs incurred are reported as expenses of the period and used as the basis for computing revenue earned on the contract by adding the constant profit margin to the costs incurred. Revenue to be recognized is computed by multiplying total contract (or element) revenue by the ratio of contract (or element) costs incurred to total estimated contract (or element) costs. The following equation illustrates this computation for the entire contract described in Example 6.1.

$$\frac{\text{Total contract costs (\$540)}}{\text{Total contract cost percentage (.54)}} = \$1,000 \ \text{(Total contract revenues)}$$

SOP 81-1 provides a series of guidelines for determining when costs incurred should not be included in the measure of progress-to-completion. In such circumstances, costs should be deferred until the activity or process associated with the cost has progressed sufficiently. Specific instances are cited in SOP 81-1, recommending that costs should not be included when

1. Because of inefficiencies or other factors, the costs incurred are not representative of progress-to-completion.

2. Disproportionate costs are incurred in the early stages of a project, such as costs of uninstalled materials not specifically produced or fabricated for the project.

3. Payments have been made that are related to subcontracts that have not been performed.

Paragraph 50 of SOP 81-1 gives an example of costs incurred that should be excluded from measuring progress-to-completion: costs of materials not unique to a project, purchased or accumulated at job sites, that have not been physically installed. Although this example, typical of SOP 81-1, generally relates to the construction industry, software companies using cost-to-cost measures should consider comparable situations in determining when to include costs incurred in measuring progress-to-completion.

Exhibit 6.3 is an illustration of how the contract described in Exhibit 6.1 would be accounted for as a single cost center in using cost-to-cost measures for the entire contract.

EXHIBIT 6.3 Illustration of Accounting for a Contract as a Single Cost Center Measuring Progress-to-Completion on an Input Cost-to-Cost Basis

| | | Accounting Period | | | |
	Total	1	2	3	4
Total revenues	$1,000	$74	$222	$667	$37
Costs incurred and recognized					
Off-the-shelf software	40		40		
Hardware	300			300	
Services	200	40	80	60	20
Total	540	40	120	360	20
Gross profit reported	$460	$34	$102	$307	$17
Gross profit margin	46%	46%	46%	46%	46%

Computations of Revenue Amounts

Costs incurred to beginning of period		$	$ 40	$160	$520
Costs incurred in period		40	120	360	20
Costs incurred to end of period		$40	$160	$520	$540
Percentage of total contract costs ($540) incurred		7.41%	29.63%	96.30%	100.00%
Percentage of total contract costs incurred, multiplied by total contract revenue ($1,000)		$74	$296	$963	$1,000
Cumulative revenue recognized to beginning of period			74	296	963
Revenue for period		$74	$222	$667	$37

If cost-to-cost measures are used for the entire contract, $307 of the total contract gross profit of $460 is reported in the period in which the cost of the hardware is incurred. As previously discussed, most software companies would attribute a minor portion of the earnings process on a contract to having incurred the hardware cost, making the result of using cost-to-cost measures for an entire contract of this nature not representative of the timing of the earnings process.

(f) Input Hours-to-Hours Measures of Progress-to-Completion

Under the hours-to-hours convention of measuring progress, the proportion of total contract hours incurred is used to measure progress. The input cost-to-cost convention does not require the use of contract cost accruals and credits to maintain the constant gross margin, because costs incurred drive the revenue amount. Yet, if input hours-to-hours measures are used, such cost accruals and reversals may be necessary to maintain the constant gross margin. Using the illustration in Example 6.1, assume that service hours are incurred on the contract as follows.

	Number of Hours Incurred
Period 1	500
Period 2	1,000
Period 3	750
Period 4	250
	2,500

Exhibit 6.4 illustrates how the contract would be accounted for if input hours-to-hours measures were used for the entire contract.

The use of input hours-to-hours measures with a constant gross margin for the entire contract seems to provide a more sensible result than the input cost-to-cost measures illustrated in Exhibit 6.3. This will usually be the case if the expenditure of hours on a project is a reasonable measure of total contract activities. Moreover, input hours-to-

EXHIBIT 6.4 Illustration of Accounting for a Contract as a Single Cost Center Measuring Progress-to-Completion on an Input Hours-to-Hours Basis

		Accounting Period			
	Total	1	2	3	4
Total revenues	$1,000	$200	$400	$300	$100
Costs incurred					
Off-the-shelf					
software	40		40		
Hardware	300			300	
Services	200	40	80	60	20
Total	540	40	120	360	20
Contract cost accruals and credits					
Accruals		68	96		34
Credits				(198)	
Costs recognized	540	108	216	162	54
Gross profit reported	$460	$92	$184	$138	$46
Gross profit margin	46%	46%	46%	46%	46%

Computations of Revenue Amounts

Hours incurred to beginning of period			500	1,500	2,250
Hours incurred in period		500	1,000	750	250
Hours incurred to end of period		500	1,500	2,250	2,500
Percentage of total contract hours (2,500) incurred		20.00%	60.00%	90.00%	100.00%
Percentage of total contract hours incurred, multiplied by total contract revenue ($1,000)		$200	$600	$900	$1,000
Cumulative revenue recognized to beginning of period			200	600	900
Revenue for period		$200	$400	$300	$100

hours will be a more sensible measure than input cost-to-cost if a single item, such as hardware, has a high cost in relation to other project costs. The next section discusses and illustrates a somewhat more sophisticated application of measures of progress-to-completion, in which different measures are used for different elements.

(g) Output Value-Added Measures

In most industries, reasonable contract accounting results can be achieved with traditional input cost-to-cost or hours-to-hours measures of progress-to-completion. In the software industry, however, in many contracts for software combined with hardware or services or both, the software is the most important item being provided, but input measures do not provide a sound basis for measuring progress-to-completion for the software element. If input measures are used, the revenue properly assignable to the software element is essentially spread over the revenue recognition driven entirely by the other elements of the contract. SOP 81-1 provides for the use of output measures of progress-to-completion, which is available to rectify this problem, but there has not been much use of output measures in practice, and little guidance has been provided on the use of output measures.

The software industry is one industry in which output measures have substantial applicability in obtaining sensible measures of progress-to-completion. Specifically, value-added output measures are applied by determining the portion of the revenue of the entire contract that is attributable to software, and by recognizing that revenue when appropriate criteria have been met for measuring progress-to-completion. Paragraph 102 of SOP 91-1 describes a way of using value-added output measures that is very important to the software industry.

> If a reasonable approximation of progress-to-completion can be obtained by measuring the application of software to the contract, the software should be included in the measurement of progress-to-completion based on output measures before delivery to the user's site.

In various paragraphs of SOP 91-1, there are references to measuring progress-to-completion on contracts for the software element upon delivery or installation. Although such events can be used for measuring progress, the place of occurrence need not be the customer's site. Depending on the circumstances, progress may be determined to have occurred at the software company's site. Paragraph 102 makes this clear in the discussion of output measures, as does paragraph 97 in the discussion of input measures.

> ... [S]ome contract activities may take place at the vendor's site rather than at the user's. Therefore, the act of delivering a completed package to the user's site may not be a good indicator of when value has been added to the contract.
>
> —SOP 91-1, paragraph 102

> If the measurement of progress-to-completion is primarily based on costs, the contribution of hardware or software to that progress may be measurable before delivery to the user's site. For example, the configuration of hardware, customization of core software, installation of off-the-shelf software or customized software, and similar activities may occur at the vendor's site. In such cases, progress-to-completion based on cost-to-cost measures should be measured as the related costs are incurred at the vendor's site, rather than on delivery to the user's site.
>
> —SOP 91-1, paragraph 97

This notion is not an invention of SOP 91-1—it goes back to the roots of contract accounting as described in ARB No. 45, *Long-Term Construction-Type Contracts*.

> While such contracts are generally carried on at the job site, the bulletin would also be applicable in appropriate cases to the manufacturing or building of special items on a contract basis in a contractor's own plant.
>
> —ARB No. 45, paragraph 1

Accordingly, the determination of a software company's practices for measuring progress-to-completion should be approached broadly. Instead of a concern with delivery to the customer's site, there should be a perception of achievement of progress on the contract whether it occurs at the software company's site or at the customer's site.

The use of value-added output measures, as described in SOP 91-1, paragraph 102, relates to recognition of the value of preexisting software provided to the customer as part of the contract. This approach is considered appropriate only for off-the-shelf software and hardware, which have separate exchange value. Off-the-shelf software is defined in paragraph 3 of SOP 91-1 as follows.

> Off-the-shelf software [is] software marketed as a stock item that customers can use with little or no customization.

The use of value-added output measures as described in paragraph 102 of SOP 91-1 is not considered appropriate for core software, which is defined in SOP 91-1 as follows.

> Core software [is] an inventory of software that vendors use in creating other software. Core software is not delivered as is because customers cannot use it unless it is customized to meet system objectives or customer specification.
>
> —SOP 91-1, paragraph 3

Again referring to the illustrative contract in Example 6.1, the use of output value-added measures would result in revenue reported in the periods indicated in Exhibit 6.5. In the case of single-cost-center contracts, if input measures are used, little or no revenue is effectively derived that could be identified with the off-the-shelf software element. Exhibit 6.5 illustrates how for single-cost-center contracts, output measures provide a more meaningful revenue amount to allocate to the off-the-shelf software element.

The illustration in Exhibit 6.5 yields results that many believe are the most sensible for contracts of this type if segmentation cannot be used. The following discussions should be carefully considered, however, if a software company wishes to apply this contract accounting approach.

Output measures can be applied to elements of a contract other than software. For example, output measures may be used to value revenue for the hardware element, or even for establishing the value of a labor-intensive element of a contract. The use of an output measure for a labor-intensive element would tend to delay revenue recognition, as compared with the timing of revenue recognition when using labor input measures. Therefore, most software companies would probably prefer to limit the use of output measures to software elements and, in some cases, hardware elements.

EXHIBIT 6.5 Illustration of Accounting for a Contract as a Single-Cost-Center, Using Output Value Added Measures for Off-the-Shelf Software, Input Cost-to-Cost Measures for Hardware, and Input Hours-to-Hours Measures for Services

	Total	Accounting Period 1	2	3	4
Revenues					
Element					
Off-the-shelf software	$400		$400		
Hardware	350			$350	
Services	250	50	100	75	25
Total revenue	1,000	50	500	425	25
Costs					
Costs incurred					
Off-the-shelf software	40		40		
Hardware	300			300	
Services	200	40	80	60	20
Costs incurred	540	40	120	360	20
Contract cost accruals and credits					
Accruals			216		
Credits		(13)	(66)	(131)	(7)
Costs recognized	540	27	270	230	14
Gross profit reported	$460	$23	$230	$196	$12
Gross profit margin	46%	46%	46%	46%	46%

Computations of Revenue Amounts

Off-the-shelf software, based on output value added to the contract on application of the software to the contract		$400		
Hardware, based on input cost-to-cost measures				
Costs incurred to beginning of period	$ 0	$ 0	$300	$300
Costs incurred in period	0	300	0	0
Costs incurred to end of period	$ 0	$300	$300	$300
Percentage of total hardware costs ($300) incurred	.00%	100.00%	100.00%	100.00%
Percentage of total hardware costs incurred, multiplied by total hardware element revenue ($350)	$ 0	$350	$350	$350
Cumulative revenue recognized to beginning of period	0	0	350	350
Revenue for period	$ 0	$350	$ 0	$ 0
Services, based on input hours-to-hours measures				
Hours incurred to beginning of period		500	1,500	2,250
Hours incurred in period	500	1,000	750	250
Hours incurred to end of period	500	1,500	2,250	2,500
Percentage of total contract hours (2,500) incurred	20.00%	60.00%	90.00%	100.00%
Percentage of total contract hours incurred, multiplied by total service element revenue ($250)	$50	$150	$225	$250
Cumulative revenue recognized to beginning of period		50	150	225
Revenue for period	$50	$100	$75	$25

The approach of using value-added output measures in application of "as is" software to a contract is relevant only to off-the-shelf software, as opposed to core software. A software company should be able to demonstrate that the off-the-shelf software has been and is being licensed separately to customers for their use without modification, in transactions that do not include the services and other elements contained in the contracts for software combined with hardware or services or both.

Another key aspect of applying value-added output measures is the determination of when to recognize progress-to-completion for the software element, which results in recognition of the software revenue. Delivery to the client can be used as the measure of progress. In many of these contracts, however, the software is not delivered to the client, or is not intended for use by the client until the end of the project, because the project services must be performed first. If a copy of the software is delivered to the client but not used by the client, and another copy is retained by the software company for the project work, then, in the absence of other compelling circumstances, it is unlikely that progress on the project has been made as a result of the delivery of the copy to the client.

The software is often retained by the software company at its site and used in, or "applied to," the contract. This represents progress as a result of the value added to the contract. A precise meaning of *application of the software to a contract* is not provided in SOP 91-1. The AICPA Task Force wanted to set the broad principle and allow guidelines to develop in practice, based on facts and circumstances. It is clear, however, that it was intended that application of the software to the contract, in order to trigger the recognition of the software revenue, would have to consist of the software being used in a substantive or significant way so that it had clearly become part of the work product of the contract.

Thus, it would not be appropriate to recognize software revenue at the beginning of a project upon producing and giving a copy of the software to the project manager for use on the project, even if the project manager then sets up the software in a separate work space for the client and begins some initial use of the software.

It has been suggested that an appropriate level of use on the project could be established by some quantitative measure of use of the software on the project—for example, a man week, a man month, or 5 percent or 10 percent of the project hours. In its initial work with SOP 91-1 in practice, however, the SEC has expressed a preference that the measure of application be event-based—that a software company be able to demonstrate evidence of progress on the project using the software.

(h) Off-the-Shelf Software, Core Software, and Value-Added Output Measures

Evaluation of whether software is off-the-shelf software may have some interesting twists. A software product could be considered off-the-shelf software for one project but not for another, depending on whether the services performed for the project involve adding to or changing the functionality of the off-the-shelf software. Exhibit 6.6 describes four types of contracts for software combined with services. It is important to determine which of these types of contracts is being considered.

(i) **TYPE 1 CONTRACTS:** It appears clear that the Task Force intended that paragraph 102 of SOP 91-1 permit recognition of revenue for a

EXHIBIT 6.6 Software and Services

Type	
1	Services do not include significant changes to the existing code or significant additions to the code of the off-the-shelf software.
2	Services include significant additions of code to add functionality, but no significant changes to the existing code of the off-the-shelf software.
3	Services include both significant changes to existing code and significant additions of code to add functionality to the off-the-shelf software.
4	Services include significant additions of code to add functionality and, possibly significant changes, to the existing code of core software.

Type 1 contract's off-the-shelf software element, based on output value-added measures of progress, when the off-the-shelf software is applied to the contract. For Type 1 contracts, progress is achieved on the software element by providing preexisting off-the-shelf software. Although integration and other services may be provided in the contract, there is no programming of significant changes to the code of the off-the-shelf software, or of significant additional functionality. Type 1 contracts, as well as the other types, may include additional services that are not "software" services such as integration; for instance, using the client's data in implementation of the software.

(ii) TYPE 4 CONTRACTS: At the other end of the spectrum, it appears clear that the AICPA Task Force intended that Type 4 contracts should not be accounted for by applying paragraph 102 to recognize revenue based on an output value-added measure of progress, when the core software is applied to the contract—meaning, when the core software is being used in the contract for the programming of changes to code or additional functionality. Type 4 contracts are clearly software development projects, in that the projects begin without any software that is usable in its existing form.

(iii) TYPE 2 AND TYPE 3 CONTRACTS: Whether the accounting described for Type 1 contracts can be used for Type 2 or Type 3 contracts, or both, is less clear.

Some believe it is important to focus on the degree of change to the software, whether by way of modification to existing code or the addition of code. They tend to measure progress-to-completion only to the extent that obligations associated with the output do not preclude revenue recognition because of their significance to the particular output. Thus, adding functionality or features to the software would delay revenue recognition for that output until the remaining functionality or features to be added are no longer significant. On the other hand, other software programming services that do not relate directly to the software being provided, such as interfacing or data conversion, would not be considered directly relevant to the timing of inclusion of the off-the-shelf output in measurement of progress-to-completion.

Others believe that the accounting described for Type 1 contracts should be permitted for Type 2 contracts, which do not include significant changes to the code of off-the-shelf software, even though there may be programming of significant additional functionality. Their view is that providing off-the-shelf software in the contract, a product with separate exchange value, constitutes completion of a key distinguishable element of a contract. They believe that even though the contract includes development of significant additional functionality, that should not taint the integrity of the off-the-shelf software as a separate contract element for which the accounting contemplated for Type 1 contracts would be permitted.

Some also believe that the accounting described for Type 1 contracts should be permitted for Type 3 contracts, even though there are significant changes to the code of the off-the-shelf product. Their view is that off-the-shelf software should always be considered a separable contract element for which progress is measured separately when provided in a contract, even if the code is significantly changed because of the specifications of the project. They believe that providing off-the-shelf software constitutes the provision of a significant element of value, and that software development work should be considered another matter, which should not taint the integrity of the off-the-shelf software as a separate element.

Opposing views would (1) not permit the accounting described for Type 1 contracts for either Type 2 or Type 3 contracts, or (2) permit that accounting for Type 2 contracts, but not for Type 3. Those who would not permit that accounting for either Type 2 and Type 3 contracts believe that if there is programming of significant changes to the code of off-the-shelf software, or of significant additional functionality, that the off-the-shelf software should be considered core software in the contract. This view is partly based on a concern that there may be technical uncertainty about whether the software, including changes to code and additional functionality, can be made to function as required under the contract and other obligations that survive delivery, which should preclude revenue recognition. Some would permit the accounting described for Type 1 contracts to be allowed for Type 2 contracts, but not for Type 3, based on the view that the off-the-shelf software should be characterized as core software only if there are significant changes to its code.

The views that would not permit the such accounting for either Type 2 or Type 3 contracts, or both, is based on different concepts of contract elements, contract milestones, and contract risks. As there are presently no definitive guidelines, in considering a Type 2 or Type 3 contract, one should determine whether, based on the specifics of the contract, the software development project should be viewed as a project for which measures of progress such as input cost-to-cost, input hours-to-hours, milestones, or another method should be used.

(iv) THE AUTHOR'S VIEW: The author's personal view would permit the accounting described for Type 1 contracts to be used for Type 2 contracts, but not for Type 3. This position is based on the view that off-the-shelf software that is not changed significantly as to existing code should be accounted for as a discrete element of a contract, separate from the development work to create additional functionality. As to Type 3 contracts, the author believes that off-the-shelf software that is changed significantly in a contract is substantively core software for purposes of that project.

The author and contributing authors have discussed the question of whether the accounting described for Type 1 contracts should be permitted for both Type 2 and Type 3 contracts, Type 2 but not Type 3 contracts, or neither. Among the group, there are different leanings. All recognize that this is an untested area in need of more study and debate. Accounting for these transactions will no doubt receive attention during the next few years as various Type 2 and 3 transactions arise in practice within the software industry.

(i) Output Value-Added Measures for Core Software

Paragraph 101 of SOP 91-1 permits the use of output value-added measures for core software, with progress measured on an output value-added basis when the software development work is complete.

> Value added by the customization of core software generally should be measured on completion of the customization and installation at the user's site. However, if the installation and customization processes are divided into separate output modules, the value of core software associated with the customization of a module should be included in the measurement of progress-to-completion when that module is completed.

The value to be recognized would consist of the value added to the software by the customization work, as well as a factor for value of the core software prior to the customization work. The value of the core software can be broken down into its constituent modules if there is a basis for such a breakdown.

Paragraph 99 of SOP 91-1 describes a way to identify the total value of core software, as well as off-the-shelf software, if values are otherwise difficult to identify.

> If output values for off-the-shelf software or core software are difficult to identify, they should be estimated by subtracting the known or reasonable estimable output values of other elements of the contract, such as hardware, from the total contract price.

(j) Separately Enforceable Obligation for Software Accounted for Using Value-Added Output Measures and Other Implementation Questions

In its early working with SOP 91-1, the SEC required that in order for a software company to use the output value-added accounting provided for in paragraph 102, the customer must be separately liable for the software, even if the software company fails to complete the services and other elements of the contract. The view that there should be a separate obligation for the software is partly based on concern that the software company could provide the off-the-shelf software, recognize the related revenue, and then fail to complete the services (or otherwise complete the contract) and be unable to collect the revenue that was recorded for the software element.

The author disagrees with this view and is of the opinion that such an obligation is not required by generally accepted accounting principles for contract accounting. It is not consistent with the reasons for using percentage-of-completion accounting.

> The buyer can be expected to satisfy his obligations under the contract. . . . The contractor can be expected to perform his contractual obligations.
>
> —SOP 81-1, paragraph 23

Nowhere in ARB No. 45 or SOP 81-1 is there a notion that any part of a contract to be accounted for as a separate identifiable element must have a separately enforceable obligation. Indeed, even if segmentation accounting is used, there is no requirement for a separate contractual obligation to pay for one of the elements. Generally accepted accounting principles for contract accounting were designed to provide sensible accounting for products and services that are bundled into a single enforceable obligation. Because the FASB and SEC were both so insistent that the software industry conform its accounting practices to those of other industries, including compliance with contract accounting requirements as applied to other industries, it does not seem appropriate now to expect the software industry to comply with requirements for contract accounting that are far beyond those expected of other industries.

There are numerous implementation issues in contract accounting within the software industry, some of which have been discussed in this chapter. These will no doubt be resolved as transactions arise and are discussed and debated by software companies, software industry organizations and advocates, standard-setting organizations, auditors, and the SEC.

CHAPTER SEVEN

Capitalization, Amortization, and Net Realizable Value Testing of Software Development Costs

7.1 CAPITALIZATION

(a) Broad Applicability of FASB Statement No. 86

FASB Statement No. 86, *Accounting for the Costs of Computer Software to Be Sold, Leased, or Otherwise Marketed,* applies to the costs of both internally developed and produced software and purchased software to be sold, leased, or otherwise marketed.

Statement 86 does not cover costs of developing software for internal use. A few months before its issuance, the FASB received an Issues Paper prepared by the Management Accounting Practices Committee of the National Association of Accountants, *Accounting for Software*

Used Internally, which proposed that in some cases costs of software developed for internal use should be capitalized. After considering whether Statement 86 should apply to software developed for internal use, the FASB decided not to so broaden the scope of Statement 86 and not to undertake a separate project on costs of software developed for internal use, because the FASB believed it was not then a significant problem in financial reporting. The FASB perceived that most companies expense such costs and did not believe that this was incorrect accounting. In recent years computer technology has continued to increase in importance to most businesses. Consequently, the perception that accounting for costs of software developed for internal use is not a significant issue has been changing. Many prominent constituents of the FASB are now including this issue high on their list of matters in need of specific accounting standards, as the costs of software developed for internal use have continued to escalate and are being accounted for in many different ways. Sometimes the issue of costs of software developed for internal use is described as part of a broad area in need of accounting standards—that is, how to account for the costs of self-constructed assets, sometimes called "soft costs." Many of those concerned about accounting for such costs cite the costs of software developed for internal use as a primary example of the self-constructed assets about which they are concerned. The author expects that, at some time in the future, accounting standards for the costs of software developed for internal use will be specifically addressed in some way.

FASB Interpretation No. 6, *Applicability of FASB Statement No. 2 to Computer Software*, paragraph 4, indicates that costs of acquiring or developing software for use in selling or administrative activities are excluded from the definition of research and development activities. Moreover, because Statement 86 does not apply to software acquired or developed for internal use, only normal research and development and asset capitalization accounting practices apply to software acquired or developed for internal use. Nevertheless, in Statement 86 the FASB said the following:

> This Statement clarifies activities that are research and development activities and establishes a high capitalization threshold that is likely to be applied to costs incurred in developing software for internal use as well as for sale or lease to others.
>
> —FASB Statement No. 86, paragraph 26

Accordingly, there seems to be a broad spectrum of alternatives in accounting for costs of software acquired or developed for internal use.

(b) Software Products

Statement 86's accounting applies to costs of computer software products to be sold, leased, or otherwise marketed. The software products may be marketed separately or as firmware (as part of a product or process), even if the software is contained in a product having a software component that cannot function or be marketed separately from the overall product. Examples are software included in calculators and products of robotic technologies.

It is sometimes difficult to determine the exact scope of Statement 86 in some situations in which software is used to derive revenue. For example, software used in telephone switching equipment, credit card clearing operations, or computer-aided design and manufacturing are considered by some to be software for internal use and therefore not accounted for under Statement 86. Others consider such software to be covered by Statement 86. The line between software for marketing to others and software for internal use is not always clear. The author believes that the dividing line should be that Statement 86 should apply to software to which the customer acquires the software or the right to use the software and that Statement 86 should not be applied to software that is used by a vendor in the production of a product or the providing of a service.

This issue has particular applicability to service bureaus, where practice is mixed as to whether Statement 86 is applied. Using the author's view, Statement 86 would be applied if the service bureau is renting time to use its software, since the software is being used by the customer, but not if the service bureau is only providing a service, such as payroll processing, even though the customer is fully aware that the service bureau is dependent on the software for providing its service. Although the author has expressed his view, there is no clear answer in Statement 86 or in practice about the line dividing software for marketing to others and software for internal use.

Software products covered by Statement 86 include enhancements, which are defined as

improvements to an existing product that are intended to extend the life or improve significantly the marketability of the original product. Enhancements normally require a product design and may require a redesign of all or part of the existing product.
—FASB Statement No. 86, paragraph 52

An issue of *FASB Highlights of Financial Reporting Issues* published in February 1986 contained unofficial FASB staff guidance on application of FASB Statement 86 in a question-and-response format. In that publication, the response to question 1 provides the following additional descriptive notions about software products contemplated by Statement 86.

A software product is most easily defined by describing its necessary qualities. As a product, it is complete and has exchange value. As software, it is a set of programs that interact with each other. A program is further defined as a series of instructions or statements that cause a computer to do work.

(c) Computer Software Research and Development Costs

Costs incurred prior to establishing technological feasibility of a software product are research and development costs and should be charged to expense in accordance with FASB Statement No. 2, *Accounting for Research and Development Costs.* These costs include costs of planning, designing, coding, and the testing that is necessary to establish that the product can be produced to meet its design specifications, including functions, features, and technical performance requirements.

The FASB used the following definition of development in defining activities that should be considered software research and development.

The translation of research findings or other knowledge into a plan or design for a new product or process or for a significant improvement to an existing product or process whether intended for sale or use. It includes the conceptual formulation, design, and testing of product alternatives, construction of prototypes, and operation of pilot plants. It does not include routine or periodic alterations to existing products, production lines, manufacturing processes, and other ongoing operations even though those alterations may represent improvements, and it does not include market research or market testing activities.

—FASB Statement No. 2, paragraph 8

Another reference considered by the FASB as descriptive of activities that should be charged to expense as software research and development activities follows.

Engineering activity required to advance the design of a product to the point that it meets specific functional and economic requirements and is ready for manufacture.

—FASB Statement No. 2, paragraph 9

Even though all other criteria for capitalization have been met, if a high-risk development issue remains, all costs incurred with regard to a software product should be charged to research and development expense. If subsequent to the establishment of technological feasibility a high-risk development issue is discovered, any development costs that were capitalized for that product, and future costs incurred until the high-risk development issue is resolved, should be charged to research and development expense. After the high-risk development issue is resolved, and provided all other conditions for capitalization are met, capitalization should resume; previously written off capitalized costs, however, remain expensed as research and development costs.

(d) Determination of Technological Feasibility in General

The criteria for determination of technological feasibility and commencement of capitalization of software development costs may vary, depending on whether the development process includes or does not include the preparation of a detail program design. The basis for determination of technological feasibility in both cases is discussed in the following paragraphs.

The determination of technological feasibility must be made for an entire software product. If a product includes more than one module and the modules are not marketable separately, the determination of technological feasibility must be made for the entire product, including all the modules, and not on a module-by-module basis.

If the criteria for capitalization are met, including technological feasibility and net realizable value, software development costs must be capitalized. A company may not elect to use an accounting policy in which it applies more stringent criteria than those set forth in Statement 86. For example, a software company may not elect to use the working model criteria for commencement of capitalization if it meets the detail program design criteria.

(e) Determination of Technological Feasibility If a Detail Program Design Is Used

If the software development process includes the preparation of a detail program design, technological feasibility is determined and capitalization of software development costs begins when the criteria specified in paragraph 4 of Statement 86 are met (see Exhibit 7.1).

EXHIBIT 7.1   Criteria for Establishing Technological Feasibility If the Software Development Process Includes a Detail Program Design

1.	The product design and detail program design have been completed, and the enterprise has established that the necessary skills, hardware, and software technology are available to the enterprise to produce the product.
2.	The completeness of the detail program design and its consistency with the product design have been confirmed by documenting and tracing the detail program design to product specifications.
3.	The detail program design has been reviewed for high-risk development issues (for example, novel, unique, unproven functions and features or technological innovations), and any uncertainties related to identified high-risk development issues have been resolved through coding and testing.

A product design is defined in Statement 86 as follows:

> A logical representation of product functions in sufficient detail to serve as product specifications.
>
> —FASB Statement No. 86, paragraph 52

A product design should include a description and objectives of the product, an explanation of how data will be input into the product (such as by on-line input or by batch processing), a description of the data and reports to be generated by the product, the major processing and data transformation definitions, data storage and data structure requirements, and a general description of the data flow and interaction of modules and transforming processes.

Statement 86 defines a detail program design as follows:

> The detail design of a computer software product that takes product function, feature, and technical requirements to their most detailed, logical form and is ready for coding.
>
> —FASB Statement No. 86, paragraph 52

A detail program design should describe the product function, features, and technical requirements in a detailed, logical way, ready for coding activities. The detail program design should normally include a description of the logic, file layouts, report definitions, field definitions, algorithms, special routines, and specific arrays of data. Ordinarily, the combined documentation package of the product design and detail program design should be in the form of outlines, narratives, flowcharts, or a combination. The precise form of the documentation can vary widely from company to company, partly depending on the development process, the individuals involved, the maturity of the company's technology, and other factors. If new products are involved, it is generally expected that there will be more documentation than, for example, for enhancements to established products.

An important step in meeting these criteria is ensuring that the information in the product design and the detail program design are consistent and that the technical features and functions described in the detail program design will meet the product specification in the product design.

(f) Technological Feasibility If a Detail Program Design Is Not Prepared

If the development process does not include preparation of a detail program design meeting the previously described criteria, then capitalization of software development costs should begin when the criteria specified in paragraph 4 of Statement 86 are met (see Exhibit 7.2). A working model is described in Statement 86 as follows.

> An operative version of the computer software product that is completed in the same software language as the product to be ultimately marketed, performs all the major functions planned for the product, and is ready for initial customer testing (usually identified as beta testing).
> —FASB Statement No. 86, paragraph 52

The term *working model* has sometimes been used to refer to a prototype with the important portions of a product written in pseudocode. Because Statement 86 requires that a working model be written in the same computer language as the product to be marketed, such prototypes are not working models for purposes of applying Statement 86.

The working model should be compared with the product design for consistency and completeness before capitalization commences.

If the working model is the basis for technological feasibility, the amount capitalized will generally be significantly less than under the detail program design approach. Most significantly, under the working model approach, much of the coding activities in creating the software product will be charged to research and development. Most of the costs capitalized under the working model approach will relate to testing, bug fixing, final coding, and preparation of documentation.

EXHIBIT 7.2 Criteria for Establishing Technological Feasibility If the Software Development Process Does Not Include a Detail Program Design

1.	The product design and a working model of the software product have been completed.
2.	The completeness of the working model and its consistency with the product design have been confirmed by testing.

(g) Projects That Do Not Precisely Employ Either a Detail Program Design or a Working Model Approach

Sometimes software companies do not use a software development process that clearly follows a detail program design approach or a working model approach. For example, a software company may not prepare a detail program design prior to starting work on constructing a working model, but a detail program design may emerge as a by-product of the working model development. In such cases, the criteria of a detail program design are met, and capitalization should commence when the detail program design has been completed, rather than waiting to start capitalization until the working model is completed.

Once technological feasibility is established and capitalization commenced, there may be refinements to the detail program design that evolve during the development process—for example, as better ideas are discovered and minor development issues arise and are resolved. Costs of refining the detail program design and related activities not specifically contemplated in the original detail program design should be capitalized. If, however, there are substantial changes to the original detail program design that indicate that the original logic or conception of the technical features of the product was not feasible, consideration should be given to whether technological feasibility had in fact been determined. If it is ascertained that technological feasibility was not determined, capitalized costs incurred should be charged to research and development up to the point that the detail program design was consistent with the technical features that will be used in developing the final product.

(h) Determination of Market Feasibility

The term *market feasibility* is not used in Statement 86. However, it is sometimes used in practice when considering whether a new software product or an enhancement of an existing product will be accepted in the marketplace, generating revenues to enable passing the net realizable value test of Statement 86. Statement 86 requires a net realizable value test (discussed in more detail later in this chapter), as of each balance sheet date for all software products for which costs have been capitalized, including new products and enhancements of existing products for which sales have not yet occurred. The notion of market feasibility points out that in order to capitalize software development costs for a product or a product enhancement, in addition to determination of technological feasibility, the software company must also be able to demonstrate that the net realizable value test will be passed for the costs of the product or enhancement that will be capitalized.

(i) Aggregating the Direct Labor Component

Software development is a labor-intensive activity. Accordingly, most software companies base the accumulation of software development costs on hours incurred. Some companies have sophisticated project cost systems that are administered with time-reporting procedures by which employees submit time sheets or time cards with hours charged to individual projects. Separate job codes may be set up for a project after the criteria for capitalization have been met. Sometimes one job code is used to accumulate all hours on a project, and hours charged to the project after the criteria for capitalization are met are isolated for computation of amounts to be capitalized.

Personnel whose hours are normally capitalized usually include programmers, systems analysts, project managers, and, in some cases, administrative personnel involved in the software development process. Most hours incurred will be directly chargeable; however, there may be some supervisory and management time that is appropriate to include in capitalized amounts. In many software companies, executive personnel are technically oriented and actively involved in the development process. In some cases it is appropriate to include a portion of their hours in software development cost accumulation on a direct charge basis, and sometimes as an overhead factor. For example, in a large software company, there may be an executive who is the company's technical director, who is active in software development, managing the projects on a full-time basis. In such a company, all other executive personnel may be performing general management or other management functions, but not directly involved in the development process. In smaller companies, all executives, including the chief executive officer, may participate in software development activities.

Although costs have been accumulated for software capitalization in diverse ways, most often software development costs are developed using direct labor as the basis. The software company tabulates the number of hours a particular employee has incurred in working on a capitalizable project, then multiplies the hours by the employee's compensation rate. Software developers frequently work more than the standard number of hours because of the time pressures involved in bringing a new product or enhancement to the marketplace. The author believes that if the number of hours worked by a software developer significantly exceeds the standard number of work hours, the hourly rate should be adjusted to the actual rate paid.

Assume that a senior programmer is paid $62,400 per year, or $30 per hour based on a work year of 2,080 hours. The programmer is entitled to 120 hours of vacation and 80 hours of holiday time, so that in a standard work year the programmer would work a net of 1,880 hours. The author recommends that the rate of $30 per hour be used in valuing the hours incurred in capitalizable projects. Appropriate recognition of the cost of the vacation and holiday time can be built into the fringe rate included in the overhead factor, as discussed in the following section of this chapter.

Assume, further, that the programmer actually works 2,400 hours during the year instead of 1,880 hours. The result is that essentially there are 2,600 hours attributable to the programmer's salary of $62,400—the 2,400 hours worked, the 120 hours of vacation time, and the 80 hours of holiday time. The author would base the amount to be capitalized on $24 per hour ($62,400 divided by 2,600). An extreme illustration shows why this is necessary. Assume that all 2,400 hours of the programmer's work time was spent on capitalized projects, and the company's accountants by rote priced out the time at the programmer's standard rate of $30 per hour. The company would have capitalized a total of $72,000 (2,400 multiplied by $30), when it paid only $62,400. The error would be further compounded by inclusion of a vacation and holiday factor in the fringe rate included in an overhead factor.

(j) Overhead Rates

Overhead rates should be computed using the general approach used in practice for inventory costing or for computing the cost of self-constructed assets. Therefore, an appropriate amount of indirect costs should be allocated to capitalized software. General and administrative costs should not be allocated to capitalized software.

The author has found it effective to develop an overhead rate to apply to capitalized direct labor, which includes the following three factors:

1. Fringe costs

2. Facilities and office expenses

3. Management and supervision

Fringe costs include factors for vacation and holiday time, employer payroll taxes, medical insurance, pension and retirement contributions, and other fringe benefits. Using the example of the senior programmer discussed in the preceding section, and assuming standard hours (1,880 hours) worked, Exhibit 7.3 shows how the fringe rate would be computed, assuming the data included therein.

(k) Other Direct Costs

The preceding two sections discuss accumulation of direct costs based on labor hours and computation of an overhead rate. In addition, capitalized costs should include other direct costs that are generally not appropriate for inclusion in an overhead rate. Examples are costs of outside consultants, purchased software to be included in the software product being developed, travel expenses, materials and supplies, and other direct costs. Costs of computer usage in development activities should also be capitalized. Sometimes these costs can be determined by multiplying the number of hours of computer usage by the average hourly cost of operating the company's computer facility. Computer hardware depreciation should be included in capitalized costs to the extent that the computers were used in development activities. This depreciation is often included in the hourly cost of computer usage of the company's computer facility. There may also be computers outside a central computer facility that are used, sometimes exclusively, in the development process, for which appropriate amounts of depreciation and other costs should be included in capitalized

EXHIBIT 7.3 Overhead Rate Computations

	Hours	Pct. of Total Hours
Net Salary for Overhead Rate Computations		
Total hours	2,080	1.000
Vacation hours	(120)	
Holiday hours	(80)	
Nonwork hours	(200)	.096
Net hours worked	1,880	.904
Total salaries (assume the company has 50 employees at an average salary of $62,400)		$3,120,000
Net hours worked percentage		.904
Net salary for overhead rate computations		$2,820,480 (A)
Fringe rate		
Vacation and holiday time		
Total salary	$3,120,000	
Nonwork hours percentage	.096	
Payroll taxes, health and life insurance, pension, and other fringe benefits		$ 299,520
		600,000
		$ 899,520 (B)
Fringe rate (A)/(B)		.319 (C)

Facilities and office rate

Facilities and office expense	$ 500,000	(D)
Facilities and office expense rate (D)/(A)	.177	(E)

Management and supervision rate

Total management and supervision salaries	$ 300,000	
Net hours worked percentage	× .904	
Percentage related to capitalizable development activities	× .100	
Management and supervision net salaries allocable to capitalized development activities	27,120	
Fringe rate factor ($27,120 × .319)	8,651	
Facilities and office expense factor ($27,120 × .177)	4,800	
Management and supervision cost to be included in overhead rate	$ 40,571	(F)
Total direct labor charged to development activities (assume the equivalent of 5 full-time programmers at net salary for overhead rate computations of $56,400 each)	$ 282,000	(G)
Management and supervision rate	.144	(H)

Summary of overhead rate

Fringe rate	.319	(C)
Facilities and office rate	.177	(E)
Management and supervision rate	.144	(H)
Total overhead rate	.640	

amounts. The specific procedures for accumulating these costs should be based on the company's internal operations and accounting systems.

Outside consultants may be engaged to perform software development activities at a software company's site. In such cases, it is appropriate to add to the consultant's fee an overhead factor for the consultant's use of the company's office and other facilities. If this is done, however, in computing the company's facilities overhead rate, a factor for the use of facilities by outside consultants should be included in the facilities overhead rate to be used for employees. This can be accomplished by adding a factor for fees paid to consultants using the facilities to the net salaries in the denominator of the computation of the facilities overhead rate. The amount added should generally not be the entire amount of the consulting fees, because such fees are usually higher than net salaries paid to employees on an hourly basis. If outside consultants are engaged to work on software development projects, depending on the circumstances, it may be appropriate to include a management and supervision overhead factor if the company executives supervised and participated in the consultants' work.

As for all costs, capitalization of other direct costs should not occur until technological feasibility of the product has been determined. For example, purchased software to be included as part of a product under development, which is acquired before technological feasibility of the entire product is determined, should be charged to research and development expense.

(l) Capitalization of Interest

Software development activities are projects for which interest cost must be capitalized under FASB Statement No. 34, *Capitalization of Interest Cost.*

(m) Recapitulation of Costs to Be Capitalized

This section summarizes each of the types of costs to be capitalized discussed in the preceding sections. The summary is based on data included in previous illustrations as if those items represented the components of capitalized software for the year for a project. Assume that the project required direct labor hours equivalent to those of two full-time programmers at the gross salary rate of $62,400 (assumed in the illustration of overhead rate computations in Exhibit 7.3). Assumed amounts are included in Example 7.1 for components of costs that were discussed but not illustrated numerically.

EXAMPLE 7.1 Summary of Capitalized Costs for Project ABC

Direct salaries, based on hours charged	
(1,880 hours × 2 programmers × $30 per hour)	$ 112,800
Overhead	
($112,800 × overhead rate of .640)	72,192
Computer usage	
(400 hours at $50 per hour)	20,000
Outside consulting fees, offsite	8,000
Outside consulting fees, onsite	
($10,000 of fees plus .177 facilities overhead rate and	
.149 management and supervision overhead rate)	13,260
Purchased software component	10,000
Travel costs and other direct costs	5,000
Total project costs	241,252
Capitalized interest	9,000
Total capitalized costs	$ 250,252

(n) Availability for General Market Release– Cessation of Capitalization

Capitalization of development costs of a software product should cease when the product is available for general market release.

(o) Enhancements

Product enhancements are defined in Statement 86 as follows:

> Improvements to an existing product that are intended to extend the life or improve significantly the marketability of the original product.

Enhancements normally require a product design and may require a redesign of all or part of the existing product.
—FASB Statement No. 86, paragraph 52

Bug fixes are included in maintenance under Statement 86, and should therefore be accounted for as period costs and not capitalizable enhancements. This distinction is sometimes missed in practice.

How to account for product enhancements was one of the first significant issues on implementation of Statement 86. In EITF Issue 85-35, in September 1985, the EITF considered the question of how Statement 86 should be applied to product enhancements. The EITF was not asked to reach a consensus—the FASB staff provided information on how to apply Statement 86 to product enhancements. The FASB staff indicated that if an original product is no longer to be marketed, the net book value of the original product should be allocated to the cost of the enhancement (perhaps more appropriately called the enhanced product). The costs of the enhanced product, including costs "allocated up" from the original product, are amortized over the life of the enhancement, and all costs are included in net realizable value testing of the enhancement.

If the software company develops an enhanced product and continues to market the original product, then a portion of the net book value of the original product should be "allocated up" to the enhancement, based on a systematic and rational allocation method. It has been suggested that lines of code could be used in some way to develop a calculation of the allocation. Relative projected revenues could also be used. Various other bases have been seen in practice. In certain circumstances, it may be appropriate to allocate to an enhanced product the value of a third-party development license. For example, this may be appropriate if the original product is the basis of a proprietary technology and will continue to have greater integrity and longevity than the enhancement, and if the technology in the original product may be transferred into other enhancements in the future.

Some software companies continually enhance their products to extend their life and to maintain their marketability in light of competition in the marketplace. In such cases it is impractical to "allocate up" the net book value of the product into the costs of the enhanced product and start a new amortization life every time an enhancement is completed. In these circumstances, the author recommends an "allocation down" approach, in which the cost of enhancements is added to the cost of the original product. This approach should not be used, however, if the enhancement is major and results in the release of a new product that is marketed as a new product.

(p) Capitalization of Funded Development Costs

Some software companies develop software for a customer under a contract pursuant to which the customer pays some or all of the cost of development, and the software company retains the right to market the product to others. In such cases, assuming that there is a viable market for the product, the software company should capitalize the costs of development of the software, provided the criteria for capitalization are met, and should recognize contract revenues for amounts earned under the contract. The software company should recognize an appropriate amount of amortization of the software being developed as the contract revenues are recognized. Costs that are not capitalizable should be recognized as contract expenses.

The accounting for funded development contracts as described can yield a beneficial result to the reported profits of a software company, in that the costs of completing the contract after determination of technological feasibility are capitalized, and yet all the contract revenue is recognized.

If, in a funded development arrangement, the costs of software development that must be expensed as research and development and other contract costs exceed the amount of contract revenue, the contract should be accounted for as a research and development project and not as a loss contract, assuming that the product being developed will have sufficient value to the company in the future.

7.2 AMORTIZATION

(a) Amortization in General

Statement 86 requires amortization of capitalized software costs for both internally developed and purchased software. Amortization should commence when capitalization ceases upon the availability of the product for general market release. Amortization should begin when a product is available for general market release, even if the software company decides to delay market release because of its competitive situation or other factors.

Amortization must be computed on a product-by-product basis using the greater of straight-line amortization or revenue-based amortization. Because amortization is computed on a product-by-product basis, within a particular period, some products may be amortized by using straight-line amortization and others by revenue-based amortization. Straight-line amortization may be used for a particular product in one period, and revenue-based amortization in another, depending on the level of revenue realized in each period.

(b) Straight-Line Amortization

Straight-line amortization should be computed by dividing the net book value of a product at the beginning of a period by the product's remaining useful life at the beginning of the period. Statement 86 does not provide any guidance on lives to be used for straight-line amortization. Based on industry practice and SEC views, however, lives in the range of 3 to 7 years are the norm. The SEC has, in fact, indicated that it may challenge lives longer than 5 years for personal computer-based software and longer than 7 years for other software. If the estimate of useful life of a software product changes from the life originally used in computing further amortization, the new estimated useful life should be used in computing amortization. However, the convention of using the most current estimate of useful life should not be employed to unduly extend the amortization period of a software product.

(c) Revenue-Based Amortization

The computation of revenue-based amortization is based on the percentage of current-period gross revenues for the product to the total of current period and estimated future gross revenues for the product. Estimated future gross revenue streams should be based on management's most realistic prediction of future revenues for the software product. Each year, actual revenues should be compared with revenues projected in the past, and present predictions should be compared with revenue levels and trends in the past few years to determine whether they are reasonable.

Statement 86 does not specify how many years into the future the revenue stream should be projected in computing revenue-based amortization. The author believes that it is appropriate to use projected revenues only for the remaining useful life used for straight-line amortization, even if the software company believes the revenue stream will continue further.

The projected gross revenue stream for revenue-based amortization should be consistent with the projected revenue stream used in the net realizable value test, discussed later in this chapter.

Because in practice many revenue projections for the net realizable value test and amortization take the shape of a bell curve, almost all amortization is ultimately determined on a straight-line basis, rather than a revenue-basis. Projected revenue curves tend to grow from the initial year leading to the straight-line minimum in initial periods, and straight-line and revenue-based amortization are generally equal in later periods.

(d) Combined Work Sheet for Straight-Line and Revenue-Based Amortization

Exhibit 7.4 gives an example of a work sheet for computing straight-line and revenue-based amortization on a product-by-product basis, and determining the company's amortization expense for the year.

(e) Amortization of Enhanced Products

If a software company has developed an enhanced product, and the net book value of the original product has been fully "allocated up" to the enhancement, the estimated life of the enhancement is used to compute straight-line amortization of the net book value "allocated up," as well as the capitalized cost of the enhancement.

If only a portion of the net book value of an original product was "allocated up," straight-line amortization of the portion of the net book value left with the original product continues to be based on the

EXHIBIT 7.4 Amortization

	Product A	Product B	Product C	Total
Capitalized cost at beginning of Year 1	$250,000	$150,000	$400,000	$800,000
Remaining useful life (in years) at beginning of Year 1	4	5	3	
Straight-line amortization	$ 62,500	$ 30,000	$133,333	$225,833
Actual gross revenue Year 1	$150,000	$ 40,000	$200,000	
Projected gross revenue				
Year 2	200,000	65,000	150,000	
Year 3	250,000	85,000	100,000	
Year 4	175,000	110,000		
Year 5		90,000		
Total gross revenue	$775,000	$390,000	$450,000	
Percentage of Year 1 gross revenue to total gross revenue	19.35%	10.26%	44.44%	
Revenue-based amortization	$ 48,387	$ 15,385	$177,778	
Greater of straight-line or revenue-based amortization	$ 62,500	$ 30,000	$177,778	$270,278

estimated life of the original product. Straight-line amortization of the portion of the original product's net book value that was "allocated up" to the enhancement and the capitalized cost of the enhancement is computed based on the life of the enhancement.

If a company's software products are continually enhanced, and the company follows the convention of adding the cost of the enhancements to the cost of the original products, the company may continue to use the life of the original product to compute straight-line amortization of both the net book value of the original product and the enhancements. If the enhancements continually extend the useful life of the product, and the costs of the enhancements are sufficiently significant that amortizing them over the life of the original product would distort amortization expense, the author recommends an alternative convention seen in practice. Using this convention, straight-line amortization of the original product continues to be computed over the original product's estimated useful life, and straight-line amortization of the enhancements is computed using the same life as that used for the original product, but starting with the year in which the enhancements were completed. In such situations, the software company might be justified in "allocating up" all net book value each year and starting the original estimated useful life over again each year. By using this "vintage account" approach, the software company does not have to go through the "allocation up" approach each year, and is, furthermore, probably amortizing its capitalized software somewhat more quickly than if it had selected the "allocation up" approach.

(f) Reporting Amortization in Interim Periods

Some companies allocate amortization to interim periods in a practical way, by computing the estimated total amortization for the year and recognizing the total amount on a straight-line basis throughout the year. However, if revenue levels vary substantially from quarter to quarter and amortization amounts are significant, it may be necessary to allocate more precisely the annual estimated amortization to quarters, based on the amount of revenues for each quarter in relation to estimated annual revenues.

7.3 NET REALIZABLE VALUE TESTING

(a) Net Realizable Value Testing in General

Paragraph 10 of Statement 86 requires an evaluation of net realizable value of capitalized costs of computer software on a product-by-product basis, at each balance sheet date. Net realizable value of a product is defined as

the estimated future gross revenues from that product reduced by the estimated future costs of completing and disposing of that product, including the costs of performing maintenance and customer support to satisfy the enterprise's responsibility set forth at the time of sale.
—FASB Statement No. 86, paragraph 10

A software product should be written down to net realizable value if its net book value exceeds its net realizable value. The written-down amount becomes the new cost of the software product—the writedown is not restored even if future net realizable value tests indicate net realizable value in excess of net book value for the software product.

The net realizable value test should be applied to all software products for which costs have been capitalized, including those that are under development.

The following sections discuss specific aspects of implementing the net realizable value test.

(b) Estimating the Future Revenue Stream

Estimating the future revenue stream for a software product can be rather subjective, as can other aspects of the net realizable value test. The estimate of the future revenue stream should take into consideration the size of the overall market for the product and the share of the market the company expects to realize, pricing, competitive products, effects of expected technological advances, the effects of hardware developments, and any other factors that could have an impact on future revenues. Projected future revenue trends should be viewed in light of historical trends for the product and for similar products.

The period for which future revenues should be projected is not addressed in Statement 86. The author believes it is generally appropriate to include in the net realizable value test, projections of revenues for only the period remaining on the straight-line useful life of the software product.

The projected future revenues of a software product for the remaining period of its straight-line useful life could show one of several different patterns of trend lines. In many situations, the trend line might take the shape of a bell curve, with increasing revenues for several years, reaching a peak, followed by declining revenues. A mature product at or near market saturation could show a declining revenue trend line for the entire projection. A product that is not near market saturation could show an increasing revenue trend line for the entire period covered by the projection.

(c) Estimating Costs of Disposal and Costs to Complete

Costs of disposal should include production costs, which are usually minor, and distribution costs. Distribution costs should consist of variable marketing costs, such as advertising and sales commissions, and shipping costs. Costs of completing the product should also cover the cost of any postcontract customer support, including development of enhancements, that the software company is obligated to incur other than those derived from future postcontract customer support contracts.

(d) Effects of Assuming Enhancements vs. Not Assuming Enhancements on Revenue and Cost Projections

The question of whether to assume that a software company will enhance a software product gives rise to an interesting exercise in logic related to the net realizable value test.

Computation of a net realizable value test could assume that a software company continues to market an existing product, without enhancement. A logical implication may be a projected trend that includes at some point declining revenue, because if software products are not enhanced, they often will not continue market penetration or maintain market share. If a software company does not expect to enhance a product, the net realizable value test can be based on a revenue trend projected on the basis of expected market performance of the existing product. This avoids the complexities discussed in the following paragraphs.

The net realizable value test may include projected revenues from enhanced versions of a software product. Indeed, software companies continually enhance their products, and unless a product is at the end of its life cycle, to assume that a product will not be enhanced is often unrealistic. If such an assumption is made, as discussed in the preceding paragraph, a declining revenue curve would be likely—which could create an artificial, unrealistic projection. If for any reason a software company assumes no enhancement costs in costs to complete, projected revenues used in the net realizable value should be consistent with only future revenues that would be expected if the software company were to make no enhancements and to continue to market only the existing product.

At the other end of the spectrum are situations in which software companies continually enhance existing products year after year, and expect to continue to do so, resulting in continually increasing revenue trends. Depending on the circumstances, this could also be a somewhat unrealistic way to approach the net realizable value test. This test is intended to evaluate the recoverability of the net book value of an existing product. At some point in the future continual year-after-year enhancement, perhaps at aggregate costs far exceeding the current net book value of the product being evaluated, results in attributing revenues to the revenue stream that are too far removed from the current product to be realistically included in the net realizable value test. Furthermore, it seems appropriate to conclude that at some time the future product will be enhanced to the point that it should not be considered an enhanced version of the current product for the net realizable value test.

In such circumstances, a sensible approach is to assume a normal level of enhancement for several years, after which enhancements would cease. Revenues would be projected on the basis of expectations of what would happen should that pattern of enhancement occur. Although such an approach may imply a bell curve revenue trend, with declining revenue in the later years of the remaining straight-line life, it may be a more appropriate basis for the net realizable value test, rather than assuming an endless stream of enhancements and an ever-growing revenue trend far into the future.

Exhibit 7.5 indicates how a software company might evaluate the implications of enhancements to future revenue streams to be assumed for a net realizable value test.

In Exhibit 7.5 it is assumed that the software company selected the data in the column B for use in the net realizable value test. Assume that the software company concluded that it was comfortable in projecting enhancements, their cost, and estimated revenue effects for enhancements for 2 years into the future, but was not comfortable in projecting enhancements further into the future, which would have the effect of creating the ever-increasing revenue stream. Further, the software company believed that the enhancements in Years 4 and 5 would probably result in a version of the product that would be enhanced so much from the current product that those enhancements and revenue streams should not be included in the net realizable value test for the current product.

The net realizable value test is rather subjective and requires the exercise of judgment. Many business and computational matters may need to be addressed in developing a logical net realizable value test with consistent assumptions and estimations of their implications.

(e) Work Sheet for Net Realizable Value Testing

Exhibit 7.6 is a suggested work sheet for a net realizable value test. Because the data used in computing amortization and the net realizable value test are so closely linked, this illustration is based on the same data in the illustration of amortization computations in Exhibit 7.4.

(f) Recording a Net Realizable Value Writedown

Net realizable value writedowns are generally recorded by increasing amortization for the period, or by a direct reduction of the cost of the software product.

(g) Net Realizable Value Writedown Establishing New Cost Basis

A writedown of a software product to net realizable value establishes a new cost basis for the product. If, subsequently, market conditions improve and projected revenue increases cause the product to have net realizable value in excess of net book value in future periods, the writedown is not reversed by increasing the net carrying value of the previous writedown that could be said to be no longer needed.

EXHIBIT 7.5 Projected Enhancement Costs and Future Revenues

COLUMN A

Projected Total NBV, Enhancement, and Revenue Stream for Years 1 through 5

Existing Product, End of Year 1

	Net Book Value	Projected Revenue
	$120,000	
Year 1		$ 50,000
Year 2		40,000
Year 3		20,000
Year 4		10,000
Year 5		
	$120,000	$120,000

Year 2 Enhancement

	Cost of Enhancement	Projected Incremental Revenue
	$ 65,000	
Year 1		$ 15,000
Year 2		25,000
Year 3		50,000
Year 4		45,000
Year 5		
	$ 65,000	$135,000

COLUMN B

NBV, Enhancement, and Revenue Stream Used for NRV Test

Existing Product, End of Year 1

	Net Book Value	Projected Revenue
	$120,000	
Year 1		$ 50,000
Year 2		40,000
Year 3		20,000
Year 4		10,000
	$120,000	$120,000

Year 2 Enhancement

	Cost of Enhancement	Projected Incremental Revenue
	$ 65,000	
Year 1		$ 15,000
Year 2		25,000
Year 3		50,000
Year 4		45,000
	$ 65,000	$135,000

Year 3 Enhancement

	Cost of Enhancement	Projected Incremental Revenue
Year 1		
Year 2		
Year 3	$ 60,000	20,000
Year 4		40,000
Year 5		35,000
	$ 60,000	$ 95,000

Year 4 Enhancement

	Cost of Enhancement	Projected Incremental Revenue
Year 1		
Year 2		
Year 3		
Year 4	$ 40,000	25,000
Year 5		40,000
	$ 40,000	$ 65,000

Year 3 Enhancement

	Cost of Enhancement	Projected Incremental Revenue
Year 1		
Year 2		
Year 3	$ 60,000	20,000
Year 4		40,000
Year 5		35,000
	$ 60,000	$ 95,000

Year 4 Enhancement

	Cost of Enhancement	Projected Incremental Revenue
Year 1		
Year 2		
Year 3		
Year 4	$	
Year 5		
	$ 0	$ 0

(continued)

EXHIBIT 7.5 (Continued)

Year 5 Enhancement

	Cost of Enhancement	Projected Incremental Revenue
Year 1		
Year 2		
Year 3		
Year 4	$ 25,000	20,000
Year 5		
Total	$ 25,000	$ 20,000

	Total Cost	Projected Total Revenue
Year 1	120,000	0
Year 2	65,000	65,000
Year 3	60,000	85,000
Year 4	40,000	135,000
Year 5	25,000	150,000
Total	$310,000	$435,000

Year 5 Enhancement

	Cost of Enhancement	Projected Incremental Revenue
Year 1		
Year 2		
Year 3		
Year 4		
Year 5		
Total	$ 0	$440,000

	Total Cost	Projected Total Revenue
Year 1	120,000	0
Year 2	65,000	65,000
Year 3	60,000	85,000
Year 4	0	110,000
Year 5	0	90,000
Total	$245,000	$350,000

EXHIBIT 7.6 Net Realizable Value Test

	Product A	Product B	Product C	Total
Net book value at beginning of Year 1	$ 250,000	$ 150,000	$ 400,000	$ 800,000
Less Year 1 amortization	(62,500)	(30,000)	(177,778)	(270,278)
	$ 187,500	$ 120,000	$ 222,222	$ 529,722
Remaining useful life (in years) at beginning of Year 1	4	5	3	
Net realizable value				
Actual gross revenue Year 1*	$ 150,000	$ 40,000	$ 200,000	
Projected gross revenue:				
Year 2	200,000	65,000	150,000	
Year 3	250,000	85,000	100,000	
Year 4	175,000	110,000		
Year 5		90,000		
	625,000	350,000	250,000	
Projected distribution cost (20%)	(125,000)	(70,000)	(50,000)	
Projected enhancement costs	(75,000)	(125,000)	—	
Net realizable value	$ 425,000	$ 155,000	$ 180,000	
Net realizable value excess (deficiency)	$ 237,500	$ 35,000	$ (42,222)	
Writedown	None	None	$ (42,222)	$ (42,222)

*Inclusion of actual revenue for 1, 2, or more years along with the projection of future revenue is useful data for considering the reasonableness of the future projections.

(h) Net Realizable Value Writedowns and Capitalization of Additional Development Costs

If a software product has been subject to a net realizable value write-down, future software development costs for that product should not be capitalized, because they would create additional net book value in excess of net realizable value. If in the future, however, market conditions change and a higher net realizable value results, the software company should capitalize current period qualifying software development costs as long as the net book value of the software product does not exceed the then net realizable value.

Questionnaire for Compiling Documentation for Capitalization of Software Development Costs

1. Name of product or project

   _____

2. If the product or project is being accounted for in a project cost system, indicate the project number(s) being used on time sheets.

   _____

3. At what locations is the software development work being performed? If more than one location, describe the work being done at each location.

   _____

   _____

4. Is this a new product or an enhancement of an existing product? If an enhancement, identify the existing product.

    _____

5. Provide a brief description of the technical features of the product or enhancement.

    _____

    _____

    _____

    _____

6. If this project was in progress at the beginning of the period, describe any new information about the project that has become known during the period (e.g., expansion of the existing project, technical difficulties, etc.).

    _____

    _____

    _____

    _____

7. When was the idea for the product or enhancement conceived, and over what period were the determinations of technological feasibility and market viability carried out?

    _____

    _____

8. On what date was technological feasibility determined, and what documentation exists to support that determination?

    _____

    _____

9. On what date was market viability determined, and what documentation exists to support that determination?

   _____

   _____

10. When was (will) the product or enhancement (be) available for general market release?

    _____

11. Describe the work that was done on the project during the period.

    _____

    _____

    _____

    _____

12. If the project was in progress at the end of the period, describe the remaining work and provide an estimate of the number of man-months required to complete.

    _____

    _____

    _____

    _____

13. If there are any outside funding sources for this project, identify the parties providing the funding and the amounts being provided by each.

    _____

    _____

CHAPTER EIGHT

Financial Reporting

8.1 ADOPTION OF SOP 91-1

(a) Effective Date and Transition

All software companies are required to comply with SOP 91-1, and adoption of that pronouncement may require changes in the way many software companies account for revenue.

SOP 91-1 is effective for financial statements issued after March 15, 1992, for fiscal years and interim periods within such fiscal years beginning after December 15, 1991. Essentially, this means that SOP 91-1 is in effect as of January 1, 1992, for calendar-year companies, and must be adopted in quarterly financial statements for the 3-month periods ended March 31, 1992. Earlier application is encouraged. See Chapter 2, section 2.3(f), for further discussion about the effective date of SOP 91-1.

Accounting changes to conform with SOP 91-1 should be made by restatement of all periods presented. If the information necessary to restate is not available, accounting changes to adopt SOP 91-1 should be reported by including in income of the earliest period restated, the cumulative effect of the change on retained earnings at the beginning of that period, or at the beginning of the period in which SOP 91-1 is first applied if it is not practicable to restate any prior periods.

Unless it is not practicable, software companies are expected to restate prior financial statements in adopting SOP 91-1, even if they adopted accounting changes in the last few years to conform with expected conclusions of SOP 91-1 and reported those changes by including the cumulative effect on prior retained earnings in income of the period of change. Such companies are now expected to restate prior financial statements.

(b) Reporting Accounting Changes by Restatement

Notes to financial statements in which a company adopts an accounting change should include disclosure of the effect of the change on income before extraordinary items, net income, and related per share amounts, in conformity with APB Opinion 20, *Accounting Changes*. See the illustration in Example 8.1.

EXAMPLE 8.1 Illustrative Financial Statement Note Regarding Change in Accounting to Adopt SOP 91-1

Effective January 1, 1992, the Company changed its accounting for revenue recognition to conform to AICPA Statement of Position 91-1, *Software Revenue Recognition*. The Company now recognizes software license revenue on delivery; previously the Company recognized

---

software license revenue on contract signing. In addition, the Company now recognizes postcontract customer support revenue on a straight-line basis over the term of the contract; previously the Company recognized postcontract customer support revenue at inception of the contract term. The Company's financial statements for prior years have been restated to give effect to the accounting change. The effect of the accounting change on results of operations for the year ended December 31, 1992, was to decrease income before extraordinary items, net income, and net income per share by $250,000, $165,000, and $.17 per share, respectively. The effects of the accounting change on results of operations for the years ended December 31, 1991 and 1990, were as follows:

| | Years Ended December 31, | | | |
| | 1991 | | 1990 | |
	Previously Reported	Restated	Previously Reported	Restated
Income before extraordinary items	$462,000	$231,000	$396,000	$330,000
Net income	462,000	231,000	396,000	330,000
Net income per share	.46	.23	.40	.33

Alternatively, the effects of the restatement on results of operations for the preceding 2 years could be presented as in Example 8.2.

EXAMPLE 8.2   Effects of Restatement

The effects of the accounting change increased (decreased) income before extraordinary items, net income, and net income per share as follows:

| | Years Ended December 31, | | |
	1992	1991	1990
Income before extraordinary items	$(250,000)	$(350,000)	$(100,000)
Net income	(165,000)	(231,000)	(66,000)
Net income per share	(.17)	(.23)	(.07)

The author prefers the first presentation, as the comparison of absolute reported numbers seems to be more informative than simply displaying the increases or decreases, as in the second presentation. For accounting changes reported in interim period financial statements, the effects of the accounting change on results of operations for the current quarter and the effects of the restatement on all interim periods presented should be disclosed. The format used in Example 8.2 or another suitable format may be used.

(c) Computing the Restatement

Computing restatements to comply with SOP 91-1's delivery criteria for software license revenue recognition may be difficult in some circumstances. Some software companies that have not used delivery as the basis for revenue recognition may not have records indicating when delivery took place, or their records may not be in a form that is practical for computing a restatement. In such instances, a software company should reconstruct the data for as many periods as possible.

Exhibits 8.1 and 8.2 are suggested worksheets for computing the effect of the new method on the current period and the restatement for prior periods. The data in this illustration is consistent with amounts included in Examples 8.1 and 8.2.

(d) Auditors' Accounting Change Preferability Letters

Preferability letters will not be required by the SEC staff for accounting changes to comply with SOP 91-1, because under the new hierarchy of generally accepted accounting principles discussed in Chapter 2, the provisions of SOP 91-1 are required accounting for all companies.

8.2 DISCLOSURE OF ACCOUNTING POLICIES

(a) Requirements of SOP 91-1 and Statement 86

SOP 91-1 requires the disclosure of accounting policies for software revenue recognition. Although Statement 86 does not specifically

EXHIBIT 8.1   Restatement Computations: Restated Amounts

	December 31,		
	1992	1991	1990
Pretax income, net income, and income per share using new accounting			
Pretax income using previous accounting	$ 900,000	$ 700,000	$ 600,000
Software licenses			
Contracts signed but not delivered, beginning of year	450,000	125,000	50,000
Contracts signed but not delivered, end of year	(600,000)	(450,000)	(125,000)
Increase (decrease)	(150,000)	(325,000)	(75,000)
Postcontract customer support			
Deferred income, beginning of year	400,000	375,000	350,000
Deferred income, end of year	(500,000)	(400,000)	(375,000)
Increase (decrease)	(100,000)	(25,000)	(25,000)
Pretax income using new accounting	650,000	350,000	500,000
Provision for income taxes (34%)	221,000	119,000	170,000
Net income	$ 429,000	$ 231,000	$ 330,000
Weighted shares outstanding	1,000,000	1,000,000	1,000,000
Net income per share	$ .43	$ .23	$ .33

require disclosure of accounting policies related to capitalized software costs, such disclosure should be provided in the financial statements of software companies. Generally, software companies should disclose their accounting policies for capitalization, amortization, and net realizable value of software development costs. In addition, Statement 86 requires the following disclosures.

EXHIBIT 8.2 Restatement Computations: Effects of Change

Net income and income per share using previous accounting			
Pretax income	$ 900,000	$ 700,000	$ 600,000
Provision for income taxes (34%)	306,000	238,000	204,000
Net income	$ 594,000	$ 462,000	$ 396,000
Weighted shares outstanding	1,000,000	1,000,000	1,000,000
Net income per share	$ .59	$ .46	$ .40

Effects of accounting change			
Pretax income			
Using new accounting	$ 650,000	$ 350,000	$ 500,000
Using previous accounting	900,000	700,000	600,000
Effect of accounting change	$ (250,000)	$ (350,000)	$ (100,000)
Income before extraordinary items and net income			
Using new accounting	$ 429,000	$ 231,000	$ 330,000
Using previous accounting	594,000	462,000	396,000
Effect of accounting change	$ (165,000)	$ (231,000)	$ (66,000)
Net income per share			
Using new accounting	$ .43	$ .23	$ .33
Using previous accounting	.59	.46	.40
Effect of accounting change	$ (.17)	$ (.23)	$ (.07)

a. Unamortized computer software costs included in each balance sheet presented

b. The total amount charged to expense in each income statement presented for amortization of capitalized computer software costs and for amounts written down to net realizable value.
—FASB Statement 86, paragraph 11

Statement 86 also clarifies that software companies must disclose research and development costs charged to expense.

The disclosure requirements for research and development costs in Statement 2 apply to the research and development costs incurred for a computer software product to be sold, leased, or otherwise marketed.
—FASB Statement 86, paragraph 12

(b) Illustration of Accounting Policy Disclosure

Following is an illustration of accounting policy disclosure for a software company for revenue recognition, and for capitalization, amortization, and net realizable value testing of software development costs.

EXHIBIT 8.3 Accounting Policy Disclosure

Revenue Recognition

The Company recognizes software license revenue on delivery of the software and documentation when there are no significant remaining related obligations. The Company accrues the cost of any insignificant obligations remaining when software license revenue is recognized. Revenue from postcontract customer support is recognized on a straight-line basis over the term of the contract. Revenue from software services is recognized as the services are performed. Revenue from contracts for software combined with hardware or services or both is recognized using the percentage-of-completion method, with progress-to-completion measured based on labor hours incurred.

Capitalized Software Development Costs

The Company capitalizes software development costs in accordance with FASB Statement 86. Software development costs not qualifying for capitalization are expensed as research and development costs, which totaled $475,000 during the year ended December 31, 19XX. Capitalized costs are amortized on a product-by-product basis, based on the greater amount computed by using (a) the ratio that current gross revenues for a product bear to the total of current and anticipated future gross revenues for that product, or (b) straight-line amortization using useful lives of 3 to 7 years. The Company evaluates the estimated net realizable value of each software product at each balance sheet date and records writedowns to net realizable value for any products for which the net book value is in excess of net realizable value. During the year ended December 31, 19XX, the Company recorded writedowns of software products of $150,000.

For years in which a company reports accounting changes in adopting SOP 91-1, the accounting policy note may be a blend of the illustrative exhibits and examples in this section and in section 8.1(b).

8.3   INCOME STATEMENT PRESENTATION

Rule 5-03 of Regulation S-X requires that captions presented on the face of the income statement meet certain criteria. Any caption for which revenue exceeds 10 percent of total revenue must be presented separately, and the related costs must also be presented separately.

Net sales and gross revenues. State separately

(a) net sales of tangible products (gross sales less discounts, returns and allowances);

(b) operating revenues of public utilities or others;

(c) income from rentals;

(d) revenues from services; and

(e) other revenues

—Regulation S-X, Item 5-03(b)(1)

Costs and expenses applicable to sales and revenues. State separately the amount of

(a) cost of tangible goods sold,

(b) operating expenses of public utilities or others,

(c) expenses applicable to rental income,

(d) cost of services, and

(e) expenses applicable to other revenues.
                    —Regulation S-X, Item 5-03(b)(2)

Essentially, these regulations require software companies to prepare income statements using a gross margin approach. Although a gross profit line is not required and often not used by software companies, the presentation of the revenues and related costs enables the financial statement user to compute a gross margin for the major categories of revenues, even if a gross margin is not presented.

Software companies for which postcontract customer support (or maintenance) revenue exceeds 10 percent of total revenue, would be expected to report separate revenue and cost amounts for such in the income statement.

Following is an array of income statement presentations of revenue and expense captions, which have been derived from income statements prepared by software companies in practice:

Company A

Net revenue
   Systems
   Service

Cost of revenue
   Systems
   Service

   Gross margin

Operating expenses
   Product development
   Selling, general, and administrative

Company B

Net revenues
Cost of revenues

Gross profit

Operating expenses
   Research and development
   Sales and marketing
   General and administrative

Company C

Net revenues
   Licenses
   Services

Costs and expenses
   Cost of software distribution
   Sales and marketing
   Research and development
   General and administrative

Company D

Net revenues
   Product
   Maintenance

Costs and expenses
   Costs of product revenues
   Costs of maintenance
   Research and development
   Sales and marketing
   Administrative and general

Company E

Revenue
   Royalties
   Product sales
   Contract and other

Costs and expenses
    Direct costs
    Research, development, and contract costs
    Sales, marketing, and customer support
    General and administrative

Company F

Revenues
    License fees
    Services

Costs and expenses
    Cost of license fees
    Cost of services
    Sales and marketing
    Product development
    General and administrative

This array of income statement captions is diverse. The selection of revenue and expense captions should be made in view of the operations of the particular software company, with careful consideration of the requirements of Rule 5-03 if the company is an SEC registrant.

8.4 DEVELOPMENT STAGE COMPANIES

The software industry is characterized by many start-up companies, whose financial statements will be subject to the requirements of FASB Statement 7, *Accounting and Reporting by Development Stage Enterprises.* A development stage enterprise is one that

> is devoting substantially all of its efforts to establishing a new business and either of the following conditions exists:
>
> a. Planned principal operations have not commenced.
>
> b. Planned principal operations have commenced, but there has been no significant revenue therefrom.
>
>   —FASB Statement No. 7, paragraph 8

Development stage enterprises are required to follow the same accounting principles as established operating enterprises. In addition, Statement 7 requires development stage enterprises to include the following information in their financial statements:

- A caption in the stockholders' equity section labeling any cumulative net losses as "deficit accumulated during the development stage"

- In addition to income statements for the periods presented, a cumulative income statement showing revenues and expenses since inception of the enterprise

- In addition to statement of cash flows for the periods presented, a cumulative statement of cash flow since inception of the enterprise

- A statement of stockholders' equity from the enterprise's inception, indicating:

  - For each issuance, the date and number of shares of stock, warrants, rights, or other equity securities issued for cash and for other consideration (issuances within the same period for the same type of consideration and the same amount per equity unit may be combined).

  - For each issuance, the dollar amounts (per share or other equity unit and in total) assigned to the consideration received for shares of stock, warrants, rights, or other equity securities. Dollar amounts shall be assigned to any noncash consideration received.

  - For each issuance involving noncash consideration, the nature of the noncash consideration and the basis for assigning amounts.

The financial statements of a development stage enterprise must be identified as such. This is usually done by including a notation in the heading of the financial statement, such as the following:

ABC Software Company
(an entity in the development stage
as defined in FASB Statement 7)
Balance Sheet
December 31, 199X

In addition, a development stage enterprise should normally include, in its financial statement footnotes, a description such as the following:

> Since inception, the Company's activities have consisted primarily of raising equity and debt financing and the development of several proprietary software products. The Company's planned principal operations of marketing software and related services have not yet commenced. The Company is considered to be a development stage enterprise as defined in FASB Statement 7.

The preceding discussion is sometimes applicable to disclosures required by companies whose continuance as going concerns may be in doubt. In such cases, the previously discussed footnote may be extended to include information such as the following:

> The financial statements have been prepared with the assumption that the Company will continue in existence as a going concern, which is dependent on obtaining additional financing as discussed in Note X, on completing the development of its proprietary software products, bringing the products to market, and achieving profitable operations. The financial statements do not include any adjustments relating to the recoverability and classification of recorded asset amounts, or the classification of liabilities that might be necessary if the Company is unable to continue as a going concern.

8.5   REPORTING AFTER THE DEVELOPMENT STAGE

In the first year in which a company is no longer a development stage enterprise, the financial statements should indicate that in prior years, the company was a development stage enterprise. Data presented for prior years (when the company was a development stage enterprise), the cumulative amounts since inception, and other disclosures required by development stage enterprises need not be included in the financial statements for the prior years reissued in comparative form with the post development stage financial statements.

CHAPTER NINE

Auditing Financial Statements of Software Companies

Richard P. Graff
Coopers & Lybrand

The views expressed in this chapter reflect those of the individual author and do not necessarily represent those of the other contributing authors.

9.1   GENERAL CONSIDERATIONS: CHARACTERISTICS OF THE INDUSTRY

The unique characteristics of the software industry and its specialized accounting must be considered by auditors in planning and carrying out audit procedures and in assessing risk.

The SEC as well as various professional organizations have identified the software industry as a high-risk business in comparison with other industries. This is a comparatively young industry, and many software companies do not have long operating histories. Many new software companies are started every year that require audits; a large number of those companies initially or soon after formation seek equity financing in the public capital markets.

For some software companies that are in the start-up phase, questions will be raised about accounting recognition of both software revenue and capitalized software development costs. Uncertainty about a young software company's ability to finance the completion of software development projects and to successfully bring the products to market may create a concern about the propriety of capitalizing software development costs.

The auditor may face more going concern issues and more rapid obsolescence of products in the software industry than in other industries.

9.2   AUDITING CAPITALIZED SOFTWARE DEVELOPMENT COSTS
(a)   Nature of Assets

FASB Statement No. 86 (discussed in Chapter 7) established standards for accounting for computer software costs, including costs to be capitalized. Capitalized software development costs are different from most assets in traditional industries. Software is intangible, intellectual property, and its existence cannot be determined by physical examination as can inventory, fixed assets, or other tangible assets. Moreover, most assets are acquired from third parties, and their cost is evidenced by third-party payments and other documentation of third-party transactions, making auditing much easier than for self-constructed assets such as software. See Chapter 7 for a detailed discussion of capitalization of software development costs. Auditing self-constructed assets entails the need to audit cost accumulation systems or work papers designed to capture capitalized costs. In addition, the auditor must be satisfied as to the technical aspects and marketability of the software for which costs are capitalized, requiring procedures not normally necessary for auditing traditional tangible assets. Auditing the technical aspects of capitalized software may require the assistance of a software technical specialist. The need for a specialist depends on the specifics of the client's situation, including the complexity of the software, the extent to which the client has reliable control procedures, and the extent to which the auditor is familiar with the client through previous audits.

(b) Assessing Significance of Capitalized Software Development Costs

The nature and extent of procedures for auditing capitalized software development costs should be determined after assessing the significance of capitalized costs to both the balance sheet and income statement. It may also be appropriate to compare the percentage of capitalized software development costs with industry averages. Generally, software companies seem to capitalize relatively small percentages of total software expenditures—perhaps in the range of 15 to 25 percent of total software expenditures. There are exceptions, varying from some companies that capitalize minimal or no costs to those that capitalize significant percentages of total software expenditures.

The auditor should carefully evaluate the business reasons why a particular software company capitalizes significantly more or less than the general range of 15 to 25 percent of total software expenditures. For example, a particular software company might capitalize a small amount or no software expenditures, claiming that because of the nature of its products or the markets it serves, it cannot determine technological feasibility or recoverability until the product is substantially completed or on the market. For these companies, any amount of software development costs that are capitalized would be immaterial. Others may capitalize significant percentages of total software expenditures—these are often applications software companies with proven products and an established market share.

The auditor should expect higher amounts to be capitalized if the client uses the detail program design approach, and lesser amounts of the client uses the working model approach.

(c) General Approach to Auditing

A sound approach to auditing capitalized software development costs involves two parallel sets of procedures: (1) auditing cost accumulation, and (2) auditing the status of the product. The first emphasizes the accumulation of capitalized amounts through a cost system or worksheet approach, or a combination of both, the amortization of capitalized software development costs, and a net realizable value test. The second, which may require the use of a specialist, emphasizes the investigation of the technical aspects of the software products and development projects, including an evaluation of whether technological feasibility was properly determined and when a software product became or will become available for general market release.

(d) Use of a Technical Specialist

If capitalized software development costs are significant, it may be necessary for the auditor to consider using a specialist qualified to carry out the technical evaluation procedures. The technical specialist usually reads design and detail program technical documents, reviews high-risk technical issues, and/or observes a completed working model of the software product. The technical specialist's procedures may also include interviews with the company's software developers and technical staff. Generally, the work of the technical specialist does not include direct analysis of program source code.

Large accounting firms have internal technical specialists qualified to perform technical evaluations. Smaller firms without such internal expertise may use the services of an outside specialist if capitalized software development costs are significant.

Guidance for auditors using the work of an outside specialist is provided in AU Section 336 of *Codification of Statements on Auditing Standards*. In selecting a specialist, an auditor should consider the following:

a. The professional certification, license, or other recognition of the competence of the specialist in his field, as appropriate.

b. The reputation and standing of the specialist in the views of his peers and others familiar with his capability or performance.

c. The relationship, if any, of the specialist to the client.
—AU Section 336.05

The auditor should understand the methods or assumptions used by the specialist and, as appropriate, review the data provided to the specialist by the client. This data consists of technical documentation, which should be compared with other information obtained by the auditor for consistency and reasonableness. If an outside technical specialist is used, the following aspects of the specialist's work should be documented.

a. The objectives and scope of the specialist's work.

b. The specialist's representations as to his relationship, if any, to the client.

c. The methods or assumptions to be used.

d. A comparison of the methods or assumptions to be used with those used in the preceding period.

e. The specialist's understanding of the auditor's corroborative use of the specialist's findings in relation to the representations in the financial statements.

f. The form and content of the specialist's report that would enable the auditor to make the evaluation described in [a subsequent paragraph .08 entitled "Using the Findings of the Specialist"].
—AU Section 336.07

(e) Auditing Determination of Technological Feasibility

In certain cases, the auditor is able to achieve satisfaction as to the technological feasibility of a software product through available documentation. At other times, participation by a technical specialist is advisable.

In auditing technological feasibility, the auditor should initially determine what approach the client used in developing the particular software product. For purposes of applying audit procedures, software development approaches can generally be divided into two categories—the detail program design approach and the working model approach. The detail program design approach follows a traditional methodology of preparation of a detail program design. The working model approach bypasses the detail program design and demonstrates the resolution of all key technical questions through the development of a working model.

When a detail program design is used, the auditor should determine that as of the date of technological feasibility, the client had the necessary skills, hardware, and software technology to complete the development of the product. The auditor should examine the product design and detail program designs and obtain evidence that they have been completed and are consistent with each other. All high-risk development issues should be identified, such as novel, unique, and unproven functions and features or technological innovations. The auditor should obtain documentation of how, when, and by whom all high-risk issues were resolved, and should also obtain evidence that product testing confirmed the resolution of these issues prior to the capitalization of costs.

If the client used a working model approach, the auditor should, through inquiry, observation, and obtaining evidential matter, determine when the product design and working model were completed. The auditor should also obtain evidence that the working model was tested in conformity to the product design.

When auditing the determination of technological feasibility of enhancements of existing products, the auditor should obtain evidence that the enhancements will extend the original product's life or significantly improve its marketability. The auditor should also follow the procedures described above, as appropriate, depending on whether a detail program design or working model approach was used.

If purchased software is incorporated into a computer software product developed by the client, the auditor should ascertain the technological feasibility of the acquired software if its cost is to be capitalized as part of the cost of the software product.

(f) Auditing Determination of Availability for General Market Release

Both the auditor and the technical specialist can contribute to auditing the determination of completion of the software development project and availability of the product for general market release. The auditor should review documentation supporting the client's conclusions about marketability of the product, which generally includes a market study of some sort, prepared either internally or by a third party. Generally, a study prepared by a third party is more reliable, but often the only studies and market projections available are those prepared internally by the software company.

The auditor should also consider the past success of the company in bringing software to the marketplace. The auditor should determine availability for general market release by reviewing evidence of completed sales transactions if revenues from the product have been realized. The realization of some revenues, however, does not necessarily mean that a product is available for general market release. For example, revenues may be recognized from a customer who uses a software product for beta testing. The auditor should corroborate the availability for general market release by noting the cessation of capitalization of development costs for the project.

The technical specialist may be helpful in verifying completion of beta testing and customer program documentation, and in evaluating whether those events indicate availability for general market release in the specific circumstances.

(g) Auditing Accumulation of Capitalized Hours, Direct Costs, and Overhead Rates

Audit procedures for the accumulation of costs to be capitalized should be essentially the same as for client-constructed fixed assets.

Because hours incurred are generally the basis for cost accumulation in software development, a key audit procedure is to substantiate the capitalizable hours incurred on each project. This can usually be done by auditing the accumulation of hours charged on time sheets or other evidence of work performed on a project. Sometimes software companies do not have time accountability or cost systems that accumulate time incurred by individual-to-project summaries. In such cases, the software company may identify personnel who worked on a capitalizable project for specified blocks of time. The auditor should be able to corroborate this information by reviewing project files, discussing the project work with client management and project personnel, and corroborating the findings of the technical specialist. Costs accumulated should be compared to budgets for the project.

Direct charges to projects, such as for outside consultants, materials, and other costs, can be audited through the normal examination of third-party invoices, payments, and other documentation.

Overhead rates can account for a substantial portion of capitalized software development costs. The auditor should review the mathematical logic and accuracy of the overhead computation and the types of costs for consistency and conformity with generally accepted accounting principles for inventory costing, which usually apply. The auditor should also consider the discussions of computing overhead to be capitalized that appear in an *FASB Highlights* published in February 1986.

(h) Auditing Amortization and Net Realizable Value

In auditing amortization and net realizable value, the auditor's primary focus will be reviewing the client's projected revenue trends, including comparisons of actual results to prior projections. See the discussion about projected revenue trends in Chapter 7.

(i) Representation Letter

In addition to other audit procedures, it is advisable for the auditor to obtain specific written representations from appropriate client personnel as to capitalized software development costs. Following is suggested language for inclusion in the representation letter requested from a software client.

We specifically confirm the following facts as they relate to software capitalization:

Software Product	Date of Technological Feasibility	Date of Availability for General Market Release	Capitalized Cost
ABC	mm/dd/yy	mm/dd/yy	$ XXX,XXX
DEF	mm/dd/yy	mm/dd/yy	XXX,XXX
GHI	mm/dd/yy	mm/dd/yy	XXX,XXX
			$X,XXX,XXX

We also confirm that management believes such costs are recoverable.

9.3 AUDITING SOFTWARE REVENUE

(a) Unique Aspects of Auditing Software Revenue

Auditing software revenue used to be unique in comparison with auditing revenue in other industries because of diverse revenue practices in the software industry. SOP 91-1 established how generally accepted accounting principles should be applied to software revenue recognition by all companies in the software industry. Thus, auditors no longer must deal with radically different approaches to revenue recognition. Yet there is still a uniqueness to auditing software revenue because the industry-wide standard is new and there are several areas in which practice must further define specific procedures to be used in applying the principles and guidelines of SOP 91-1. In this respect, the auditor should be aware of ongoing SEC interpretations about the application of SOP 91-1.

Moreover, auditing software revenue continues to be unique because software contracts and transactions are structured in many different ways, making it difficult at times to determine what kind of transaction has occurred. These situations often arise when software products and services are included in the same agreements.

(b) Auditing Software License Revenue

Primary audit procedures for software license revenue are reading and understanding the contract or software license agreement and determining the date of delivery of the software. In audits of software companies with many transactions of small amounts, this should be done on a test basis, relying as far as possible on the uniformity of transactions and client control procedures. In audits of software companies with fewer transactions of larger amounts, it may be necessary to audit most or all transactions, especially if the terms of the contracts or license agreements vary from transaction to transaction.

In assessing whether there are other significant vendor obligations that preclude revenue recognition on delivery, the auditor should review the history of the client in successfully completing installations of its software products and obtaining customer acceptance as expected. The auditor should consider the nature of the services and their magnitude in determining whether the obligations are significant enough to require delay in recognition of revenue. If the software company is engaged in its initial marketing of a new product, the auditor should consider whether there is a basis for assuming that the company is engaged in initial marketing of a new product, the auditor should consider whether there is a basis for assuming that the com-

The auditor should be especially alert for provisions in software contracts that give the customer the right to cancel the transaction. If returns are a consideration, the auditor should ensure that the client has complied with accounting procedures required by FASB Statement No. 48. In doing so, the auditor should test client estimates of returns to be provided for.

(c) Auditing Contract Accounting Revenues and Costs

The auditor should be satisfied that the client has selected the appropriate alternative method—either the completed contract method or the percentage-of-completion method of accounting for contracts. As discussed in Chapter 6, there is a presumption that companies engaging in contracting activities are able to make the estimates of project revenues and costs that would require the use of the percentage-of-completion method.

If a company accounts for percentage-of-completion contracts for software combined with hardware or services or both, using input cost-to-cost or hours-to-hours measures of progress, the auditor's considerations are comparable to those in auditing contracts in other industries. If the client uses different measures of progress-to-completion for elements of a contract, such as output value-added measures of progress for software and input hours-to-hours measures for services, the auditor will face additional issues. These include identifying and valuing of the contract elements, determining that the software company has had sufficient separate transactions with off-the-shelf software (if the accounting treatment is dependent on the software being off-the-shelf software), timing of the measure of progress on the output value-added element, and other issues that may surface as more of these transactions are addressed and interpreted in practice.

The auditor should consider the nature of the services being performed in a contract if this is a factor in the accounting treatment. The auditor should read the contractual descriptions of services to be performed and may need the assistance of a technical specialist to determine whether a project is a software development project. The nature of the services may determine what measures of progress-to-completion may be used and when progress can be determined to have occurred.

As in all audits involving contract accounting, the auditor should review the client's estimates of remaining revenues and costs-to-complete to assess whether a contract loss reserve is needed.

If a software company has used segmentation in accounting for contracts for software combined with hardware or services or both, the auditor will need to determine that the transactions meet the segmentation criteria of SOP 81-1. For contracts accounted for by segmentation, the auditor should be satisfied as to the costs identified with each element. If a contract is accounted for as a single cost center, the auditor should ensure that a constant profit margin has been reported in each period of the contract.

(d) Auditing Postcontract Customer Support Revenue

Audit procedures should include substantiation that, where required, all postcontract customer-support arrangements have been identified and unbundled from license transactions that include postcontract customer support. The auditor should determine that the amortization schedules used by the software company appropriately allocate postcontract customer support revenue over the period of the contract.

(e) Reporting on Accounting Changes to Adopt SOP 91-1

SOP 91-1 requires adoption of its recommendations by retroactive restatement for all periods for which restatement is practicable. Following is an example of a paragraph that would follow the opinion paragraph of an audit report on financial statements in which the provisions of SOP 91-1 have been adopted by retroactive restatement.

As discussed in Note 1, effective January 1, 1991, the Company adopted the provisions of AICPA Statement of Position 91-1, *Software Revenue Recognition*, and the financial statements for 1990 and 1989 have been restated for the changes in revenue recognition policy to adopt the provisions of SOP 91-1.

If restatement of prior periods is not practicable, SOP 91-1 provides that accounting changes to adopt its recommendations may be made by a cumulative-effect accounting change. The auditor may report on a cumulative-effect accounting change by including a paragraph such as the following after the opinion paragraph.

As discussed in Note 1, effective January 1, 1991, the Company changed its method of accounting for revenue to adopt the provisions of AICPA Statement of Position 91-1, *Software Revenue Recognition*.

All software companies are required to adopt SOP 91-1 for fiscal years, and interim periods in such fiscal years, beginning after December 15, 1991.

9.4 GOING CONCERN CONSIDERATIONS

(a) Industry and Company Characteristics

In the software industry, a relatively few individuals with technological capability are able to conceive an idea for one or more software products and start a company. Generally, initial development work on such products can be financed to some extent through "sweat equity," with the principals doing much of the development and programming themselves. As the project takes shape, other investors may provide financing. At this stage, however, the financing is rarely sufficient to complete development, bring the product to market, and make the company a self-sustaining entity. Conventional financing, such as bank financing, is more difficult to obtain in the software industry than in other industries, because the primary assets of a software company are not tangible resources, such as inventory and fixed assets, and are generally not given the same consideration as collateral.

Software companies often face critical times in their development when survival is uncertain and the ability to continue in business depends on incurring additional debt or obtaining equity financing, or achieving profitable operations and cash flow, or both. The auditor is required to express opinions on the financial statements of developing software companies during these times. Moreover, some of the same issues arise from time to time in audits of established software companies.

(b) Going Concern Audit Procedures

The software industry includes many new, developing companies, some of which are development stage enterprises as defined in FASB Statement 7, *Accounting and Reporting by Development Stage Enterprises*. The auditor will therefore be faced with going concern issues in the software industry more often than in other industries. Essentially, a going concern issue exists if there is information indicating that the entity may be unable to continue to meet its obligations as they become due, without substantial disposition of assets outside the ordinary course of business, restructuring of debt, externally forced revisions of its operations, or similar actions. The auditor is responsible for determining whether there is any doubt about the entity's ability to continue as a going concern for 1 year after the date of the financial statements being audited.

AU Section 341.03 provides the following guidelines for determining whether there is substantial doubt about an entity's ability to continue as a going concern.

a. The auditor considers whether the results of his procedures performed in planning, gathering evidential matter relative to the various audit objectives, and completing the audit identify conditions and events that, when considered in the aggregate, indicate there could be substantial doubt about the entity's ability to continue as a going concern for a reasonable period of time. It may be necessary to obtain additional information about such conditions and events, as well as the appropriate evidential matter to support information that mitigates the auditor's doubt.

b. If the auditor believes there is substantial doubt about the entity's ability to continue as a going concern for a reasonable period of time, he should (1) obtain information about management's plans that are intended to mitigate the effect of such conditions or events, and (2) assess the likelihood that such plans can be effectively implemented.

c. After the auditor has evaluated management's plans, he concludes whether he has substantial doubt about the entity's ability to continue as a going concern for a reasonable period of time. If the auditor concludes that there is substantial doubt, he should (1) consider the adequacy of disclosure about the entity's possible inability to continue as a going concern for a reasonable period of time, and (2) include an explanatory paragraph (following the opinion paragraph) in his audit report to reflect his conclusion. If the auditor concludes that substantial doubt does not exist, he should consider the need for disclosure.

Audit procedures that generally provide information relevant to the evaluation of an entity as a going concern are identified in AU Section 341.05, including analytical procedures, review of subsequent events, review of compliance with the terms of debt and loan agreements, reading of minutes, inquiry of legal counsel, and confirmation with related and third parties of the details of arrangements to provide or maintain financial support.

AU Section 341.06 describes conditions or events that may indicate doubt about an entity's ability to continue as a going concern. Generally, they include such factors as cash flow difficulties, defaults on loans or similar agreements, denial of credit, need to seek new financing or to dispose of assets, substantial revisions of operations, and losses of key customers or suppliers.

If a going concern issue is present, the auditor's evaluation of management's plans is a key procedure. AU Sections 341.07 to 341.09 describe how an auditor should evaluate management's plans. As many going concern issues involve the question of cash flow, the auditor should request a cash flow projection for at least 1 year after the date of the financial statements being audited, and should carefully evaluate the assumptions used.

If the auditor concludes that there is substantial doubt about an entity's ability to continue as going concern, the auditor should consider the possible effects on the financial statements and the adequacy of disclosures. AU Section 341.10 suggests that the following information might be disclosed in the financial statements: the conditions and events giving rise to the going concern issue, the possible effects, management's evaluation of their significance and mitigating factors, possible discontinuance of operations, management's plans, and information about the recoverability of recorded asset amounts or classification of liabilities. The auditor's report should include an explanatory paragraph, following the opinion paragraph, such as the following.

The accompanying financial statements have been prepared on the assumption that the Company will continue as a going concern. As discussed in Note 1 to the financial statements, the Company has a net working capital deficiency that raises substantial doubt about its ability to continue as a going concern. Management's plans in regard to these matters are also described in Note 1. The financial statements do not include any adjustments that might result from the outcome of this uncertainty.

Following is another example of a going concern qualification paragraph that could have relevance to software companies.

The accompanying financial statements have been prepared on the assumption that the Company will continue as a going concern. As discussed in Note 1 to the financial statements, the Company presently anticipates that it has working capital to meet its needs through at least June 30, 19X3. Commercial product sales of software licenses are not expected to produce positive cash flow until at least the first quarter of 19X4. Therefore, the Company must raise additional equity or debt capital in order to fund its operations. There is no assurance that sufficient equity or debt capital can be raised. Those circumstances raise substantial doubt about the Company's ability to continue as a going concern. The financial statements for the year ended December 31, 19X2, do not include any adjustments that might result from the outcome of this uncertainty.

If a going concern issue is present, but it is determined that management's plans are adequate to remove doubt about the entity's ability to continue as a going concern for 1 year after the date of the financial statements, it may still be necessary to disclose the conditions that gave rise to the going concern question, along with the mitigating factors, such as management's plans, that alleviated the question.

9.5 CONCLUSION: A CHALLENGING INDUSTRY FOR AUDITORS

The software industry continues to be one of the fastest-growing industries. The business issues characterizing this industry—continued dependence on research and development owing to short product life cycles, the intellectual component of the products, and high gross margins connected with incremental revenues, to name a few—lead to unique issues in both accounting and auditing.

Specific guidance on software capitalization is provided by Statement 86. In addition, the auditor must have knowledge of the software industry and a specific understanding of the client's business to conclude as to the appropriateness of software capitalization, which includes determining the point at which technological feasibility of the product is established. That determination is subjective, based on the software developer's approach and interpretation of information about the development project. Once technological feasibility is determined and capitalization begins, the capitalized costs must be evaluated for recoverability based on estimated future revenue streams. That estimate is also subjective and can be uncertain for new companies lacking preestablished markets.

Specific guidance on revenue recognition is provided in SOP 91-1. That statement will be subject to interpretation over the next few years, as related implementation issues are encountered and resolved.

In summary, the software industry provides unique opportunities and challenges for auditors. Auditors must be technically proficient in the application of the specific industry accounting pronouncements and, have an in-depth understanding of the industry and the client. The merging of these two knowledge bases is essential in carrying out the auditor's responsibility.

As the business community continues to evolve into an increasingly information-based infrastructure, further opportunities for audit practice development will arise in the software industry.

Appendix A

Statement of Position

91–1

Software Revenue Recognition

December 12, 1991

Prepared by the AICPA Task Force
on Accounting for the Development
and Sale of Computer Software

American Institute of
Certified Public Accountants

AICPA

NOTE

Statements of position of the Accounting Standards Division present the conclusions of at least a majority of the Accounting Standards Executive Committee, which is the senior technical body of the Institute authorized to speak for the Institute in the areas of financial accounting and reporting. Statements of position do not establish standards enforceable under rule 203 of the AICPA Code of Professional Conduct. However, SAS No. 69, *The Meaning of "Present Fairly in Conformity With Generally Accepted Accounting Principles" in the Independent Auditor's Report* (AICPA, *Professional Standards*, vol. 1, AU sec. 411), includes AICPA statements of position among the sources of established accounting principles that an AICPA member should consider if the accounting treatment of a transaction or event is not specified by a pronouncement covered by rule 203. If an established accounting principle from one or more of these sources is relevant to the circumstances, the AICPA member should be prepared to justify a conclusion that another treatment is generally accepted. If there is a conflict between accounting principles relevant to the circumstances from one or more of the sources of established accounting principles, the auditor should follow the treatment specified by the source in the higher category—for example, follow the guidance in an SOP over prevalent practice in a particular industry—or be prepared to justify a conclusion that a treatment specified by a source in the lower category better presents the substance of the transaction in the circumstances.

Table of Contents

Page

Page

SUMMARY

This statement of position (SOP) provides guidance on applying generally accepted accounting principles in recognizing revenue on software transactions. The basic principle is that revenue is recognized on delivery of software; however, this SOP provides for some exceptions. Briefly, it recommends the following:

a. *Software licenses with no other vendor obligations.* If collectibility is probable and the vendor has no obligations remaining under the sales or licensing agreement after delivering the software, revenue from the software licensing fee should be recognized on delivery of the software.

b. *Software licenses with other insignificant vendor obligations.* If the vendor has insignificant obligations remaining under the sales or licensing agreement after delivering the software, revenue from the software licensing fee should be recognized on delivery of the software if collectibility is probable. The remaining obligations should be accounted for either (a) by accruing the remaining costs or (b) by deferring a pro rata portion of revenue and recognizing it either ratably as the obligations are fulfilled or on completion of performance.

c. *Software licenses with other significant vendor obligations.* If, in addition to the obligation to deliver the software, the sales or licensing agreement includes other significant vendor obligations, the agreement should first be examined to determine whether it should be accounted for using contract accounting or as a service transaction. For agreements with significant vendor obligations beyond delivery of the software that are not accounted for using contract accounting or as service transactions, revenue should not be recognized until all of the following conditions are met:

- Delivery has occurred.
- Other remaining vendor obligations are no longer significant.
- Collectibility is probable.

d. *Software transactions structured as leases.* If a lease of software involves property, plant, or equipment, the revenue attributable to the property, plant, or equipment should be accounted for in conformity with Financial Accounting Standards Board (FASB) Statement of Financial Accounting Standards No. 13, *Accounting for Leases,* and any revenue attributable to the software, including postcontract customer support (PCS), should be accounted for separately in conformity with the guidance set forth in this SOP. However, if the property, plant, or equipment contains software that is incidental to the property, plant, or equipment as a whole, the software should not be accounted for separately. The allocation of revenues between the software and the property, plant, or equipment should be based on fair values. If the fair values are not readily determinable, other reasonable methods of allocation should be used. The costs of the software should be accounted for as set forth in FASB Statement No. 86, *Accounting for the Costs of Computer Software to Be Sold, Leased, or Otherwise Marketed.*

e. *Significant uncertainties about customer acceptance.* If, after delivery, there is significant uncertainty about customer acceptance of the software, license revenue should not be recognized until the uncertainty becomes insignificant.

f. *Absence of a reasonable basis for estimating the degree of collectibility of receivables.* Revenues associated with software transactions for which there is no reasonable basis of estimating the degree of collectibility of related receivables should be accounted for using either the installment method or the cost recovery method of accounting.

g. *Contract accounting.* If a contract to deliver software or a software system, either alone or together with other products, requires significant production, modification, or customization of software, a system, or the other products, that contract should be accounted for in conformity with Accounting Research Bulletin (ARB) No. 45, *Long-Term Construction-Type Contracts,* using the relevant guidance in SOP 81-1, *Accounting for Performance of Construction-Type and Certain Production-Type Contracts.* However, transactions that are normally accounted for as product sales should not be accounted for as long-term contracts merely to avoid the delivery requirements for revenue recognition normally associated with product sales.

h. *Service transactions.* If, in addition to the obligation to deliver the software, the sales or licensing agreement includes obligations to perform services that (a) are not essential to the functionality of any other element of the transaction and (b) are separately stated and priced such that the total price of the agreement would be expected to vary as a result of the inclusion or exclusion of the services, the services and the sales or licensing component should be accounted for separately.

If collectibility is probable, revenue from software services generally should be recognized as the services are performed or, if no pattern of performance is discernible, ratably over the period during which the services are performed. If significant uncertainty about customer acceptance of the services exists, revenue should not be recognized until the uncertainty becomes insignificant.

i. *Postcontract customer support.* If collectibility is probable, revenue from PCS, including revenue that is bundled with an initial licensing fee, generally should be recognized ratably over the period of the PCS arrangement. Revenue attributable to PCS, however, may be recognized together with the initial licensing fee on delivery of the software if all of the following conditions are met:

- The PCS fee is bundled with the initial licensing fee.
- The PCS bundled with the initial license is for one year or less.
- The estimated cost of providing PCS during the initial period of the PCS arrangement is insignificant.
- Enhancements offered during the initial period of the PCS arrangement have historically been minimal and are expected to be minimal during the initial period of the PCS arrangement.
- Collectibility is probable.

PCS fees that meet the above conditions should be accounted for in a manner similar to that used in accounting for insignificant obligations. If revenue is recognized together with the initial licensing fee on delivery of the software, all estimated costs of providing the PCS, including costs of services and enhancements, should be (*a*) charged to expense as incurred or (*b*) accrued and charged to expense at the time the revenue is recognized, whichever occurs first.

j. *Disclosure of accounting policies.* Software revenue recognition policies should be disclosed in the notes to the financial statements.

k. *Effective date.* This SOP is effective for financial statements issued after March 15, 1992, that are for fiscal years, and interim periods in such fiscal years, beginning after December 15, 1991. Earlier application is encouraged.

Software Revenue Recognition

Scope

1. This statement of position (SOP) provides guidance on when revenue should be recognized and at what amounts for licensing, selling, leasing, or otherwise marketing computer software. It applies to all entities that earn revenue from those activities. It does not apply, however, to revenue earned on a product containing software that is incidental to the product as a whole.

2. Selling all rights to products already developed is the same as selling such rights in other industries and is not addressed in this SOP. However, if the sale is accompanied by a variable pricing arrangement of the kind described in paragraph 52 of this SOP, the conclusions of this SOP should be applied in accounting for the variable pricing arrangement.

Definitions

3. This SOP uses the following terms with the definitions indicated:

Core software. An inventory of software that vendors use in creating other software. Core software is not delivered as is because customers cannot use it unless it is customized to meet system objectives or customer specifications.

Customer. A user or reseller.

Delivery. A transfer of software accompanied by documentation to the customer. It may be by—

a. A physical transfer of tape, disk, integrated circuit, or other medium;

b. Transmission by telecommunications;

c. Making available to the customer software that will not be physically transferred, such as through the facilities of a computer service bureau;

d. Authorization for duplication of existing copies in the customer's possession.

If a licensing agreement provides a customer with the right to multiple copies of a software product in exchange for a fixed fee, delivery means transfer of the product master, or the first copy if the product master is not to be transferred.

Fixed fee. A fee required to be paid at a set amount that is not subject to refund or adjustment. A fixed fee includes amounts designated as minimum royalties. Factors to consider in determining whether a fee is fixed are discussed in paragraphs 57 and 58 of this SOP.

Licensing. Granting the right to use but not to own software through leases or licenses.

Off-the-shelf software. Software marketed as a stock item that customers can use with little or no customization.

Performance milestone. A task associated with long-term contracts that, when completed, provides management with a reliable indicator of progress-to-completion on those contracts.

Platform. The hardware architecture of a particular model or family of computers, the system software, such as the operating system, or both.

Postcontract customer support (PCS). The right to receive services or product enhancements, or both, offered after the software license period begins or after another point as provided for by the PCS arrangement. PCS does not include installation and other services directly related to the initial license of the software. PCS is typically provided at no additional cost for the initial license period and is offered for a fee in succeeding periods.

PCS arrangements include patterns of providing services or enhancements, or both, although the arrangements may not be evidenced by a written contract signed by the vendor and the customer, as discussed in paragraph 116 of this SOP.

PCS is generally referred to in the software industry as *maintenance*, a term that is defined, as follows, in paragraph 52 of Financial Accounting Standards Board (FASB) Statement of Financial Accounting Standards No. 86, *Accounting for the Costs of Computer Software to Be Sold, Leased, or Otherwise Marketed*:

> Activities undertaken after the product is available for general release to customers to correct errors or keep the product updated with

current information. Those activities include routine changes and additions.

However, the term *maintenance* is not used in this SOP because it has taken on a broader meaning in the industry than the one described in FASB Statement No. 86; it may be confused with hardware maintenance or *maintenance* as it is used elsewhere in accounting literature, and its meaning varies from company to company.

The right to receive services and enhancements provided under PCS is generally specified by the PCS arrangement. Typical PCS arrangements include services, such as telephone support and correction of errors (bug fixing or debugging), and product enhancements developed by the vendor during the period in which the PCS is provided.

Reseller. Entity licensed by a software vendor to market the vendor's software to users or other resellers. Licensing agreements with resellers typically include arrangements to sublicense, reproduce, or distribute software. Resellers may be distributors of software, hardware, or turnkey systems, or they may be other entities that include software with the products or services they sell.

Site license. A license that permits a customer to use either specified or unlimited numbers of copies of a software product either throughout a company or at a specified location.

Turnkey system. An integrated group of hardware and software that is built, supplied, or installed complete and ready to operate. Many contracts for turnkey systems define solutions in terms of meeting functionality and performance criteria; others specify basic hardware and software configurations. The vendors represent to the users that the systems will perform stipulated tasks; significant customization of software is often required.

User. Party that ultimately uses the software in an application.

Background

4. The FASB encouraged the American Institute of Certified Public Accountants (AICPA) to develop this statement of position from a 1987 AICPA issues paper, *Software Revenue Recognition.*

5. Although FASB Statement of Financial Accounting Concepts No. 5, *Recognition and Measurement in Financial Statements of Business*

Enterprises, provides guidance on when to recognize revenue in general, authoritative accounting literature provides no specific guidance on when to recognize revenue on licensing, selling, leasing, or otherwise marketing computer software.

6. At this SOP's printing, the financial statements of publicly held companies indicated a wide range of revenue recognition practices. It is difficult to determine the extent to which that wide range represented diverse application of generally accepted accounting principles (GAAP) in the same circumstances. It appeared that at least some similar transactions were being accounted for diversely; however, the variety of ways in which software is licensed or sold, as discussed in the following section, also contributed to the apparent diversity.

7. Descriptions of historical practice for various software licensing arrangements are included in the following section solely to illustrate the diversity in accounting methods in use at this SOP's printing.

Product Marketing and Historical Revenue Recognition Practices

8. Vendors transfer rights to software products to customers using a variety of marketing arrangements, including the following:

- Licenses and leasing arrangements with users for their own use, with no right to reproduce for sale or sublicense, or with the right to reproduce and use only at designated sites or machines
- Licenses of software to resellers that allow the resellers to distribute or reproduce software and market it to users
- Sales of all rights to products already developed, which are not considered in this SOP except as noted previously in paragraph 2
- Contracts to develop software combined with services or hardware products or both and service transactions with some or all of the rights passing to the customer
- PCS arrangements

Licensing and Leasing Off-the-Shelf Software to Users

9. Licensing and leasing arrangements with users of off-the-shelf software take a variety of forms. In general, the kinds of activities

software vendors may be required to perform before and after delivery of software products are affected by the needs of customers and the kinds of software. Some software products may involve virtually no vendor obligations beyond delivery and are sold and delivered much like other packaged goods. Other software products require installation, bug fixing, enhancements, warranty support, training, provision of additional copies, and other support. To be useful to users, some software products require extensive modifications, involving the addition of new modules or the integration of modules already in use. Such modifications may be included in the installation or may be contracted for separately.

Pricing and Payment Terms

10. For some software products, the user's obligation to pay is tied to the signing of a licensing contract or lease. Some payments may be spread over vendor performance milestones or may vary with the amount of use of the product. The costs of services and ancillary products, such as hardware, are sometimes included—bundled— with the price of the software product; sometimes those services and products are priced separately. Some companies have policies under which the user may return the software or exchange one product for another.

Historical Revenue Recognition Practices

11. At this SOP's printing, the following revenue recognition methods were found in practice for licenses and leases of off-the-shelf software to users with substantially no vendor obligations beyond delivery of the software:

a. Recognition in income of all revenue and related expenses, if any, at contract signing

b. Recognition in income of all revenue and related expenses, if any, at delivery

c. Recognition in income of a percentage of revenue and profit attributable to the software generally at contract signing, with the balance recognized during or on completion of installation and acceptance (percentage-of-completion based on milestones)

d. Recognition in income of all revenue and profit over the installation period based on the installation effort (percentage-of-completion based on labor measures)

e. Recognition in income of all revenue and related expenses at completion of installation or acceptance by the user (completed-contract)

f. Accounting for arrangements with characteristics of leases as operating or sales-type leases under FASB Statement No. 13, *Accounting for Leases*, as amended (hereinafter referred to as FASB Statement No. 13).

Licensing Software to Resellers

12. Licensing software to resellers to market to users or other resellers includes arrangements to sublicense, reproduce, or distribute software. Terms of those arrangements may be perpetual or for fixed periods. They may also provide for—

a. Exchange rights (that is, vendors agree with resellers to exchange unsold or returned products for other products).

b. Rights to obtain licenses to distribute additional selected products with a fixed minimum purchase required for—

- Existing products.

- Products being developed.

- Some combination of both.

c. Reproduction of the software by the vendor under the same contract or under a separate contract.

13. Licenses to reproduce do not necessarily grant resellers exclusive rights to copy software. For example, some licensing agreements require vendors to copy software at the option of the resellers.

Pricing and Payment Terms

14. The following are typical pricing terms found in software licensing arrangements with resellers:

- Fixed price

- Royalty, based on the passage of time, the volume of use, or some other variable pricing arrangement

- Fixed price plus royalty

Royalty arrangements may include noncancelable obligations or non-refundable advance payments.

15. Some licenses have fixed fees or minimum royalties that are small in relation to anticipated total payments under the arrangements. Under other licenses, fixed fees or minimum royalties are all that the vendor expects to receive, but the vendor retains the right to receive additional amounts if the products are more successful than expected.

Historical Revenue Recognition Practices

16. At this SOP's printing, entities that license software to resellers were recognizing fixed fees at contract signing, on delivery of the software master or first copy, over the estimated life of the distribution arrangement, by the terms of a royalty arrangement, or based on payment (cash basis).

Contracts for Software Combined With Services or Hardware or Both and Service Transactions

17. Contracts with customers to develop software or contracts to develop software combined with services or hardware or both are similar in certain respects to long-term contracts or service transactions.

18. Typical products and services provided by vendors under such arrangements include hardware and software, software development, system installation and integration, and turnkey systems. Some vendors sell a package of existing software and hardware elements without customization or integration. Other vendors contract with customers to customize the software products and, in addition, they may package the software with hardware elements.

19. All goods and services to be provided are generally contracted for in a single document, although the parties sometimes negotiate separate contracts for software, labor, and hardware. Under many agreements with hardware manufacturers, software vendors can sell hardware only with software and cannot enter into separate contracts to supply hardware. Such vendors are referred to as *value-added resellers* or *value-added distributors*.

Pricing Terms

20.   Software may be developed under contract for a fixed price or for a variable fee, such as on a time-and-materials basis. If hardware is included, its contractually stated price is generally lower than if purchased directly from the manufacturer. In addition, the stated price generally attributes a lower profit margin to the hardware than to the software.

Historical Revenue Recognition Practices

21.   At this SOP's printing, use of the percentage-of-completion method was predominant practice for revenue recognition on software contracts requiring significant vendor performance beyond delivery of the software or customer acceptance of modifications of the vendor's ordinary specifications after delivery. However, the completed-contract method was also used by some vendors if the percentage-of-completion method could not be applied. In addition, some vendors recognized all contract revenue on delivery of the hardware, regardless of other obligations remaining on the contract.

22.   For turnkey systems, the following were the most commonly used methods of recognizing revenue and profit:

- Ratably over the period of development and installation
- Separately (segmented) for hardware on delivery and software on delivery or contract signing
- On completion and installation of software
- On completion of all tasks and delivery of systems
- On a percentage-of-completion basis

23.   Companies that described revenue recognition practices for service transactions in their financial statements generally reported a policy of recognizing revenue on the services ratably over the period of performance.

Providing Postcontract Customer Support

24.   As defined in paragraph 3 of this SOP, PCS consists of the right to receive services or product enhancements, or both, offered after the license period begins or after another point as provided for by the PCS arrangement. PCS does not include installation and other

services directly related to the initial license of the product. PCS is an important source of revenue for software vendors because of the demand by customers for services and updates to enhance product performance. PCS arrangements generally have three distinct elements: telephone support, bug fixing, and product enhancements.

25.   Under PCS arrangements, vendors are generally required to provide telephone support and bug fixing. The demand for those services tends to be constant over long periods, but typically increases after new enhancements or products are released. In contrast, vendor discretion over whether to release product enhancements tends to make that element of PCS far less predictable than telephone support and bug fixing.

26.   Vendors develop product enhancements in response to competitive market forces, which tend to change as products age. Early in products' life cycles, vendors generally seek to increase market penetration by producing enhancements that encourage sales to new customers. As products mature and markets become saturated, the vendors increasingly rely on sales of PCS to previous customers for additional revenue. PCS arrangements become principal revenue sources, and mature products are often enhanced primarily to attract subscribers to PCS.

27.   After the initial license period, access to product enhancements tends to be more important to PCS customers than access to bug fixing or telephone support services. Consequently, if a vendor does not provide enhancements over a continued period of time, PCS arrangements are not likely to be renewed.

Pricing Terms

28.   PCS for first-year product licenses is often included in the initial licensing fee, but ongoing PCS is generally sold separately. However, some vendors bundle both initial and ongoing PCS in the software licensing fee and do not sell PCS separately. Such bundled licenses are usually for fixed terms ranging from six months to five years or longer, whereas other licenses tend to have unlimited terms.

Historical Revenue Recognition Practices

29.   At this SOP's printing, predominant practice for separately priced PCS arrangements was to recognize revenue on the PCS ratably

over the period in which the PCS was provided. Other practices included recognizing all revenue on contract signing or recognizing it at the start of the contract year either when billed or when billable. For PCS arrangements bundled with initial software licenses, PCS revenue was generally recognized at the same time as the licensing revenue, but some companies unbundled PCS revenue and recognized it ratably over the period in which the PCS was provided.

30.   For initial and ongoing PCS arrangements that were not available separately from software licenses, vendors generally recognized all PCS revenue at the same time as the licensing fee. However, some recognized all revenue, including the licensing revenue, ratably over the PCS period. The three distinct elements of PCS arrangements — telephone support, bug fixing, and product enhancements — generally were not accounted for separately.

Conclusions

31.   The following conclusions should be read in conjunction with the "Discussion of Conclusions and Implementation Guidance," beginning with paragraph 45 of this SOP, which explains the bases for the conclusions and provides guidance for implementing them.

Software Licenses With no Other Vendor Obligations

32.   If collectibility is probable and the vendor has no obligations remaining under the sales or licensing agreement after delivering the software, revenue from the software licensing fee should be recognized on delivery of the software.

Software Licenses With Other Insignificant Vendor Obligations

33.   If the vendor has insignificant obligations remaining under the sales or licensing agreement after delivering the software, revenue from the software licensing fee should be recognized on delivery of the software if collectibility is probable. The remaining obligations should be accounted for either (a) by accruing the remaining costs or (b) by deferring a pro rata portion of revenue and recognizing it either ratably as the obligations are fulfilled or on completion of performance.

Software Licenses With Other Significant Vendor Obligations

34. If, in addition to the obligation to deliver the software, the sales or licensing agreement includes other significant vendor obligations, the agreement should first be examined to determine whether it should be accounted for using contract accounting or as a service transaction. For agreements with significant vendor obligations beyond delivery of the software that are not accounted for using contract accounting or as service transactions, revenue should not be recognized until all of the following conditions are met:

a. Delivery has occurred.

b. Other remaining vendor obligations are no longer significant.

c. Collectibility is probable.

Software Transactions Structured as Leases

35. If a lease of software involves property, plant, or equipment, the revenue attributable to the property, plant, or equipment should be accounted for in conformity with FASB Statement No. 13, and any revenue attributable to the software, including PCS, should be accounted for separately in conformity with the guidance set forth in this SOP. However, in conformity with paragraph 1 of this SOP, if the property, plant, or equipment contains software that is incidental to the property, plant, or equipment as a whole, the software should not be accounted for separately. The allocation of revenues between the software and the property, plant, or equipment should be based on fair values. If the fair values are not readily determinable, other reasonable methods of allocation should be used. The costs of the software should be accounted for as set forth in FASB Statement No. 86.

Significant Uncertainties About Customer Acceptance

36. If, after delivery, there is significant uncertainty about customer acceptance of the software, license revenue should not be recognized until the uncertainty becomes insignificant.

Absence of a Reasonable Basis for Estimating the Degree of Collectibility of Receivables

37. Revenues associated with software transactions for which there is no reasonable basis of estimating the degree of collectibility

of related receivables should be accounted for using either the installment method or the cost recovery method of accounting.

Contract Accounting

38. If a contract to deliver software or a software system, either alone or together with other products, requires significant production, modification, or customization of software, a system, or the other products, that contract should be accounted for in conformity with Accounting Research Bulletin (ARB) No. 45, *Long-Term Construction-Type Contracts*, using the relevant guidance in SOP 81-1, *Accounting for Performance of Construction-Type and Certain Production-Type Contracts*. However, transactions that are normally accounted for as product sales should not be accounted for as long-term contracts merely to avoid the delivery requirements for revenue recognition normally associated with product sales.

Service Transactions

39. If, in addition to the obligation to deliver the software, the sales or licensing agreement includes obligations to perform services that (*a*) are not essential to the functionality of any other element of the transaction and (*b*) are separately stated and priced such that the total price of the agreement would be expected to vary as a result of the inclusion or exclusion of the services, the services and the sales or licensing component should be accounted for separately.

40. If collectibility is probable, revenue from software services generally should be recognized as the services are performed or, if no pattern of performance is discernible, ratably over the period during which the services are performed. If significant uncertainty about customer acceptance of the services exists, revenue should not be recognized until the uncertainty becomes insignificant.

Postcontract Customer Support

41. If collectibility is probable, revenue from PCS, including revenue that is bundled with an initial licensing fee, generally should be recognized ratably over the period of the PCS arrangement. Revenue attributable to PCS, however, may be recognized together with the initial licensing fee on delivery of the software if all of the following conditions are met:

a. The PCS fee is bundled with the initial licensing fee.

b. The PCS bundled with the initial license is for one year or less.

c. The estimated cost of providing PCS during the initial period of the PCS arrangement is insignificant.

d. Enhancements offered during the initial period of the PCS arrangement have historically been minimal and are expected to be minimal during the initial period of the PCS arrangement.

e. Collectibility is probable.

PCS fees that meet the above conditions should be accounted for in a manner similar to that used in accounting for insignificant obligations. If revenue is recognized together with the initial licensing fee on delivery of the software, all estimated costs of providing the PCS, including costs of services and enhancements, should be (a) charged to expense as incurred or (b) accrued and charged to expense at the time the revenue is recognized, whichever occurs first.

Disclosure of Accounting Policies

42. Software revenue recognition policies should be disclosed in the notes to the financial statements.

Effective Date and Transition

43. This SOP is effective for financial statements issued after March 15, 1992, that are for fiscal years, and interim periods in such fiscal years, beginning after December 15, 1991. Earlier application is encouraged. Accounting changes to conform to the recommendations of this SOP should be made retroactively by restating the financial statements of prior periods. Such restatements should be made regardless of any changes in software revenue recognition methods reported previously. In the year that this SOP is first applied, the financial statements should disclose the nature of accounting changes adopted to conform to the provisions of this SOP and their effect on income before extraordinary items, net income, and related per share amounts for the current year and for each restated year presented.

44. If the information for restatement of prior periods is not available, the cumulative effect on retained earnings at the beginning of the earliest period restated (or at the beginning of the period in

which the SOP is first applied if it is not practicable to restate any prior periods) should be included in determining net income for that period. In addition, the effect on income before extraordinary items, net income, and related per share amounts should be disclosed, in conformity with Accounting Principles Board (APB) Opinion 20, *Accounting Changes.*

Discussion of Conclusions and Implementation Guidance

45. The following discussion explains the bases for the conclusions reached in this SOP and provides implementation guidance.

Software Licenses With no Other Vendor Obligations

46. The principle of revenue recognition on delivery applies to both software licensed to users and software licensed to resellers. However, as stated in paragraph 3 of this SOP, if a licensing agreement provides a customer with the right to multiple copies of a software product in exchange for a fixed fee, delivery means transfer of the product master or the first copy if the product master is not to be delivered. The effects of various contract terms on revenue recognition for software licensed to resellers are discussed in paragraphs 59 to 64 and 73 to 75 of this SOP.

Underlying Concept

47. The recognition of revenue from product sales on delivery is consistent with paragraphs 83 and 84 of FASB Concepts Statement No. 5. Paragraph 84 states that in recognizing revenues and gains,

> [t]he two conditions [for revenue recognition] (being realized or realizable and being earned) are usually met by the time product or merchandise is delivered...to customers, and revenues...are commonly recognized at time of sale (usually meaning *delivery*). [*Emphasis added.*]

48. Transfers of rights to software by licenses rather than outright sales protect vendors from unauthorized duplication of their products. However, because the rights transferred under software licenses are substantially the same as those normally expected to be transferred in sales of other kinds of products, the legal distinction between

a license and a sale should not cause revenue recognition on software products to differ from revenue recognition on the sale of other kinds of products.

49.   The following sections discuss the principle of revenue recognition on delivery and provide guidance on its application to specific situations. They consider the effects on revenue recognition of—

- Signed contracts.

- License restrictions that benefit the vendor or the reseller.

- Provisions for additional payments beyond fixed fees.

- Customer cancellation privileges.

- Exchange rights.

- Discounting receivables.

- Factors that affect the determination of whether a fee is fixed.

- Rights to multiple copies of software products under site licenses or reseller arrangements.

- Delivery other than to the customer.

- Licensing and leasing transactions that include PCS.

Except as otherwise indicated, the following sections pertain solely to fixed fees. Paragraph 41 of this SOP provides guidance on accounting for PCS that is included as part of a software license.

Signed Contracts

50.   Some software licenses are evidenced by a written contract signed by the vendor and the customer. Even if all other requirements set forth in this SOP for recognition of revenue are met, revenue should not be recognized on those licenses until persuasive evidence of the agreement exists. Such evidence is usually provided by the signed contract.

License Restrictions That Benefit the Vendor or the Reseller

51.   Fixed fees should be recognized on delivery even if the licenses to reproduce, distribute, or use software are for a limited quantity, a limited period, or a limited number of users. Revenues should not be recognized on limited licenses later than on unlimited

licenses, because, all other things being equal, limited licenses are more advantageous than unlimited licenses to vendors or resellers to the extent that they provide for the possibility of additional revenues in the form of license renewal fees or fees for additional copies.

Provisions for Additional Payments Beyond Fixed Fees

52.   Some software transactions provide for fees payable to vendors or resellers in addition to a fixed fee. Such additional fees may be based on use, reproduction, or distribution of software by the customers. The additional fees should be recognized as revenue when they are earned. As in the transactions with restrictions that benefit vendors or resellers, discussed in the previous paragraph, there is no basis for deferring recognition of the fixed fees beyond delivery of the software if the vendors' or resellers' obligations for the fixed fees are completed.

Customer Cancellation Privileges

53.   Revenue from cancelable licenses should not be recognized until the cancellation privileges lapse. Revenue from licenses with cancellation privileges expiring ratably over the license period should be recognized ratably over the license period as the cancellation privileges lapse. That is consistent with customer obligations to pay only one monthly or periodic payment at a time. In applying the provisions of this paragraph, warranties that are routine, short-term, and relatively minor and short-term rights of return, such as thirty-day, money-back guarantees, should not be considered cancellation privileges; they should be accounted for in conformity with FASB Statement No. 5, *Accounting for Contingencies*, and FASB Statement No. 48, *Revenue Recognition When Right of Return Exists*.

Exchange Rights

54.   As part of their standard sales terms or as matters of practice, vendors may grant resellers rights to exchange unsold software for other software. Such exchanges, including those referred to as "stock balancing arrangements," are returns and should be accounted for in conformity with FASB Statement No. 48 even if the vendors require the resellers to purchase additional software to exercise the exchange rights.

55.   Exchanges of software products by users—but not by resellers— for products with the same price and functionality are analogous to

the exchanges "by ultimate customers of one item for another of the same kind, quality, and price...[that] are not considered returns" according to footnote 3 of FASB Statement No. 48. Examples of such exchanges include exchanges of a program for—

- The same program designed to run on another platform.

- A slightly modified version of the program with minimal enhancements. A minimal enhancement is an improvement to an existing product that makes only small changes in product functionality and features.

- The same program on a different software medium of approximately the same cost, such as a different size floppy disk.

Conversely, exchanges of software products for different software products or for similar software products with more than minimal differences in price, functionality, or features are considered returns that should be accounted for in conformity with FASB Statement No. 48.

Discounting Receivables

56. Receivables resulting from software transactions may generally be reported at their face amounts if they occur in the normal course of business and if they are due in customary trade terms not exceeding approximately one year. The kinds of trade terms that are customary for a particular software transaction should be determined based on trade terms for similar kinds of transactions with similar kinds of customers; customary trade terms should not automatically be presumed to extend for a full year. Receivables that do not result from transactions in the normal course of business or that are not due in customary trade terms should be reported at their discounted amounts in conformity with APB Opinion 21, *Interest on Receivables and Payables*.

Factors That Affect the Determination of Whether a Fee Is Fixed

57. Some agreements that call for fixed payments, including minimum royalties, specify a payment period that is short in relation to the period during which the customer expects to use or market the related products, whereas others have payment terms that extend over the entire period during which the customer expects to use or market the related products. Collection issues, such as those

described in paragraph 78 of this SOP, may result from extended payment terms because of uncertainties surrounding enforceability of the agreement, the customer's credit rating, or the vendor's reluctance to pursue collection in the interest of continuing a business relationship with the customer. In general, a fee should be presumed not to be fixed if—

- The amount of the fee or the timing of payments is based on the number of units distributed or the customer's use of the product.

- The vendor has a contingent liability to refund a portion of the fee or to provide product credit, such as in a transaction with a reseller that provides for adjustment of the fee based on the number of units sold.

- Payment of a significant portion of the licensing fee is not due until after expiration of the license.

- Payment is not due until more than twelve months after delivery.

However, a presumption that payment terms are not fixed may be refuted by persuasive evidence to the contrary.

58. In addition, for reseller arrangements, the following factors should be considered:

- Business practices, the reseller's operating history, competitive pressures, formal or informal communication, or factors that indicate that payment is contingent on the reseller's success in distributing individual units of the product may lead to a decision not to recognize revenue.

- Uncertainties about the potential number of copies to be sold by the reseller because of such factors as the newness of the product or marketing channel, competitive products, or dependence on the market potential of another product offered by the reseller, may indicate that profit cannot be reasonably estimated on delivery. If so, revenue should not be recognized until the vendor can reasonably determine that the transaction is viable for both parties or that the reseller is willing to honor and is capable of honoring the commitment to make the fixed payments.

- Resellers that are new, undercapitalized, or in financial difficulty generally cannot demonstrate an ability to honor a commitment to make fixed payments until they collect cash from their customers.

The ability to honor the commitment should be considered in determining whether to recognize revenue.

Rights to Multiple Copies of Software Products Under Site Licenses or Reseller Arrangements

59.   Sales of rights to market or use multiple copies of a software product under site licenses, reseller arrangements, and similar arrangements should be distinguished from sales of multiple single licenses of the same software. In the former, the licensing fee is payable even if no additional copies are requested by the reseller or user, and the obligation to deliver additional copies is generally insignificant, as discussed in paragraph 75 of this SOP. In the latter, the licensing fee is solely a function of the number of copies delivered to the reseller or user, and revenue should be recognized ratably as the copies are delivered if the other criteria in this SOP for revenue recognition are met.

60.   *Multiple Product Arrangements.*   Some fixed-fee site license or reseller arrangements provide customers with the right to reproduce or obtain copies at a specified price per copy of two or more software products up to the total amount of the fixed fee. For example, for a $10,000 fixed fee, a customer may obtain the right to 100 copies of Product A at $100 each or, at the customer's option, 50 copies of Product B at $200 each, or any combination of the two up to a combined amount of $10,000. Some of the products covered by the arrangement may not be deliverable at the inception of the arrangement but may be developed while the arrangement is in effect. Furthermore, such arrangements may not specify the products to be developed.

61.   Although the revenue per copy is fixed at the inception of the arrangement, the total revenue attributable to each software product is unknown and depends on choices to be made by the customer while the arrangement is in effect. Therefore, revenue should not be fully recognized until at least one of the following conditions is met:

- Delivery is complete for all products covered by the arrangement. As defined in paragraph 3 of this SOP, delivery means transfer of the product master, or the first copy if the product master is not to be transferred.

- The aggregate revenue attributable to all software delivered is equal to the fixed fee, provided that the vendor is not obligated to deliver additional software under the arrangement.

62.   If all of the products covered by the arrangement are deliverable at the inception of the arrangement, but some have not been delivered, revenue from licensing fees should be recognized either (*a*) as copies are reproduced by the customer from any product master or first copy that has been delivered or (*b*) as copies are furnished to the customer, if the vendor is duplicating the software. When the arrangement terminates, the vendor should recognize any licensing fees not previously recognized for which collectibility is probable.

63.   If some products covered by the arrangement are not deliverable at the inception of the arrangement, revenue should be recognized as described in the previous paragraph, provided that the vendor is not obligated to deliver the products unless they are developed while the arrangement is in effect.

64.   If one or more of the products is not deliverable at the inception of the arrangement and the vendor is obligated to furnish the product or products, the obligation should be considered significant and accounted for in conformity with paragraph 34 of this SOP.

Delivery Other Than to the Customer

65.   For purposes of applying the revenue recognition criteria in this SOP, delivery should not be considered complete unless the destination to which the software is shipped is the customer's place of business or another site specified by the customer. In addition, if a substantial portion of the payment by the customer is not payable until delivery by the vendor to a particular site specified by the customer, revenue should not be recognized until delivery is made to that site.

Licensing and Leasing Transactions That Include Postcontract Customer Support

66.   If a software licensing or leasing transaction includes a PCS arrangement, the recognition of the licensing fee may be affected by the PCS arrangement, as discussed in paragraphs 120, 124, and 125 of this SOP.

Determining the Significance of Other Vendor Obligations

67. Paragraph 83(b) of FASB Concepts Statement No. 5 provides the following guidance for recognition of revenues:

Revenues are not recognized until earned. An entity's revenue-earning activities involve delivering or producing goods, rendering services, or other activities that constitute its ongoing major or central operations, and revenues are considered to have been earned when the entity has substantially accomplished what it must do to be entitled to the benefits represented by the revenues. [*Footnote omitted.*]

68. If a transaction is substantially completed on delivery, revenue should be recognized on delivery, and any insignificant other vendor obligations remaining should be accounted for by either deferring a pro rata portion of revenue for the remaining tasks or by accruing the costs related to the remaining obligations. Accounting for insignificant obligations in that manner is consistent with accounting practices in other industries. If other vendor obligations remaining after delivery are significant, revenue should not be recognized, because the earnings process is not substantially completed.

69. If a sales or licensing agreement provides for obligations in addition to delivery of the software, assessments of potential risks, estimates of related costs, and the probability that the vendor will be able to fulfill those obligations within cost estimates should be considered in determining whether the obligations are significant or insignificant. If a reasonable estimate of the costs to fulfill remaining obligations cannot be made, it should be presumed that those costs are significant. The vendor's ability to make a reasonable estimate of the significance of remaining potential risks, obligations, and costs depends on many factors and circumstances that may vary among transactions and among vendors. The following factors may impair the ability to make a reasonable estimate:

- Absence of historical experience of fulfilling similar kinds of obligations
- Prior history of inability to fulfill similar kinds of obligations to the satisfaction of customers
- Absence of a history of relatively homogeneous contracts to be used as a measure of past performance
- Relatively long performance periods

The existence of one or more of the preceding conditions should not be presumed to preclude the ability to make a reasonable estimate. Conversely, conditions other than those described above may prevent a reasonable estimate from being made.

70.   The following are examples of service obligations that may be part of a software transaction and may be significant or insignificant in relation to the transaction as a whole:

- *Installation.* Compiling, linking, and loading software modules onto hardware or software platforms so that the software product will execute properly on the system.

- *Testing.* Executing installed software products, applying test routines and data, and evaluating the results against desired or expected results. It may involve adjusting installation or application parameters until the desired or expected results are achieved.

- *Training.* Educating users or resellers to operate or maintain a software system or to teach others to operate or maintain the system. For purposes of this definition, users may consist of personnel who will be operating the system, in-house technical support staff, or both.

- *Data conversion.* Making data from different sources compatible by changing the presentation format or the physical recording medium.

- *Interface.* Establishing communication between independent elements, such as between one program and another, between a computer operator and the computer, and between a terminal user and a computer.

- *System integration.* Organizing a sequence of data processing steps or a number of related data processing sequences to reduce or eliminate the need to duplicate data entry or processing steps.

- *Porting.* Translating a computer program from one machine language to another so that software designed to operate on one platform can operate on another platform.

71.   Each of the above functions can be insignificant or significant depending on the software tools and automated processes used by the vendor, the frequency of work performed, past experience, and

the level of staff required in the process. For example, a complex task of porting to another operating system can be made routine by use of a software tool that translates all or most of the original code to the new system code.

72.   Installation, testing, conversion of specified data, and inter-facing are more often done at insignificant cost than are porting, system integration, or general data conversion. However, normally routine testing can be made lengthy and complex by including customer-prescribed routines, data, and sign-offs or by being subject to an integrated system test in which the vendor's product must be shown to integrate with several other new applications.

Other Vendor Obligations Associated With Site Licenses and Reseller Arrangements

73.   Certain fixed-fee site license or reseller arrangements for software products may provide for the vendor to furnish the following:

- Porting that can be accomplished at insignificant cost and is not significant to customer acceptance.

- A slightly modified version of the software with minimal enhance-ments. A minimal enhancement is an improvement to an existing product that makes only small changes in product functionality and features.

- A copy of the product from a different software medium of approximately the same cost, such as a different size floppy disk.

Any obligations associated with those items should be accounted for as insignificant vendor obligations, as described in paragraph 33 of this SOP. Revenue should be recognized as described in paragraphs 46 and 59 to 64 of this SOP.

74.   *Vendor Duplication of Software.* When dealing with site licenses with users and distribution arrangements with resellers, some vendors insist on duplicating the software to maintain quality control or to protect software transmitted by telecommunications. Others agree to duplicate the software as a matter of convenience to the customer. The vendors may, therefore, be obligated to furnish up to a specified number of copies of the software, but only if the copies are requested by the user.

75. Duplication of the software is generally an insignificant obligation that should be accounted for as described in paragraph 33 of this SOP. The contract is primarily the sale of rights to market or use the software and, although reproduction and delivery of the software may be important to the reseller's use of the rights, the arrangement to reproduce is incidental to the software license. Revenue should be recognized as described in paragraphs 46 and 59 to 64 of this SOP.

Software Transactions Structured as Leases

76. Some agreements that transfer rights to use software are structured as leases. Revenue attributable to transfers of software rights, including PCS, should be recognized in conformity with this SOP, rather than in conformity with FASB Statement No. 13, because paragraph 1 of that Statement indicates that it does not apply to "licensing agreements for items such as motion picture films, plays, manuscripts, patents, and copyrights." Although there may be certain legal differences between leases and licensing agreements, those differences should not affect the recognition of revenue on transactions involving software and should be accounted for in conformity with this SOP.

77. Leases of software, however, may also include property, plant, or equipment (typically hardware) that are in the scope of FASB Statement No. 13, as described in paragraph 1 of that Statement. Revenues attributable to such items should be included in the determination of minimum lease payments, as defined in paragraph 5(j) of that Statement. Revenues attributable to the software elements, including PCS, should be accounted for separately in conformity with the guidance for software transactions set forth in this SOP.

Absence of a Reasonable Basis for Estimating the Degree of Collectibility of Receivables

78. The guidance in this SOP on accounting for revenues associated with software transactions for which no reasonable basis exists to estimate the degree of collectibility of receivables is consistent with footnote 8 of APB Opinion 10, *Omnibus Opinion—1966*, which states:

> [T]here are exceptional cases where receivables are collectible over an extended period of time and, because of the terms of the transactions or other conditions, there is no reasonable basis for estimating

the degree of collectibility. When such circumstances exist, and as long as they exist, either the installment method or the cost recovery method of accounting may be used. (Under the cost recovery method, equal amounts of revenue and expense are recognized as collections are made until all costs have been recovered, postponing any recognition of profit until that time.)

Contract Accounting

79.   ARB No. 45 established the basic principles for measuring performance on contracts for the construction of facilities or the production of goods or the provision of related services with specifications provided by the customer. Those principles are supplemented by the guidance in SOP 81-1.

Distinguishing Transactions Accounted for Using Contract Accounting From Product Sales

80.   SOP 81-1 suggests that transactions that are normally accounted for as product sales should not be accounted for using contract accounting merely to avoid the delivery requirements for revenue recognition normally associated with product sales. Paragraph 14 of that SOP states the following:

> Contracts not covered...include...[s]ales by a manufacturer of goods produced in a standard manufacturing operation, even if produced to buyers' specifications, and sold in the ordinary course of business through the manufacturer's regular marketing channels if such sales are normally recognized as revenue in accordance with the realization principle for sales of products and if their costs are accounted for in accordance with generally accepted principles of inventory costing.

Application of ARB No. 45 and SOP 81-1

81.   SOP 81-1 provides guidance on the application of ARB No. 45 that applies to a broad range of contractual arrangements. Paragraph 1 of SOP 81-1 describes contracts that are similar in nature to software contracts, and paragraph 13 includes the following kinds of contracts within the scope of that SOP:

- Contracts to design, develop, manufacture, or modify complex...electronic equipment to a buyer's specification or to provide services related to the performance of such contracts.

- Contracts for services performed by. . .engineers. . .or engineering design firms.

82. Although the kinds of software contracts discussed in this SOP were not considered when SOP 81-1 was written, SOP 81-1 provides guidance that can be applied to software contracts because software contracts are similar in many respects to contracts explicitly covered by SOP 81-1. The determination of whether to measure progress-to-completion using the percentage-of-completion method or the completed-contract method should be made according to the recommendations in paragraphs 21 through 33 of SOP 81-1. Evidence to consider in assessing the presumption that the percentage-of-completion method of accounting should be used includes the technological risks and the reliability of cost estimates, as described in paragraphs 25, 26, 27, 32, and 33 of SOP 81-1.

83. ARB No. 45 presumes that percentage-of-completion accounting should be used provided that the contractor is capable of making reasonable estimates. Paragraph 15 of ARB 45 states:

> [I]n general when estimates of costs to complete and extent of progress toward completion of long-term contracts are reasonably dependable, the percentage-of-completion method is preferable. When lack of dependable estimates or inherent hazards cause forecasts to be doubtful, the completed-contract method is preferable.

84. Paragraph 24 of SOP 81-1 specifies a further presumption that a contractor is capable of making reasonable estimates and states the following:

> [T]he presumption is that [entities]. . .have the ability to make estimates that are sufficiently dependable to justify the use of the percentage-of-completion method of accounting. *Persuasive evidence to the contrary is necessary to overcome that presumption. [Emphasis added and footnote omitted.]*

Segmentation

85. Some software contracts have discrete elements that meet the criteria for segmenting in paragraphs 39 to 42 of SOP 81-1. When a contract is segmented, each segment is treated as a separate profit center. Segmentation of contractual elements in conformity with

SOP 81-1 often provides the best available combination of verifiability and representational faithfulness to measure progress-to-completion on software contracts. Progress-to-completion for each segment should be measured in conformity with the section of this SOP that best describes the characteristics of that segment.

86. Some vendors of contracts for software combined with services or hardware or both do not unbundle the elements and do not sell them separately because of agreements with their suppliers. Other vendors who are not restricted by such agreements nevertheless bid or negotiate software and other products and services together. Contracts that do not meet the segmentation criteria in paragraph 40 of SOP 81-1 are precluded from being segmented, unless the vendor has a history of providing the software and other products and services to customers under separate contracts, as set forth in paragraph 41 of that SOP.

Measuring Progress-to-Completion Under the Percentage-of-Completion Method

87. Paragraph 46 of SOP 81-1 describes the approaches to measuring progress on contracts under the percentage-of-completion method. Those approaches are grouped into input and output measures:

> Input measures are made in terms of efforts devoted to a contract. They include. . . methods based on costs and on efforts expended. Output measures are made in terms of results achieved. They include methods based on units produced, units delivered, contract milestones, and value added. For contracts under which separate units of output are produced, progress can be measured on the basis of units of work completed.

For software contracts, an example of an input measure would be labor hours; an example of an output measure would be contract milestones, such as completion of specific program modules.

88. Output measures, such as value-added or contract milestones, may be the best measures of progress-to-completion on software contracts, but many companies, nevertheless, use input measures because they are more easily verified than output measures. However, as noted in paragraph 47 of SOP 81-1, "The use of either type of

measure requires the exercise of judgment and the careful tailoring of the measure to the circumstances." Paragraph 51 continues: "The acceptability of the results of input or output measures deemed to be appropriate to the circumstances should be periodically reviewed and confirmed by alternative measures that involve observation and inspection."

89. SOP 81-1 provides extensive guidance on the measurement of progress-to-completion using input measures, but it provides little guidance on the use of output measures. This SOP provides guidance on the application of both kinds of measures to the various elements of software contracts and analyzes the results of such accounting. In particular, it considers the timing and amounts of revenue recognized on hardware, off-the-shelf software, and core software elements.

90. The method chosen to measure progress-to-completion on an individual element of a software contract should be the method that best approximates progress-to-completion on that element. Progress-to-completion on different elements of the same software contract may thus be measured by different methods. The software vendor should apply the criteria for choosing measurement methods consistently to all of its software contracts, so that it uses similar methods to measure progress-to-completion on similar elements.

91. *Input Measures.* Input measures of progress-to-completion on contracts are made in terms of efforts devoted to the contract and, for software contracts, include methods based on costs, such as cost-to-cost measures, and on efforts expended, such as labor hours or labor dollars. Progress-to-completion is measured indirectly, based on an established or assumed relationship between units of input and productivity. A major advantage of their use is that inputs expended are easily verifiable. A major disadvantage is that their relationship to progress-to-completion may not hold if there are inefficiencies or if the incurrence of the input at a particular point in time does not indicate progress-to-completion.

92. Although cost-to-cost measures may be verified easily, they tend to attribute excessive profit to the hardware elements of bundled software and hardware contracts. Although the hardware elements of such contracts have high cost bases, they generally yield relatively

low profit margins to vendors. Furthermore, if excessive revenue is attributed to the hardware element, revenue recognition on the contract becomes overly dependent on when that element is included in the measurement of progress-to-completion.

93. For off-the-shelf software elements, application of the cost-to-cost method produces the opposite effect. The cost basis of the software tends to be low, because frequently most of the costs associated with software are charged to expense when incurred in conformity with FASB Statement No. 86. Although profit margins associated with software are generally higher than for other contractual elements, application of cost-to-cost measures with a single profit margin for the entire contract would attribute little or no profit to the off-the-shelf software. Similarly, application of cost-to-cost to contracts that include core software, which also has a relatively low cost basis, would attribute a disproportionately small amount of profit to the software.

94. Costs incurred should be included in measuring progress-to-completion only to the extent that they relate to contract performance. Items not specifically produced for the contract, such as hardware purchased from third parties or off-the-shelf software, should not be included in the measurement of progress-to-completion until installation is complete if inclusion would tend to overstate the percentage-of-completion otherwise determinable. The cost of core software should be included as the software is customized.

95. Labor hours are often chosen as the basis for measuring progress-to-completion, because they approximate closely the output of labor-intensive processes. However, if progress-to-completion is measured solely in labor hours, profit attributable to the hardware and off-the-shelf software elements of bundled contracts may be understated when included in the measurement of progress-to-completion, because the hardware and off-the-shelf software elements of most software contracts are not labor intensive.

96. Core software requires labor-intensive customization. Therefore, labor hours may provide good measures of progress-to-completion on elements of software contracts that involve customization of core software.

97. If the measurement of progress-to-completion is primarily based on costs, the contribution of hardware or software to that progress may be measurable before delivery to the user's site. For example, the configuration of hardware, customization of core software, installation of off-the-shelf or customized software, and similar activities may occur at the vendor's site. In such cases, progress-to-completion based on cost-to-cost measures should be measured as the related costs are incurred at the vendor's site, rather than on delivery to the user's site.

98. *Output Measures.* Progress on contracts that call for production of identifiable units of output can be measured in terms of value added or milestones reached. Conceptually, progress-to-completion based on output measures is measured directly from results achieved, thus providing for a better approximation of progress. However, a major disadvantage of output measures is that they may be somewhat unreliable because of the difficulties associated with verifying them.

99. Value-added output measures often would provide the best approximation of progress-to-completion, but little has been written about how to apply such measures. Conceptually, value is added to a contract at every step of performance. However, for the value added to be verifiable, contractual elements or subcomponents of those elements must be identified. If output values for off-the-shelf software or core software are difficult to identify, they should be estimated by subtracting the known or reasonably estimable output values of other elements of the contract, such as hardware, from the total contract price. If output measures are not known or reasonably estimable, they should not be used to estimate percentage-of-completion.

100. If value added is used as the basis for measuring progress-to-completion, progress is generally not considered to take place until the outputs are delivered to the user's site in a manner consistent with paragraph 32 of this SOP. In addition, progress should be measured on delivery only to the extent that remaining obligations associated with the output do not preclude revenue recognition. That limitation is consistent with the guidance provided in paragraphs 33 and 34 of this SOP.

101. Value added by the customization of core software generally should be measured on completion of the customization and installa-

tion at the user's site. However, if the installation and customization processes are divided into separate output modules, the value of core software associated with the customization of a module should be included in the measurement of progress-to-completion when that module is completed.

102.   As noted in paragraph 97 of this SOP, some contract activities may take place at the vendor's site rather than at the user's. Therefore, the act of delivering a completed package to the user's site may not be a good indicator of when value has been added to the contract. If a reasonable approximation of progress-to-completion can be obtained by measuring the application of software to the contract, the software should be included in the measurement of progress-to-completion based on output measures before delivery to the user's site.

103.   Contract milestones may be based on contractual provisions or project plans. Contractual provisions generally require performance of specific tasks with approval or acceptance by the customer; project plans generally schedule inspections in which the project's status is reviewed and approved by management. Such inspections are natural points to establish milestones because they are subject to relatively independent review as an intrinsic part of the project management process.

104.   The challenge in using milestones is to translate the completed milestone into a meaningful measure of progress-to-completion. It is relatively easy to verify what tasks have been completed to date; it is more difficult to determine what completion of those tasks means in terms of overall progress on the contract, because there is generally uncertainty in predicting the level of difficulty that may be encountered in performing a particular task.

105.   Although achievement of contract milestones may cause contract revenues to become billable under the contract, the amounts billable should be used to measure progress-to-completion only if such amounts indeed indicate such progress. Considerations other than progress-to-completion affect when amounts become billable under many contracts.

106.   Although many different milestones may be selected, those used to measure progress-to-completion should be part of the manage-

ment review process. The percentage-of-completion designated for each milestone should be determined by considering the experience of the vendor on similar projects. The milestones should be validated by comparing them with estimates of the results that would be obtained by applying other measures of progress-to-completion.

Service Transactions

107.   Footnote 1 to paragraph 11 of SOP 81-1 excludes service transactions from the scope of the SOP, as follows:

> This statement is not intended to apply to "service transactions" as defined in the FASB's October 23, 1978 Invitation to Comment, *Accounting for Certain Service Transactions*. However, it applies to separate contracts to provide services essential to the construction or production of tangible property, such as design . . . [and] engineering. . . .

108.   The Invitation to Comment on service transactions, which was based on an AICPA-proposed SOP, was issued in 1978. The FASB later included service transactions as part of its project to develop general concepts for revenue recognition and measurement. The resulting FASB Concepts Statement No. 5, however, does not address service transactions in detail. Nevertheless, some of the concepts on service transactions developed in the Invitation to Comment are useful in accounting for certain software transactions.

109.   A service transaction is defined in paragraphs 7 and 8 of the Invitation to Comment as

> a transaction between a seller and a purchaser in which, for a mutually agreed price, the seller performs . . . an act or acts . . . that do not alone produce a tangible commodity or product as the principal intended result. . . . A service transaction may involve a tangible product that is sold or consumed as an incidental part of the transaction or is clearly identifiable as secondary or subordinate to the rendering of the service.

The term *service transaction* is used in the same sense in this SOP but, as used in this SOP, does not apply to PCS. Items classified as tangible products in software service transactions generally should be limited to off-the-shelf software or hardware.

110. Service transactions, like contracts covered by SOP 81-1, may include product and service elements. However, the characteristic that distinguishes service transactions from contracts covered by SOP 81-1 is the existence of a discrete service element. A service element is discrete if both of the following conditions are met:

a. Performance of the service is not essential to the functionality of any other element of the transaction.

b. The service is separately stated and priced such that the total price of the transaction would be expected to vary as a result of the inclusion or exclusion of the service.

An example of a service transaction with a discrete service element is one in which a vendor agrees to evaluate and redesign the user's account structure and in the same transaction agrees to provide off-the-shelf software to make a minor enhancement in the report preparation software already in use by the customer.

111. A service element may be considered discrete although the customer would not likely purchase the service separately from the other transaction elements. For example, a vendor of a software product may also provide optional training in the use of that product at an additional cost to the customer. Because the separately priced training is not required as a condition of the product sale and because the product's functionality does not depend on the training, the training would be considered a discrete service element, although it may be unlikely that the service would be provided in the absence of the software sale. In addition, such a service may be available from other vendors as well as from the vendor of the software.

112. If the vendor provides both a service and a software license in a single transaction and if including or excluding the software would not affect the total agreement price, the software license is incidental to the rendering of the service, and the transaction should be accounted for as a service transaction.

Accounting for Service Transactions

113. This SOP, like the Invitation to Comment, recommends separation of such transactions with discrete elements into their

product and service elements. Paragraph 8(b) of the Invitation to Comment states:

> If the seller of a product offers a related service to purchasers of the product but separately states the service and product elements in such a manner that the total transaction price would vary as a result of the inclusion or exclusion of the service, the transaction consists of two components: a product transaction that should be accounted for separately as such and a service transaction. . . .

Revenue from the service element generally should be recognized as performed or, if no pattern of performance is discernible, ratably over the period during which the service is rendered, and revenue from the product element generally should be recognized on delivery. However, revenue from an element should be recognized only if collectibility is probable and all significant obligations associated with that element have been fulfilled.

Postcontract Customer Support

114.   An obligation to perform PCS is incurred at the inception of a PCS arrangement and is discharged by performing services, delivering enhancements, or both, over the period of the PCS arrangement. The obligation may also be discharged by the passage of time. Because estimating the timing of expenditures under a PCS arrangement is generally not practicable, revenue from PCS generally should be recognized in income on a straight-line basis over the period of the PCS arrangement.

115.   However, if sufficient historical evidence indicates that costs to provide PCS are incurred on other than a straight-line basis and the vendor anticipates that the costs incurred in performing under the current arrangement will follow a similar pattern, revenue should be recognized over the period of the PCS arrangement in proportion to the amounts expected to be charged to expense during the period. Such amounts include costs of PCS services and allocated portions of costs accounted for as research and development costs and amortization of costs capitalized in conformity with FASB Statement No. 86. Because the timing, frequency, and significance of enhancements can vary considerably, the point at which enhancements are delivered should not be used to support income recognition on other than a straight-line basis.

116. A vendor that is not specifically obligated to provide PCS may, nevertheless, develop historical patterns of regularly providing all customers or certain kinds of customers with significant services or enhancements normally associated with PCS. For purposes of applying the guidance in this SOP, PCS includes a vendor's expected performance based on such patterns, even if performance is entirely at the vendor's discretion. However, the presumption that such a pattern of performance will continue may be refuted by persuasive evidence to the contrary.

117. Although PCS and software may be sold together as part of the same transaction, they are generally considered to be separate items that should be accounted for separately, except as indicated in paragraphs 120 to 125 of this SOP.

Initial Licenses That Are Not Offered Separately From Postcontract Customer Support Arrangements

118. *Separate Recognition of Fees.* Revenue from PCS fees, including revenue that is bundled with an initial licensing fee, should generally be recognized ratably over the period of the PCS arrangement. In measuring revenue from a PCS fee bundled with an initial licensing fee, consideration should be given to the level of PCS expected to be offered. If the level of services and enhancements offered in the initial period of the PCS arrangement is the same as in subsequent periods under separate PCS arrangements, the bundled license and PCS fees should be unbundled by allocating an amount to each component in proportion to its normal separate price.

119. If the level of services and enhancements offered in the initial period of the PCS arrangement is not the same as in subsequent periods under separate PCS arrangements, the price of the subsequent PCS should not be used as a surrogate for the price of the initial PCS in determining the amount to be allocated to each of the unbundled components. Instead, similarly objective evidence should be used to derive separate prices for the PCS and the initial licensing fee.

120. However, if there is insufficient information to derive the separate prices, revenue from both the PCS and the initial licensing fee components should be recognized ratably over the period of the PCS arrangement.

121. *Recognition of Licensing Fee and Postcontract Customer Support Revenue on Delivery of the Software.* Revenue attributable to PCS that is bundled with an initial licensing fee may be recognized together with the initial licensing fee on delivery of the software if all of the following conditions are met:

- The PCS bundled with the license is for one year or less.

- The estimated cost of providing PCS during the initial period of the PCS arrangement is insignificant.

- Enhancements offered during the initial period of the PCS arrangement have historically been minimal and are expected to be minimal during the initial period of the PCS arrangement. A minimal enhancement is an improvement to an existing product that makes only small changes in product functionality and features.

- Collectibility is probable.

PCS fees that meet the above conditions should be accounted for in a manner similar to that used in accounting for insignificant obligations, as described in paragraph 33 of this SOP.

122. A determination that PCS enhancements offered during the initial period of the PCS arrangement are expected to be minimal should be evidenced by similar patterns on previous PCS arrangements spanning a period of at least several years. A pattern of offering minimal enhancements would not be overcome by occasional departures from a predominant pattern of offering minimal enhancements in the initial period. However, a conclusion that enhancements in the initial period are minimal should not be reached simply because enhancements are offered less frequently than on an annual basis. Regardless of the vendor's history of offering enhancements to initial licensees, PCS should be accounted for separately from the initial licensing fee if the vendor expects to offer greater than minimal enhancements to the initial licensees during the initial period of the PCS arrangement.

123. If PCS bundled with the initial licensing fee is accounted for as insignificant and the revenue is recognized on delivery of the software, all costs of providing the PCS should be (a) charged to expense as incurred or (b) accrued and charged to expense at the time the

revenue is recognized, whichever occurs first. Such costs should include estimated costs of services and, in conformity with FASB Statement No. 86, amortization of capitalized enhancement costs and amounts to be charged to expense as research and development costs. Enhancements are generally not developed solely for distribution to PCS customers; revenues are generally expected to be earned from providing the enhancements to other customers, as well. Costs should, therefore, be allocated between PCS arrangements and other licenses.

Continuing Licenses That Are Not Offered Separately From Postcontract Customer Support Arrangements

124.   Sometimes vendors provide PCS with their software licenses but do not make PCS generally available to customers separately from the software licenses. Revenue from such PCS arrangements should be accounted for in the same manner as revenue from PCS bundled with an initial licensing fee, as follows:

- If enhancements offered are expected to be, and have historically been, minimal and the arrangement meets all of the other conditions in paragraph 121, revenue from both the licensing fee and the PCS may be recognized on delivery with all associated costs charged to expense as incurred or accrued at the time the revenue is recognized, whichever occurs first, as described in paragraph 123.

- If enhancements offered are expected to be, or have historically been, greater than minimal, or if the other conditions in paragraph 121 are not met, and there is sufficient information to derive a separate price for the two components, the revenue from the licensing fee should be recognized on delivery of the software, as described in paragraph 32 of this SOP, and the revenue on the PCS arrangement should be recognized separately, as described in paragraphs 114 and 115.

- If enhancements offered are expected to be, or have historically been, greater than minimal, or if the other conditions in paragraph 121 are not met, and there is insufficient information to derive a separate price for the PCS and the initial licensing fee, revenue from both components should be recognized ratably over the period in which the PCS is provided, as described in paragraph 120.

125. Some vendors charge substantially less to renew a license bundled with PCS than they do to provide the initial bundled arrangement. Such renewal fees generally should be accounted for in their entirety as PCS and recognized as set forth in paragraph 41 of this SOP, although the license would lapse without the renewal.

126. Vendors should recognize, however, the license renewal separately from the PCS if they have a history of providing PCS separately to other customers for similar products at a price lower than that of the bundled arrangement or if they have other similarly objective evidence of what the prices of the components would be if offered separately.

Product Updates

127. Some PCS arrangements may in fact be subscriptions to annual updates to a product if (a) the vendor takes on an explicit obligation to provide the updates, (b) the utility of the product becomes severely limited with the passage of time for reasons other than technological changes, and (c) the primary objective of the updates is not to incorporate new technology or improve operating performance. An example is an income tax preparation product that must be updated annually to reflect changes in income tax rules; the product itself basically has only a one-year life and limited, if any, utility thereafter. Those arrangements should be accounted for annually as sales of software licenses and not as PCS arrangements.

Revenue Recognition on Software Transactions (Flowchart)

Revenue Recognition on Software Transactions*

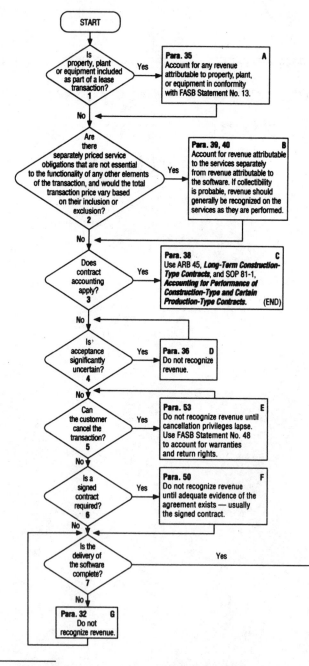

*This flowchart does not illustrate revenue recognition on postcontract customer support arrangements, multiple copy site licenses, or reseller arrangements.

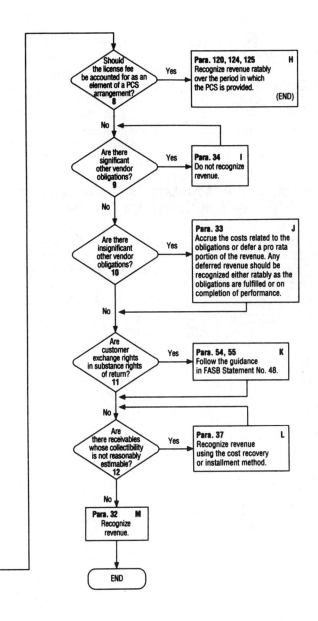

Accounting Standards Executive Committee
(1990–1991)

JOHN L. KREISCHER, *Chairman*
G. MICHAEL CROOCH
PETER S. DYE
ANDREW D. FINGER
WILLIAM J. IHLANFELDT
PAUL W. KARR
GREGORY D. KOSCHINSKA
JOHN M. LACEY

MARJORIE MARKER
JAMES C. MEEHAN
FRANCIS J. O'BRIEN
BARRY P. ROBBINS
WALTER SCHUETZE
WILLIAM JERRY SNOW
REVA STEINBERG

Task Force on Accounting for the Development and Sale of Computer Software

JOSEPH D. LHOTKA, *Chairman*
NAOMI S. ERICKSON
JAMES I. GILLESPIE
I. SIGMUND MOSLEY, JR.

FRANCIS J. O'BRIEN
LAWRENCE J. SCHOENBERG
PAUL K. WILDE

AICPA Staff

JOHN F. HUDSON, *Vice President*
Technical Standards and Services

CLIFFORD H. SCHWARTZ,
Technical Manager
Accounting Standards

FREDERICK R. GILL,
Senior Technical Manager
Accounting Standards

Appendix B

Statement of Financial Accounting Standards No. 86

Accounting for the Costs of Computer Software to Be Sold, Leased, or Otherwise Marketed

August 1985

Financial Accounting Standards Board
of the Financial Accounting Foundation
HIGH RIDGE PARK, PO BOX 3821, STAMFORD, CONNECTICUT 06905-0821

For additional copies of this Statement
and information on applicable prices and
discount rates contact:

Order Department
Financial Accounting Standards Board
High Ridge Park
P.O. Box 3821
Stamford, Connecticut 06905-0821

FINANCIAL ACCOUNTING SERIES (ISSN 0149-8452)
is published monthly except for occasional special issues by
the Financial Accounting Foundation. Second-class postage paid at Stamford, CT and at additional mailing offices.
The full subscription rate is $115 per year. POSTMASTER:
Send address changes to Financial Accounting Series, High
Ridge Park, P.O. Box 3821, Stamford, CT 06905-0821.

Summary

This Statement specifies the accounting for the costs of computer software to be sold, leased, or otherwise marketed as a separate product or as part of a product or process. It applies to computer software developed internally and to purchased software. This FASB project was undertaken in response to an AICPA Issues Paper, "Accounting for Costs of Software for Sale or Lease," and an accounting moratorium imposed by the Securities and Exchange Commission precluding changes in accounting policies related to computer software costs pending FASB action.

This Statement specifies that costs incurred internally in creating a computer software product shall be charged to expense when incurred as research and development until technological feasibility has been established for the product. Technological feasibility is established upon completion of a detail program design or, in its absence, completion of a working model. Thereafter, all software production costs shall be capitalized and subsequently reported at the lower of unamortized cost or net realizable value. Capitalized costs are amortized based on current and future revenue for each product with an annual minimum equal to the straight-line amortization over the remaining estimated economic life of the product.

This Statement is applicable, on a prospective basis, for financial statements for fiscal years beginning after December 15, 1985. The conclusions reached in this Statement change the predominant practice of expensing all costs of developing and producing a computer software product.

Statement of Financial Accounting Standards No. 86

Accounting for the Costs of Computer Software to Be Sold, Leased, or Otherwise Marketed

August 1985

CONTENTS

Statement of Financial Accounting Standards No. 86

Accounting for the Costs of Computer Software to Be Sold, Leased, or Otherwise Marketed

August 1985

INTRODUCTION

1. This project was undertaken in response to requests by the Securities and Exchange Commission (SEC) and the Accounting Standards Executive Committee (AcSEC) of the American Institute of Certified Public Accountants (AICPA) to clarify the accounting for the costs of internally developed and produced computer software to be sold, leased, or otherwise marketed. They indicated that existing accounting pronouncements contain only general guidance that has been interpreted inconsistently.

SCOPE

2. This Statement establishes standards of financial accounting and reporting for the costs of computer software to be sold, leased, or otherwise marketed as a separate product or as part of a product or process, whether internally developed and produced or purchased. It identifies the costs incurred in the process of creating a software product that are research and development costs and those that are production costs to be capitalized, and it specifies amortization, disclosure, and other requirements. As used in this Statement, the terms *computer software product, software product,* and *product* encompass a computer software program, a group of programs, and a **product enhancement.**[1] This Statement does not address the accounting and reporting of costs incurred for computer software created for internal use or for others under a contractual arrangement.

---

[1]Terms defined in the glossary (Appendix C) are in **boldface type** the first time they appear in this Statement.

STANDARDS OF FINANCIAL ACCOUNTING AND REPORTING

Research and Development Costs of Computer Software

3. All costs incurred to establish the technological feasibility of a computer software product to be sold, leased, or otherwise marketed are research and development costs. Those costs shall be charged to expense when incurred as required by FASB Statement No. 2, *Accounting for Research and Development Costs.*

4. For purposes of this Statement, the technological feasibility of a computer software product is established when the enterprise has completed all planning, designing, **coding,** and **testing** activities that are necessary to establish that the product can be produced to meet its design specifications including functions, features, and technical performance requirements. At a minimum, the enterprise shall have performed the activities in either (a) or (b) below as evidence that technological feasibility has been established:

a. If the process of creating the computer software product includes a **detail program design:**
   (1) The **product design** and the detail program design have been completed, and the enterprise has established that the necessary skills, hardware, and software technology are available to the enterprise to produce the product.
   (2) The completeness of the detail program design and its consistency with the product design have been confirmed by documenting and tracing the detail program design to product specifications.
   (3) The detail program design has been reviewed for high-risk development issues (for example, novel, unique, unproven functions and features or technological innovations), and any uncertainties related to identified high-risk development issues have been resolved through coding and testing.
b. If the process of creating the computer software product does not include a detail program design with the features identified in (a) above:
   (1) A product design and a **working model** of the software product have been completed.
   (2) The completeness of the working model and its consistency with the product design have been confirmed by testing.

Production Costs of Computer Software

5. Costs of producing **product masters** incurred subsequent to establishing technological feasibility shall be capitalized. Those costs include coding and testing performed subsequent to establishing technological feasibility. Software production

costs for computer software that is to be used as an integral part of a product or process shall not be capitalized until both (a) technological feasibility has been established for the software and (b) all research and development activities for the other components of the product or process have been completed.

6. Capitalization of computer software costs shall cease when the product is available for general release to customers. Costs of **maintenance** and **customer support** shall be charged to expense when related revenue is recognized or when those costs are incurred, whichever occurs first.

Purchased Computer Software

7. The cost of purchased computer software to be sold, leased, or otherwise marketed that has no alternative future use shall be accounted for the same as the costs incurred to develop such software internally, as specified in paragraphs 3-6. If that purchased software has an alternative future use, the cost shall be capitalized when the software is acquired and accounted for in accordance with its use.

Amortization of Capitalized Software Costs

8. Capitalized software costs shall be amortized on a product-by-product basis. The annual amortization shall be the greater of the amount computed using (a) the ratio that current gross revenues for a product bear to the total of current and anticipated future gross revenues for that product or (b) the straight-line method over the remaining estimated economic life of the product including the period being reported on. Amortization shall start when the product is available for general release to customers.

Inventory Costs

9. The costs incurred for duplicating the computer software, documentation, and training materials from the product masters and for physically packaging the product for distribution shall be capitalized as inventory on a unit-specific basis and charged to cost of sales when revenue from the sale of those units is recognized.

Evaluation of Capitalized Software Costs

10. At each balance sheet date, the unamortized capitalized costs of a computer software product shall be compared to the net realizable value of that product. The amount by which the unamortized capitalized costs of a computer software product exceed the net realizable value of that asset shall be written off. The net realizable

value is the estimated future gross revenues from that product reduced by the estimated future costs of completing and disposing of that product, including the costs of performing maintenance and customer support required to satisfy the enterprise's responsibility set forth at the time of sale. The reduced amount of capitalized computer software costs that have been written down to net realizable value at the close of an annual fiscal period shall be considered to be the cost for subsequent accounting purposes, and the amount of the write-down shall not be subsequently restored.

Disclosures

11. The following shall be disclosed in the financial statements:

a. Unamortized computer software costs included in each balance sheet presented
b. The total amount charged to expense in each income statement presented for amortization of capitalized computer software costs and for amounts written down to net realizable value.

12. The disclosure requirements for research and development costs in Statement 2 apply to the research and development costs incurred for a computer software product to be sold, leased, or otherwise marketed.

Amendments to Other Pronouncements

13. The following sentence in paragraph 31 of Statement 2 is deleted:

For example, efforts to develop a new or higher level of computer software capability intended for sale (but not under a contractual arrangement) would be a research and development activity encompassed by this Statement.

14. The following portions of FASB Interpretation No. 6, *Applicability of FASB Statement No. 2 to Computer Software,* are deleted:

a. The sentence in paragraph 3 that states:

For example, efforts to develop a new or higher level of computer software capability intended for sale (but not under a contractual arrangement) would be a research and development activity encompassed by this Statement.

b. The phrase in the first sentence of paragraph 6 that states:

> or as a product or process to be sold, leased, or otherwise marketed to others for their use

c. Paragraphs 7 and 9

d. The two sentences in paragraph 8 that state:

> Developing or significantly improving a product or process that is intended to be sold, leased, or otherwise marketed to others is a research and development activity (see paragraph 8 of Statement 2). Similarly, developing or significantly improving a process whose output is a product that is intended to be sold, leased, or otherwise marketed to others is a research and development activity.

15. This Statement supersedes FASB Technical Bulletin No. 79-2, *Computer Software Costs.*

Effective Date and Transition

16. This Statement shall be effective for financial statements for fiscal years beginning after December 15, 1985 and shall be applied to costs incurred in those fiscal years for all projects including those in progress upon initial application of this Statement. Earlier application in annual financial statements that have not previously been issued is permitted.

17. Costs incurred prior to initial application of this Statement, whether capitalized or not, shall not be adjusted to the amounts that would have been capitalized if this Statement had been in effect when those costs were incurred. However, the provisions of paragraphs 8 (amortization), 10 (net realizable value test), and 11 (disclosures) of this Statement shall be applied to any unamortized costs capitalized prior to initial application of this Statement that continue to be reported as assets after the effective date.

**The provisions of this Statement need
not be applied to immaterial items.**

This Statement was adopted by the affirmative votes of five members of the Financial Accounting Standards Board. Messrs. Kirk and Mosso dissented.

Mr. Kirk and Mr. Mosso dissent from this Statement because (a) it unduly restricts capitalization of software costs, (b) it extends the research and development classification of Statement 2 to a major class of routine production activities, and (c) it permits significantly different amounts of capitalization depending upon a company's choice of production methods.

In discussing the first point, the requirement in this Statement that either a detail program design or a working model be completed before capitalization can begin is likely to result in expensing most computer software costs, even though software is a significant, and often the only, revenue-generating asset of many companies. Assessing the probability of future benefits from computer software is difficult in the software industry, but no more difficult than in some tangible output industries such as fashion clothing and oil and gas drilling, or even in other creative process industries such as motion pictures. In each of these cases, capitalization of costs is accepted despite the inherent uncertainties.

The second point is related. This Statement sets the stage for extending the reach of Statement 2, with its mandatory expensing requirement, to a broad sweep of routine production activities because it assigns the bulk of computer programming activities (detail program design, coding, and testing) to the classification of research and development. Certainly, much research and development-type activity does take place in the computer software industry. However, most detail program design and coding activities are not discovery- or design-oriented in the sense of Statement 2; they are just the meticulous execution of a plan—skilled craftsmen applying proven methods as in any production process.

The third point is that this Statement makes capitalization dependent upon how the programming process is arranged, that is, the extent to which detail program design is separated from or integrated with coding and testing. The amount capitalized could differ significantly for comparable program outputs and, within the range of permitted capitalization, results would be essentially a matter of choice of approach to the programming process.

Mr. Mosso's dissent is based on the view that computer software is a key element in the ongoing shift of emphasis in the U.S. economy from tangible outputs and physical processes to intangible outputs and creative processes. Changes of that nature are evident in both emerging and old-line industries. In his view, accounting should accommodate this transition by reporting the results of creative processes on the balance sheet when those results comprise reasonably probable future economic benefits. Otherwise, financial statements will lose relevance as creative activities proliferate.

Messrs. Kirk and Mosso would support capitalization of costs incurred after an entity had completed the software product design and determined that proven technology is available to produce a deliverable product. The research and development classification of Statement 2 would apply only to those costs of designing the product and determining the availability of proven technology.

Members of the Financial Accounting Standards Board:

Donald J. Kirk, *Chairman*
Frank E. Block
Victor H. Brown
Raymond C. Lauver
David Mosso
Robert T. Sprouse
Arthur R. Wyatt

Index